the vegetarian kitchen

PRUE LEITH + PETA LEITH

the vegetarian kitchen

PRUE LEITH + PETA LEITH

bluebird
books for life

CONTENTS

introduction

Why are we writing a vegetarian book? It's not only because vegetarianism is gaining ground for environmental reasons, health concerns and on compassionate grounds. It's also because as a life long vegetarian (Peta) and a cook who loves to eat and wants to do right by the planet (Prue), it seemed a great thing to do. Plant-based cooking is undergoing a renaissance, and the new flavours and combinations excite us both hugely. Also, we are closely related, we like each other and we thought it would be fun!

Most curious cooks will know how to make a handful of vegetarian dishes: the perfect stew, omelette or risotto … but how about making a Red Dragon Pie, Cheese and Marmite Soufflé or spicy Paneer Curry? Even resolute meat eaters will love these. Flavour, texture, colour and balance is what makes a good dish, and originality and surprise don't half help. So that's what we have here: a collection of easy-to-make, great-tasting recipes for everyone: vegetarians, vegans, flexitarians or meat eaters who want a change or to have a bigger repertoire for visiting veggie and vegan friends and relatives.

Prue was brought up in South Africa, where the only vegetarian numbers were side-affairs or afterthoughts, perhaps delicious toasted cheese-and-apricot-jam sandwiches or charred 'mielies' (sweetcorn). It wasn't until Prue opened her own restaurant, Leith's, in London, that she became truly enamoured of veg. Now she finds herself cooking and eating more and more vegetarian dishes. So the dream project was to combine forces with her niece, chef Peta.

Peta, a pastry chef, has been vegetarian for her whole life, so is in the rare position of never having knowingly tried meat or fish. She decided to pursue a career in pastry because she knew she wanted to work in kitchens but didn't want to limit herself to working only in vegetarian restaurants. She worked for a year with Claire Ptak at Violet Cakes, before leaving to study bread-making at the French Culinary Institute in New York. On her return to London, she found a job in the pastry section of the Ivy, where she stayed and honed her skills over the next seven years. When Prue approached Peta to work on this book, the timing couldn't have been better to collaborate on their love of vegetarian cooking.

our recipes

If you are reading this book as a vegetarian, you will be very familiar with using tofu, nuts and pulses, but we understand that many non-veggies struggle to imagine what they would eat if they gave up meat, wondering what on earth they would replace it with. Our aim in writing this book is to address that need, as well as providing existing vegetarians with some fresh inspiration. The dishes are so delicious you won't miss the meat and we've given you precise instructions on how to handle any ingredients that might be new to you. Bringing our combined experiences to the table, our hope is that this book might help to quell some of those fears and inspire people to try something new.

Our style of vegetarian cooking is simple, rustic and flavoursome. We're not interested in foams and gels and edible flowers in every mouthful. Of course that style of cuisine has its place, but food is about nourishment, comfort and enjoyment. We use really good-quality, seasonal ingredients, and do only what's necessary to them in order to make them taste fantastic. Nothing pleases us more than when we cook for staunch carnivores, and find them asking for second helpings and wanting to know the recipe. Vegetarian and vegan food should not be about compromising or missing out on anything; a really well-devised and well-executed plant-based meal should be just as delicious (if not more so!) than any unrestricted meal.

We hope that these pages fit the description above, and appeal not only to vegetarians and vegans, but to everybody who cares about good food.

vegetarian and vegan basics

Having been brought up vegetarian, I knew my mung beans from my lentils from a pretty young age, but there are so many ingredients out there, so I can understand it might all be a bit overwhelming for those who are new to plant-based cooking. On the following pages you'll find a few basics, which I hope will help you to understand the various components that make up a balanced vegetarian or vegan meal, and show you how to make the most of them. *Peta*

Sources of protein

One of the main concerns people have when considering switching to a plant-based diet is whether they will get enough protein. There are plenty of vegetable protein sources, so it's simply a case of knowing what your options are.

Pulses and legumes

These include lentils, chickpeas and all kinds of dried beans. These are a great, inexpensive way to get protein into your diet. Tinned beans are convenient, but they are well cooked, so if you like bite to your beans, you are better off using dried.

When planning your meals in advance, I would recommend buying dried beans, and cooking them yourself – this requires a pre-soak, which takes time, however it allows you to cook them until al dente and it also makes them more easily digestible. You can either soak the beans in cold water overnight, or if you're in a hurry, pour boiling water over them, and soak them for an hour. They will swell hugely while soaking, so put them into a large container for the soak. When you want to cook them, drain and rinse them thoroughly, then put them into a pan of cold water, bring to the boil, and simmer until just tender. Never add salt to the cooking water as it makes them tough, and prevents them from softening. If you're not using the beans immediately, drain and store them in the fridge for up to 3 days before using.

Another fantastic way of using dried pulses is to sprout them. This increases their nutritional value enormously because they begin to germinate, a process which makes them less starchy, more easily digested, and richer in folate, iron, magnesium, zinc and protein. Soak your choice of dried pulses in cold water for 24 hours, then drain them and put them into a large jar, which they should fill only half way at most. Cover the top with either muslin or a piece of cling film with holes pierced in it – the idea is that air should be able to circulate within the jar. Lay the jar on its side on a sunny window sill, and leave for 3–4 days, rinsing, draining and turning them over once daily. Different beans have slightly different sprouting times, but once they have long tails, they are ready. Keep them in the fridge, and add them to salads, or just eat handfuls for a really nutritious snack. Beware, raw sprouts are unsuitable for pregnant women, due to a small listeria risk.

Tofu

Tofu is a curd made from soy beans. It's bland, so it is always used as a textural base, and then flavoured. The main two kinds you will find in UK supermarkets are silken and firm.

You usually press firm tofu to dry it out and then marinate it ahead of baking or frying in a stir-fry or curry. The easiest way to do this is to place the block of tofu between a few sheets of kitchen paper, and then place a heavy chopping board weighed down with a stack of books (or something similarly heavy) on top of it. Leave it for a couple of hours, and you'll return to find a puddle of water surrounding your now-pressed tofu. Silken tofu has a very wet texture, and is generally blended with other ingredients to make vegan mayonnaise or desserts, such as our Chocolate and Orange Mousse on p.182.

Tofu puffs (used in the Fragrant Laksa on p.32) are deep fried and very light – like you would find in a Thai curry. They aren't as widely available as firm or silken tofu, but Asian supermarkets sell them, and of course you can find them online.

Nuts

Nuts are widely consumed in desserts and salted, as appetizers, but they can also give savoury dishes a huge nutritional boost. Hazelnuts especially have a very earthy flavour, which pairs brilliantly with mushrooms, as in our Mushroom and Hazelnut Pithivier on p.102.

Egg replacements

It is hard to find a replacement for eggs, given their unique structure. When it comes to baking, I would follow an egg-free recipe from the outset, rather than using a substitute for the egg – the texture simply won't be the same. When it comes to meringue, a common substitute for egg white is aquafaba, which is the water from a can of chickpeas. This whisked with an equal quantity of sugar will form a meringue, so if you can't live without meringue, this is your best bet but it's not a perfect substitute. It takes forever to whisk up, and when baked it won't be crunchy like a traditional meringue.

Sources of dairy

If you're vegan or simply want to cut down, there are countless dairy replacements on the market. Virtually anything can be milked these days – almonds, soy beans, coconuts, hazelnuts, rice, oats etc. Personally I prefer to use oat milk. It is the creamiest (in my opinion), and it has the lowest environmental impact of those on offer. Most large supermarkets stock not only a wide selection of dairy-free milks, but also dairy-free yoghurts, cream and créme fraîche.

sumptuous soups

ROASTED TOMATO SOUP WITH WALNUT AND PARSLEY OIL

A good tomato soup is always a treat. Amazingly versatile, it's delicious chilled or hot, and becomes party food with the addition of a dollop of plain yoghurt or a vegan substitute on the top. It's amazing with this walnut and parsley oil. *Prue*

SERVES 4

1kg large vine-ripened tomatoes, quartered

7 garlic cloves, finely chopped

2 tbsp olive oil

450ml vegetable stock

1 tsp caster sugar

salt and black pepper to season

FOR THE PARSLEY AND WALNUT OIL

30g flat-leaf parsley leaves

40g walnuts, toasted (see Tip)

1 garlic clove

4 tbsp olive oil

1. Heat the oven to 160°C/fan 140°C/gas mark 3.

2. Put the quartered tomatoes in a roasting tin with the garlic and olive oil and season with salt and black pepper. Toss them to coat them in the oil, then roast in the oven for 2–3 hours, until really soft and shrunken.

3. Remove from the oven and blend the tomatoes in a blender or liquidizer with the stock and sugar, then season to taste.

4. To make the parsley and walnut oil, blitz all the ingredients in a food processor, then season with salt and black pepper to taste.

5. Serve the soup, hot or cold, with a drizzle of the oil.

Tip

To toast the walnuts, put them in a small, dry frying pan and shake over a medium heat for a few minutes until lightly browned and fragrant.

LENTIL DHAL WITH POACHED EGGS AND ROTI CANAI

Make it Vegan

Roti canai is a Malaysian version of the better-known Indian paratha. It's flaky and tender all at once, and it's very hard to stop at eating just one. In Malaysia, they serve it freshly made with bowls of lentil dhal for breakfast – something I came to love while travelling there. The poached egg on top isn't very authentic, but it is delicious. (Image on page 25.) *Peta*

SERVES 2 GENEROUSLY

FOR THE ROTI

200g plain flour

a pinch of salt

1 tsp vegetable oil plus extra for coating, shaping and frying

FOR THE DAHL

2 tbsp vegetable oil

1 onion, diced

4 garlic cloves, finely chopped

2cm (¾in) piece of ginger, peeled and minced

a pinch of dried chilli flakes, or 1 fresh red chilli, deseeded and finely chopped

200g split red lentils

½ tsp ground turmeric

900ml boiling water

½ tsp ground cumin

½ tsp ground coriander

½ tsp garam masala

1 medium tomato, chopped

salt and black pepper to season

TO SERVE (OPTIONAL)

2 poached eggs
(see Tip on page 24)

Curried Pea and Potato Samosas (see page 48)

1. Start with the roti. Combine the flour, salt and vegetable oil with 100ml cold water in a mixing bowl to form a dough. Knead the dough for about 6 minutes until it is smooth and elastic, then divide it into four equal pieces and shape them into balls. Put them back in the mixing bowl and coat them generously with vegetable oil, so that there is oil pooling underneath them. Turn them a few times, then cover the bowl with cling film and leave it for at least 3 hours at room temperature – you could also refrigerate them overnight at this point (see Tip below).

2. Meanwhile, make the dhal. Heat the vegetable oil in a large saucepan over a medium heat and sauté the onion until softened. Add the garlic, ginger and chilli and continue to cook, stirring frequently, until the onion is soft and translucent. Tip the red lentils into the pan, add the turmeric, then stir to combine.

3. Pour half the boiling water into the pan, then add the cumin, coriander, garam masala and tomato. Bring to the boil, then reduce the heat and simmer, stirring occasionally, for 10 minutes. When the water level starts to look low, add the rest of the boiling water, a little at a time. After 20–25 minutes, taste to see if the lentils are cooked – they should be completely tender. Once the lentils are done, remove from the heat and season with salt and black pepper.

4. Shaping the roti is a messy job, so make sure you have everything you need to hand before you begin. Set a large frying pan on the hob with a little oil in it, but do not turn it on just yet. Clean and dry a large area of work surface, then oil it lightly.

Tip

If you do refrigerate the dough overnight, allow it to come back to room temperature before attempting to shape it, as it will be less elastic if it's cold.

5. Take one piece of the roti dough and press it down onto the work surface. There should be plenty of oil all over the dough, your hands, and the work surface, so nothing should stick. The aim is to stretch the dough out into a wafer-thin sheet, so press down firmly while pushing it outwards with both of your hands, working in circular motions. You can also lift the edges and stretch it a little, but be careful not to tear it.

6. Once you have stretched it out as large and as thin as you are able to, take the right third of it and fold it in towards the centre, trying to trap as much air in the fold as possible. Then take the left third, and bring it over the centre piece, again, trying to catch air as you go – do not press down to deflate it once it is folded. It should now look like a tall rectangle, so take the upper third and bring it down towards the middle, then bring the lower section up over the middle, so it should now be more square. Repeat this process with each piece of dough.

7. Heat the frying pan with a little oil in it over a medium–high heat, and when it is good and hot, lower one of the rotis into it. Cook for 1–2 minutes on each side until the rotis have deep golden patches. Once it looks crisp and well-coloured, take it out of the pan and place it on a wooden board. As soon as you can bear to touch it with your hands, bring your hands together in a clapping motion on either side of it, essentially scrunching it up between your hands. This helps to make it even more flaky. Repeat with each roti.

8. Serve the roti immediately with a piping hot bowl of dhal, and a poached egg sitting on top of the dhal. Serve with Curried Pea and Potato Samosas (see page 48), if desired.

Tips

A simple way to poach eggs is to use a wide, deep frying pan of simmering, salted water with a teaspoon of white vinegar in it. Slip the eggs in, side by side, and gently shake the pan by moving the handle from side to side to stop them catching on the bottom. Cook for about 3 minutes, or until the white is set.

To make this vegan, simply omit the poached eggs.

COURGETTE, PEA AND MINT SOUP WITH GOAT'S CHEESE TOASTS

This is a classic, inexpensive green soup that tastes good chilled or hot. The addition of the goat's cheese toasts, served on the side, turns the dish into a one-course lunch or supper dish. I've also served it on smarter occasions, taking the trouble to blend the soup to a velvety smoothness, and make mini goat's cheese toasts which I place on the top of each serving of soup. *Prue*

SERVES 4

2 tbsp vegetable oil

300g courgette, thinly sliced (about 1½ medium courgettes)

4 garlic cloves, crushed

260g frozen petits pois

1 litre vegetable stock

4 slices of bread (sourdough is ideal)

2 tsp olive oil

200g soft or crumbly goat's cheese

a small handful of fresh mint, leaves finely chopped

salt and black pepper to season

1. Heat the vegetable oil in a large saucepan over a high heat, then add the courgette and cook for a few minutes, stirring constantly. Add the garlic and cook for 2 minutes until soft and fragrant, then add the peas and stock.

2. Season the soup with salt and black pepper, bring to the boil, then reduce the heat and simmer for 5–10 minutes until the courgette is tender.

3. Use a stick blender or transfer the soup to a blender or liquidizer and blend until smooth. Heat the grill to medium-high.

4. Toast the bread well. Drizzle the olive oil over each slice, then divide the goat's cheese between the slices. Spread it out. Grind some black pepper over the top, then place under the hot grill for 10 minutes, or until nicely golden.

5. Ladle the soup into warm bowls, top with a sprinkle of chopped mint, and serve with the cheesy toasts on the side.

SPICY CHICKPEA AND KALE SOUP

Make it Vegan

When I was at the Cordon Bleu, learning to cook, I don't think chickpeas were ever mentioned. Certainly we weren't taught to cook them, and no one had heard of gram flour, which is the helpfully gluten-free flour made from chickpeas. Kale only crossed my horizon, and my taste buds, in the eighties. Now it sold as a super-food (it provides a great deal of fibre as well as essential vitamins and minerals) and is available everywhere. I prefer the curly variety. It is quick to cook, has a wonderful colour and a strong flavour. *Prue*

SERVES 2 GENEROUSLY

1 tbsp vegetable oil

2 garlic cloves, finely chopped

1 red chilli, finely chopped (with seeds)

1 onion, finely diced

1 tbsp tomato purée

1 x 400g tin chickpeas, drained and rinsed

200g tinned chopped tomatoes

500ml vegetable stock

60g kale, tough stalks removed and leaves roughly chopped

salt and black pepper to season

TO SERVE

2 tbsp plain yoghurt

1 tsp toasted coriander seeds (see Tips) or 1 tsp sweet paprika

1. Heat the vegetable oil in a large saucepan over a medium heat, add the garlic, chilli and onion and fry until softened. Add the tomato purée, chickpeas and tinned tomatoes, followed by the vegetable stock. Bring to the boil, then add the kale and simmer for a further 10 minutes. Season with salt and black pepper to taste.

2. Remove from the heat and serve immediately, ideally with a dollop of yoghurt and a few toasted coriander seeds or a shake of paprika.

Tips

To toast coriander seeds, put them in a small, dry frying pan and shake over a medium heat until you can smell the coriander flavour and the seeds are a shade browner.

If you prefer a little less heat in your soup, deseed the chilli before chopping it.

To make this vegan, simply top with a swirl of extra virgin olive oil instead of the yoghurt.

CELERIAC SOUP WITH TRUFFLE OIL

Vegan

Celeriac has a wonderfully distinctive flavour, which is best left more or less on its own to be the star of the show. When it is blended at high speed it becomes silky and creamy. It's the perfect autumnal lunch, warming and delicious with a chunk of crusty bread and a drizzle of good-quality truffle oil. *Prue*

SERVES 2 AS A MAIN OR 4 AS A STARTER

2 tbsp vegetable oil

1 small onion, diced

250g celeriac, peeled and diced

2 large celery sticks, diced

900ml light vegetable stock (see Tip)

salt and black pepper to season

TO SERVE

truffle oil (optional)

crusty bread

1. Heat the vegetable oil in a large saucepan over a medium heat, add the onion and cook until soft and translucent. Add the celeriac and celery to the pan and continue to cook for a few minutes until they start to sweat. Add the stock with a few good twists of pepper. Bring to the boil, then turn down the heat and simmer gently for 20–30 minutes until the celeriac is soft.

2. Transfer the soup to a liquidizer or blender and blend until it is completely smooth. It may be too thick at this point, so loosen it with a little boiling water, if necessary. Taste and season with salt and more pepper if needed.

3. Serve hot, with a drizzle of truffle oil on the top of each serving (if using), and crusty bread on the side.

Tip

If using stock cube or powder, simply use 1.5 times the water specified on the packet to make a lighter stock.

FRAGRANT LAKSA WITH TOFU PUFFS

Vegan

Laksa is a fragrant, Malaysian noodle soup – fresh and flavoursome with a gentle heat. My husband proposed to me while on holiday in Malaysia, so I definitely look back at all the food we ate on that holiday with rose-tinted glasses! You can vary the vegetables in this recipe – baby corn and Tenderstem broccoli both work brilliantly here. Sold in vacuum-packed bags, tofu puffs are deep-fried tofu pieces with the texture of sponge. They are very different to firm or silken tofu, so don't be tempted to substitute either. If you can't find the puffs, omit them and add another vegetable instead. *Peta*

SERVES 2

½ red chilli

1 green chilli

4 garlic cloves

2 shallots, roughly chopped

2.5cm (1in) piece of galangal, peeled and roughly chopped

1 lemongrass stem, trimmed

2 tbsp vegetable oil, plus extra

200ml full-fat coconut milk

400ml vegetable stock

1 kaffir lime leaf

½ tsp each of hot curry powder and ground turmeric

a generous pinch each of salt and caster sugar

100g dried rice noodles

60g green beans, chopped

1 pak choi, sliced

60g beansprouts

40g tofu puffs, halved

1 lime, halved

a handful of coriander

1. Put the chillies, garlic, shallots, galangal and lemongrass in a small food processor or spice grinder and blitz until you have a smooth paste.

2. Heat the vegetable oil in a wok over a low heat, then add the paste and fry it, stirring constantly, for 15 minutes. Watch carefully to ensure it doesn't burn – it should just become very aromatic.

3. Add the coconut milk, 200ml of the vegetable stock, the lime leaf, curry powder, turmeric, salt and caster sugar. Bring to the boil, then reduce the heat and simmer very gently for 10 minutes. Add the remaining vegetable stock, return it to the boil, then remove it from the heat. Pick out the lime leaf and discard it.

4. Cook the rice noodles according to the instructions on the packet, then coat them in a little vegetable oil to stop them from sticking and divide them between two soup bowls.

5. Bring a large pan of water to the boil and blanch the green beans until they are just tender. Lift them out with a slotted spoon and divide them between the two soup bowls. Into the same water, add the pak choi and blanch it for a couple of minutes, before removing with a slotted spoon and dividing it between the bowls.

6. Add the beansprouts to the water for 1–2 minutes, then drain them and divide them between the bowls.

7. Return the broth to the boil, then add the tofu puffs, and keep the wok on the heat for a moment to allow them to warm through.

8. Ladle the broth over the noodles and vegetables in the bowls, dividing the tofu pieces evenly between them. Garnish each bowl with half a lime and a scattering of chopped coriander and serve.

sunday night suppers

CHEESE AND MARMITE SOUFFLÉ

We are told everyone either loves or hates Marmite, but I've never found anyone who hates this. It is a simply delicious soufflé. The Marmite gives the cheesy flavour an umami depth and it's the ultimate Sunday night comfort food when served with baked beans (see our recipe on page 91) – trust me, it's a winning combination! *Peta*

(see our recipe on page 91)

SERVES 2 FOR A LIGHT SUPPER

15g unsalted butter plus extra for greasing

15g plain flour

150ml whole milk

45g mature Cheddar cheese, grated

20g vegetarian Parmesan-style cheese, grated

2 tsp Marmite

2 large eggs, separated

black pepper

1. Heat the oven to 210°C/fan 190°C/gas mark 6–7. Generously grease a small soufflé dish (about 15cm/6in in diameter) with butter.

2. Melt the butter in a saucepan over a medium heat, then add the flour and stir briskly for a few minutes. The roux (flour and butter mix) should look like wet sand.

3. Take the pan off the heat and gradually whisk in the milk, then return the pan to a medium heat and whisk for a couple of minutes until very thick, glossy and smooth.

4. Remove from the heat, then beat in the grated Cheddar, Parmesan-style cheese, Marmite and egg yolks. Season with pepper but not salt (the Marmite and cheese provide enough salt).

5. Whisk the egg whites separately in a clean bowl until they form soft peaks. Fold the whites into the mix using a silicone spoon, taking care not to knock the air out of the whites too much – better a few pockets of unmixed egg white than losing the air.

6. Transfer the mixture to the greased soufflé dish, then bake in the middle of the oven for 25 minutes. It should be very well risen and golden brown on top. Remove from the oven and serve immediately.

Tip

If you're a Marmite hater, substitute the Marmite for ½ teaspoon of English mustard powder, and ½ teaspoon of cayenne pepper.

TWICE-BAKED POTATOES
WITH CHILLI, GARLIC AND AVOCADO

Baked potatoes are an ideal Sunday night supper; comforting enough to keep the blues away, and so easy they don't require much more effort than it takes to turn on the oven. To ring the changes and give them an interesting twist, they can be stuffed and baked again, as in this recipe. Pretty much anything that goes on toast will be delicious mashed into the scooped out flesh of a baked potato – cheese, baked beans, fried mushrooms, tomatoes, olives, you name it. In this vegan version, creamy avocado is given a delicious kick with a good dose of chilli and garlic. If you like guacamole, you'll love these. *Prue*

SERVES 2

2 small baking potatoes

2 tsp olive oil plus extra for drizzling

1 garlic clove, finely chopped

1 red chilli, deseeded and finely chopped

6 cherry tomatoes, quartered and deseeded

1 avocado, halved, stoned, peeled and diced

salt and black pepper to season

1. Heat the oven to 210°C/190°C fan/gas mark 6–7.

2. Prick the potatoes all over with the point of a knife, then put them on a baking tray. Bake in the oven for 1 hour, or until they feel tender when pierced with a sharp knife.

3. Remove from the oven and once they are cool enough to handle cut them in half, then scoop the flesh out into a mixing bowl. Reserve the skins.

4. Mash the flesh with a fork, then add the olive oil, garlic, chilli and cherry tomatoes, and season with salt and black pepper. Mix well, then gently stir in the avocado.

5. Spoon the mixture back into the potato skins and use a fork to pack it in tightly. Drizzle a little olive oil over the top of each, then return them to the oven, on the baking tray, for 20 minutes. Serve immediately.

BRUSCHETTA TWO WAYS

Bruschetta (pronounced 'brusketta', not 'brushetta'!) is basically an Italian open sandwich made with grilled bread, rubbed with garlic and brushed with olive oil. Traditionally, they are topped with chopped raw tomatoes, but today anything goes. They are nicest, I think, when the bread is still warm and the topping cold. *Prue*

FIG, GORGONZOLA AND HONEY BRUSCHETTA

This is a classic combination, and is only worth doing when fresh figs are in season. The sweetness of the figs and the honey, alongside the sharp blue cheese is just divine. If you can get your hands on truffled honey, all the better! *Peta*

SERVES 2

2 slices of sourdough (brown or white)

extra virgin olive oil for drizzling

4 ripe figs

60g gorgonzola (piccante or dolce)

clear honey to drizzle

1. Toast the sourdough, then drizzle the olive oil over it.

2. Cut the figs into quarters and crumble the gorgonzola. Arrange the figs and gorgonzola on top of the toasts, then drizzle a little honey over the whole thing. Serve immediately, while the toast is still warm.

Tip

If your figs are not very ripe, cut them in half and sprinkle a little sugar on the cut side, then place them under a hot grill for a couple of minutes. Allow them to cool a little, then proceed as above.

1. To make the pickling liquor for the cabbage, combine the apple cider vinegar, sugar, salt, mustard seeds and peppercorns in a small saucepan with 125ml water and bring to the boil. Remove from the heat as soon as it boils. Put the shallot and cabbage into a clean, heatproof jar, then pour the hot pickling liquor over it and press the cabbage down to ensure it's all submerged. Leave it to cool, then seal with a lid and refrigerate it for at least a few hours, ideally overnight.

2. To make the falafels, cook the quinoa in a large pan of boiling water for 10 minutes or until the quinoa is tender. Drain and allow it to cool.

3. Put the chickpeas, harissa paste, garlic, spices, flour, baking powder, onion and herbs in a food processor and blitz until smooth, adding a tablespoon of warm water if it is dry and crumbly. Keep adding warm water, a tablespoon at a time, blitzing between additions, until you have a paste that will hold together (you may need up to 6 tablespoons).

4. Transfer the mixture to a bowl, then stir in the quinoa, season to taste with salt and black pepper, and chill in the fridge for at least 1 hour.

5. To make the tahini dressing, combine all the ingredients with 3 tablespoons of warm water in a small bowl and whisk until smooth. Season to taste.

6. Using clean hands, take egg-sized lumps of the falafel mixture into your hands and shape them into patties (the mixture should make around twelve). Press them together, then roll them gently in flour – they will be fragile, so handle them with care.

7. Heat the vegetable oil in a heavy-based non-stick frying pan over a medium high heat, then fry the falafels in batches, carefully flipping them over halfway through cooking, until they are golden brown on both sides. Transfer to a plate lined with kitchen paper to soak up any excess oil.

8. To assemble the wraps, spread a generous spoonful of the tahini dressing on each wrap, then divide the lettuce, avocado and falafels between them. Add some pickled cabbage to each, then drizzle over a little extra tahini dressing. Wrap them up tightly and serve immediately.

Tip

The pickled cabbage will keep for up to 10 days, covered, in the fridge.

LEFTOVER VEGETABLE FRITTATA

In our family, Sunday night means eggs on toast. It's the perfect light meal, when you're likely to have had a large lunch, plus it's comforting when you're in the grip of the Sunday blues. This is just a way of dressing up those eggs, and using up some leftover vegetables from lunch at the same time. Any cooked vegetable will work well, but my preference would be potatoes, carrots, parsnips, chard or spinach, beetroot, beans, broccoli, peas, courgette and cauliflower. *Peta*

SERVES 4

2 tbsp vegetable oil

1 onion, diced

300g leftover cooked vegetables, diced (see intro for options)

60g mature Cheddar cheese, grated

4 large eggs

40ml whole milk

salt and black pepper to season

green salad to serve

1. Heat the oven to 200°C/fan 180°C/gas mark 6.

2. Heat the vegetable oil in a 20cm (8in) ovenproof frying pan over a medium heat, add the onion and fry until soft and translucent, then add the cooked vegetables and stir them about so they are well mixed – the pan will look quite full, but that's how it should be. Scatter the cheese evenly over the top of the vegetables.

3. Beat the eggs with the milk in a jug or bowl and season with salt and black pepper. Pour this over the vegetables, then continue to cook over a medium-high heat for a couple of minutes, until it starts to set around the edges. Transfer the pan to the middle of the oven and cook for 20 minutes, by which point it should be puffed up and golden. Press the tip of a knife into the centre to ensure the egg is set all the way through.

4. Serve immediately, with a green salad.

LEEK AND CHEDDAR SAUSAGE ROLLS

My father, Prue's younger brother, makes the best Glamorgan sausages, and he used to do so in industrial quantities when I was a child, so he could pull them out of the freezer at a moment's notice to feed his vegetarian brood. He made them by eye, measuring everything in handfuls, so this is not an exact replica of his recipe, but it's a good approximation. Wrapped in flaky, buttery puff pastry, they're absolutely delicious. They are perfect served warm, fresh from the oven, or at room temperature, as part of a picnic. (Image on page 47.)

Classic Glamorgan sausages are made with the same filling ingredients, but instead of being wrapped in pastry and baked, they are carefully rolled first in flour, then beaten egg, then breadcrumbs, and are then pan-fried in a mixture of butter and oil to brown them all over. *Peta*

MAKES 8 LARGE SAUSAGE ROLLS

1 large leek, trimmed, washed and finely chopped

115g mature Cheddar cheese, grated

140g fresh breadcrumbs

a good handful of flat-leaf parsley, finely chopped

1 large egg, beaten, plus 1 large beaten egg yolk

40ml whole milk

250g all-butter puff pastry

salt and black pepper to season

1. Heat the oven to 210°C/fan 190°C/gas mark 6–7. Line a baking sheet with baking parchment.

2. In a large bowl, mix the leek, cheese, breadcrumbs, parsley, whole beaten egg and milk. Season with salt and black pepper. The mixture should be damp enough to just hold its shape when squeezed together.

3. Roll out the pastry away from you to a large 40 x 30cm (16 x 12in) rectangle, so that the shorter edge is nearest you. Divide the filling in half and spoon each down one side of the two long edges of the pastry, packing the mixture tightly with your fingers to shape it into two long sausages.

4. Brush the pastry between the two 'sausages' with the beaten egg yolk.

5. Roll the pastry in from the outer edges into the middle, so that you end up with the two rolls encased in pastry, sitting alongside each other. Use a sharp knife to cut the pastry down the middle, dividing the two rolls.

6. Press along the seam of each one to ensure it is bonded well and use a fork to mark along the seams. Transfer the rolls to the lined baking sheet, then brush them all over with the remaining egg yolk. Use a sharp knife to cut diagonal slashes into the tops at regular intervals along the length of them. If you want to freeze them, do that now.

7. Bake in the middle of the oven for 25–30 minutes, until the pastry is puffed up and golden. Check they are cooked on the undersides and cook them for a little longer if necessary. Remove from the oven and allow to cool slightly on a wire rack. Serve warm or cooled, each sausage cut into four pieces to give you eight large rolls.

Tips

These rolls are good served hot with mustard, or cold for a picnic.

If baking from frozen, allow the sausage rolls to sit at room temperature for 30 minutes before baking, and give them an extra few minutes in the oven. Use a sharp knife or skewer to check the centre is piping hot before removing from the oven.

CURRIED PEA AND POTATO SAMOSAS

These are a bit of a fiddle to assemble, but the filling is so quick and easy, the whole thing won't take you long at all. They're absolutely delicious served with a cold beer! *Peta*

MAKES 20–24 SMALL SAMOSAS

2 tbsp vegetable oil plus extra for brushing

1 onion, finely chopped

½ tsp black mustard seeds

½ tsp ground cumin

1 tsp garam masala

1 tsp ground turmeric

2 medium baking potatoes, peeled and diced

120g frozen petits pois

400ml boiling water

juice of ¼ lemon (about 2–3 tsp)

4 sheets filo pastry

3 tsp black onion seeds

salt and black pepper to season

1. Heat the vegetable oil in a large frying pan over a medium heat, then add the onion, mustard seeds, cumin, garam masala and turmeric. Sauté until the onion is soft and translucent, then add the diced potato and cook for a few minutes, stirring to combine.

2. Add the peas, followed by the boiling water. Bring everything to the boil, then reduce the heat and simmer gently, stirring occasionally, for about 15 minutes until the water has evaporated and the potato is cooked. (Add a little more water if the potato is not yet tender.)

3. Remove from the heat, add the lemon juice and season with salt and black pepper. Use a fork to mash half of the potato pieces – not so that the mixture is smooth, just to help make the mixture more cohesive. Set the mixture aside and allow to cool.

4. Heat the oven to 200°C/fan 180°C/gas mark 6. Line two baking trays with baking parchment.

5. Set a filo sheet in front of you in landscape orientation. Cut it vertically into six equal strips running from left to right. Repeat with the other filo sheets and cover with a clean, damp cloth to prevent it from drying out.

6. Taking one strip at a time, put a small amount of the cooled filling onto the pastry at the top of the strip, then bring the top right corner down to meet the other side, forming a triangle with the filling inside.

7. Brush a little oil on the rest of the strip, then roll the triangle down the strip, following the natural turns it makes – you should end up with a triangular shape that has a well-encased filling. Use the vegetable oil to seal the pastry, then brush it lightly all over.

8. Repeat this until you have used up all your filling. Arrange the samosas on the two lined baking trays, then scatter the black onion seeds over the top. Bake in the middle of the oven for 15–20 minutes until golden brown and crisp. Remove from the oven and serve immediately.

KEDGEREE WITH DARK LEAFY GREENS

For me, this is the ultimate comfort food — creamy, warming and filling, just what's called for on a cold day. It's a great option for entertaining because you can cook the rice, sauce and eggs in advance, meaning you won't have to spend long away from your guests while you're assembling it. *Peta*

SERVES 4

150g basmati rice, rinsed

70g unsalted butter

2 large brown onions, chopped

1 medium red chilli, deseeded and finely chopped

2.5cm (1in) piece of ginger, peeled and finely chopped

¼ tsp ground cumin

¼ tsp ground turmeric

½ tsp garam masala

2 tsp hot curry powder

250g fresh spinach, washed

200ml double cream

½ lemon

4 large eggs, hard-boiled (see Tips) and peeled

salt and black pepper to season

1. Cook the rice in a large pan of boiling water until tender. Drain and set aside.

2. Melt the butter in a very large saucepan over a medium heat, then add the onions, chilli and ginger and sauté until softened a little. Add the spices, cook for a further minute, then add the spinach. Cover the pan and cook for a few minutes, shaking the pan from time to time, until the spinach has wilted. Add the cream, bring to the boil, then reduce the heat and simmer gently for 5 minutes. Season with salt and black pepper, then squeeze the juice from the half lemon into the sauce. Stir the cooked rice into the sauce and check the seasoning.

3. Spoon the rice onto four plates, placing two halves of a boiled egg on top of each portion.

Tips

To hard-boil eggs, carefully slide them into a pan of boiling water set over a medium heat. Return the water to the boil, then cook for 6–7 minutes.

If you've got leftovers of the kedgeree, reheat them thoroughly in the microwave in a shallow bowl, or stir gently in a large pan until heated right through. To reheat hard-boiled eggs, drop them, peeled, into a pan of boiling water for 30 seconds.

To make it vegan, substitute the butter for olive oil, and the cream for oat cream, then serve it without the boiled eggs on top.

VEG HAGGIS WITH PARSNIP MASH AND FRIED TOMATOES

I once judged a competition for various butchery products, and was astonished that both the haggis and the black pudding competitions were won by the vegetarian versions. We judges had not been told in advance that there were veggie products in among all the meat ones. And both of us (there were two judges) declared them the best. If you can get McSweens Vegan Haggis, that's the one! *Prue*

SERVES 6

600g peeled parsnips, cut into large chunks

600g peeled potatoes, cut into large chunks

80ml olive oil

1 tbsp chopped flat-leaf parsley

1 tbsp chopped chives

1 tbsp vegetable oil

6 large ripe tomatoes

1 vegan haggis (about 500g; see Tip)

salt and black pepper to season

1. Cook the parsnips and potatoes in separate pans of boiling water until tender. Drain and mash them separately while they are still hot. (You can purée the parsnips in a food processor but the mashed potatoes go gluey if puréed, so they need a hand masher.) While they are still hot, combine the two purées in a bowl and beat in the olive oil and herbs. Season with salt and black pepper and keep warm.

2. Heat the vegetable oil in a frying pan over a medium heat. Cut the tomatoes in half across the 'equator' and place them cut side down in the pan. Let them cook without shifting them about for as long as you dare – about 4 minutes – until they are well browned, even a bit charred, then flip them over and give them another few minutes.

3. While the tomatoes are frying, cut the casing off the haggis and slice it into six pieces. Put the pieces in a heatproof dish and cover with a heatproof plate. Microwave for 4–5 minutes to heat them through. Serve the haggis with the mash and tomatoes.

 Tip

If you don't have a microwave, cook the vegan haggis in a moderate oven according to the packet instructions. You might need to do this as the first step as some varieties take over an hour to cook.

pasta and gnocchi

ORECCHIETTE WITH CALABRIAN PESTO

I was introduced to this pasta by an Italian friend who used to bring her grandmother's orecchiette back to London with her. I love it with this Calabrian pesto – the contrast of the creamy ricotta with the kick from the chilli works so well, especially with the springy 'little ears' of pasta. If you're short of time, or making this mid-week, you can substitute dried pasta and it will still be delicious. If you cannot get orecchiette, rigatoni would be a good substitute. I would urge you to make the pasta if you have the time though – it's very therapeutic once you get the hang of it. (Image of finished dish on page 61.) *Peta*

SERVES 4

500g fine semolina

plain flour for dusting

2 plum tomatoes, deseeded and chopped

green salad leaves to serve

FOR THE CALABRIAN PESTO

4 tbsp vegetable oil

1 small onion, diced

1 large garlic clove, roughly chopped

1 red pepper, deseeded and diced

1 small red chilli, deseeded and chopped

125g vegetarian Parmesan-style cheese, grated, plus extra to serve

80g ricotta

4 tbsp olive oil

salt and black pepper to season

1. For the pasta, combine the semolina with 200ml cold water in a mixing bowl and, using your hands, bring it together to form a firm but pliable dough. Add a little more water if necessary – the dough should be smooth and not at all sticky. Knead the dough vigorously for 5 minutes, then wrap it in cling film and chill in the fridge for 1 hour.

2. Unwrap the dough, place it a clean work surface and divide it into golf ball-sized pieces. Roll each piece into a rope about 1cm (½in) in diameter – you will need to press firmly to ensure the rope isn't hollow, as this dough has a tendency to create pockets of air. Don't be afraid to really work the dough – you don't need a light touch as you would with pastry.

3. Use a serrated, round-tipped knife to cut the rope into 1–2cm (½–¾in) pieces. Take each of these in turn and, holding the rounded tip of the knife at a 45-degree angle from the work surface, drag the knife across the piece of dough, pressing firmly down on it so that the dough curls up around the tip of the knife. Pick up the piece of dough, turn it over and push your thumb into it, in order to turn it inside out. It should look like a concave disk of dough, thinner in the middle, with a thicker rim around it.

4. Put the finished orecchiette onto a lightly floured board or tray while you finish shaping the rest of them. You might need a few boards or trays, as it's best not to let them touch each other too much in case they stick. Leave the pasta uncovered at room temperature to dry a bit while you make the pesto.

5. For the pesto, heat half the vegetable oil in a frying pan over a medium heat, add the onion, garlic and red pepper and sauté until softened, then remove from the heat and set aside.

6. Combine the sautéed onion, garlic and pepper with the raw chilli, vegetarian Parmesan-style cheese and ricotta in the bowl of a food processor. Add the remaining vegetable oil and the olive oil and blitz until mostly smooth, but still flecked with red. Taste and season with salt and black pepper.

7. Bring a large pan of salted water to the boil, add the orecchiette and cook for about 5 minutes. You will need to taste a piece regularly in order to assess when they are done, as they are hand-shaped and the thickness of the dough will vary a little each time you make them. They should taste cooked but still be pleasantly chewy when they are ready.

8. Transfer the pesto to a large, warmed serving bowl, then using a slotted spoon, scoop the pasta out of the boiling water and into the bowl of pesto. Toss the pasta with the pesto and add the chopped tomatoes. Serve immediately, with grated Parmesan-style cheese and salad on the side.

Tips

I often serve this with a green salad, but it's also delicious with roasted Mediterranean vegetables to make it more of a substantial meal.

My Italian friend cooks her orecchiette with garlic, chilli and *cime di rapa*, a bitter brassica that's hard to find here. Purple sprouting or green broccoli both make good substitutes.

BEST MACARONI CHEESE

Macaroni cheese has been my favourite food since I was a child, and nothing has changed over the years – I would still gladly eat it every day, if my conscience didn't prevent me from doing so! (This version is definitely 'worth the calories', as Prue would say.) Until recently I used to think it was a waste of posh Cheddar to use it in a sauce, and I would save it for cheese boards. Now I've realized the error of my ways and found what a huge difference it makes to the macaroni cheese.

Perhaps controversially, I prefer to use rigatoni or penne in place of actual macaroni when I make it, but you could use any short pasta shape and it will be delicious. *Peta*

SERVES 4–6

400g dried macaroni (or rigatoni, which is my preference)

olive oil for drizzling

900ml cold whole milk

40g unsalted butter

40g plain flour

a pinch of English mustard powder

200g mature Cheddar cheese, grated

80g vegetarian Parmesan-style cheese, grated

1 tbsp vegetable oil

1 onion, diced

40g fresh breadcrumbs

salt and black pepper to season

tomato and red onion salad to serve (optional)

1. Heat the oven to 220°C/fan 200°C/gas mark 7.

2. Bring a large pan of salted water to the boil, add the macaroni and cook for about 10 minutes until al dente (13 minutes for rigatoni). Drain the pasta and tip it into a large ovenproof dish (about 30 x 20cm/12 x 8in and 10cm/4in deep). Drizzle with a little olive oil and stir it through to prevent the pasta sticking together.

3. Combine the cold milk, butter, flour and mustard powder in a second saucepan, set it over a medium heat and whisk frequently until the butter has melted and the flour is all incorporated. Bring it to the boil and cook, continuing to whisk regularly, until the sauce has thickened enough to coat the back of a spoon.

4. Remove it from the heat, then whisk in the grated Cheddar and 60g of the grated vegetarian Parmesan-style cheese. Taste it, then season with salt and black pepper – it's best to do it this way around, as the cheese is salty, so you may not need as much salt as you would think. Pour the sauce over the pasta and stir to coat the pasta evenly.

5. Heat the vegetable oil in a frying pan over a medium heat, add the onion and sauté until it is soft and translucent. Stir the cooked onion into the pasta.

6. Scatter the breadcrumbs and remaining Parmesan-style cheese over the top of the pasta, trying to cover the surface evenly. Bake in the middle of the oven for 20 minutes, by which time it should be golden brown, crisp on top and piping hot. Remove from the oven and serve immediately.

PICI WITH WALNUT PESTO AND ROCKET SALAD

Pici is a type of hand-rolled pasta – a little like thick spaghetti. There's no doubt that this is a little time-consuming to make, but if you have the time, it's an enjoyable way to spend an hour. It's also a very easy pasta to shape, so small hands can be put to work! If you don't have the time, dried spaghetti is a perfectly good alternative, which would make this a very quick weeknight supper. A really important step in this recipe is when you combine the pesto with the pasta; the starchy pasta cooking water is a key ingredient in the pesto, turning it into a creamy, luxurious sauce. *Peta*

SERVES 6

550g fine semolina plus extra for dusting

large handful of rocket

drizzle of balsamic vinegar

FOR THE WALNUT PESTO

200g walnuts, toasted (see Tips)

2 garlic cloves

70g vegetarian Parmesan-style cheese, grated, plus extra to serve

100ml extra virgin olive oil, plus extra to serve

100ml vegetable oil

salt and black pepper to season

1. For the pici, combine the semolina with 200ml cold water in a mixing bowl and, using your hands, bring it together to form a firm but pliable dough. Add a little more water if necessary – the dough should be smooth and not at all sticky. Knead the dough vigorously for 5 minutes, then wrap it in cling film and chill in the fridge for 1 hour.

2. For the pesto, put the walnuts, garlic and vegetarian Parmesan-style cheese in the bowl of a food processor and blitz, then drizzle in the oils, as you blitz, until the pesto is fully combined but still a little grainy. Season with salt and black pepper.

3. Unwrap the dough, place it on a clean work surface, flatten it into a disc, then use a sharp knife to divide it into 3–4mm strips. Take one at a time and roll it on the work surface into a long, thin cord, 2–3mm thick. Repeat until the dough is all shaped into cords.

4. Lay out a clean tea towel dusted with semolina. Place the rolled pici on the tea towel in neat lines, ensuring they don't touch each other, as they could stick. Leave them here to dry, at room temperature, for 30 minutes before cooking.

5. Cook the pici in a large pan of boiling salted water, stirring frequently, for 4–6 minutes, until they are just cooked but still a little chewy – you will need to test them regularly during cooking.

6. Put the walnut pesto into a mixing bowl large enough to accommodate the pasta. When the pici are almost cooked, and their water is cloudy with starch, steal a good ladleful of the cooking water and stir this into the pesto, then drain the pasta, add it to the bowl and toss well.

7. Turn the pici into a warmed serving dish and serve immediately, with extra grated Parmesan-style cheese. Dress the rocket with a little balsamic, olive oil, salt and black pepper, and serve alongside.

Tips

To toast the walnuts, put them in a small, dry frying pan and shake over a medium heat for a few minutes until you can smell the nutty aroma.

The pici freeze brilliantly. If you do this, just add them to boiling water from frozen, and allow an extra couple of minutes for them to cook.

PEA GNUDI WITH ASPARAGUS AND GARLIC BUTTER

As a pasta lover I was seriously unimpressed when I first heard of gnudi, which are best described as ravioli without the pasta case. 'What on earth is the point of that?!' However, I was quickly converted once I tried them – they're soft and pillowy, full of flavour, and every bit as comforting as pasta. *Peta*

SERVES 6

400g frozen petits pois

200g ricotta

1 large egg

60g vegetarian Parmesan-style cheese, grated, plus extra to serve

2 tbsp plain flour

fine semolina for rolling

450g asparagus, trimmed and cut into 2.5cm (1in) lengths

120g unsalted butter

8 garlic cloves, crushed

salt and black pepper to season

1. Cook the frozen peas in a pan with plenty of boiling water, then drain them thoroughly. Put them in the bowl of a food processor then blitz them until they are well broken down, but not yet puréed.

2. Combine the peas, ricotta, egg, vegetarian Parmesan-style cheese, flour and some salt and black pepper in a mixing bowl. Mix to form a soft dough.

3. Sprinkle a baking tray with a generous layer of semolina and, using either wet hands or a small hinged ice-cream scoop, take walnut-sized pieces of mixture and roll them in the semolina to coat. Roll the balls between your palms to ensure they are tightly packed and place them neatly on the tray. Sprinkle more semolina on top and leave to rest at room temperature for at least 2 hours before cooking. (Overnight in the fridge is ideal, if you have time.)

4. Bring a large pan of salted water to the boil and cook the asparagus in it for 1–2 minutes until just tender, but still al dente. Remove the asparagus with a slotted spoon and set aside. Keep the water simmering, as you will use this to cook the gnudi.

5. Melt the butter in a large frying pan over a medium heat then add the garlic and sauté for about 3 minutes until it is softened and fragrant but not browned. Add the asparagus, season with salt and black pepper, stir to coat the asparagus in the garlic butter, then remove from the heat.

6. Brush the excess semolina off the gnudi, then lower them into the boiling water with a slotted spoon and stir gently to ensure none of them stick to the bottom of the pan. Return the pan to the boil, and once the gnudi rise to the top and float (around 2–3 minutes), they are done. Remove them with a slotted spoon and add them to the pan with the asparagus.

7. Set the frying pan back over the heat, then very gently (so as not to break the gnudi) turn everything over in the pan to ensure the gnudi are well coated in the butter and everything is hot.

8. Transfer the gnudi to warm pasta bowls, ensuring each portion gets plenty of butter and asparagus. Serve with grated Parmesan-style cheese.

BIG ROASTED VEGETABLE LASAGNE

Make it Vegan

This is a recipe I always turn to when I have a crowd to feed. It's hugely popular with everyone, kids adore it, and the beauty of it is that it can all be made in advance before anyone arrives, so you're free to enjoy yourself once they're there. All you need to do is remember to turn the oven on! *Peta*

SERVES 6

1 aubergine, diced

2 red onions, roughly diced

3 red peppers, deseeded and roughly diced

280g baby plum or cherry tomatoes, chopped

2 tbsp vegetable oil plus extra for coating

salt and black pepper

1 garlic bulb

1 large courgette, cut into bite-sized pieces

1 tbsp tomato purée

a good bunch of basil, leaves roughly torn, plus extra to top

450ml cold whole milk

20g unsalted butter

20g plain flour

a pinch of English mustard powder

100g mature Cheddar cheese, grated

60g vegetarian Parmesan-style cheese, grated

200g dried lasagne sheets

1. Heat the oven to 200°C/fan 180°C/gas mark 6.

2. In a large roasting tray, toss the aubergine, red onions, red peppers and tomatoes with the 2 tablespoons of vegetable oil, and season with salt and black pepper. Cut the top off the garlic bulb in order to expose each clove at the top, then wrap it in foil and add it to the roasting tray.

3. Roast the vegetables in the oven for 35 minutes, then add the courgette and stir through the tomato purée. Return to the oven for 25 minutes, then remove from the oven and stir in the torn basil leaves.

4. When cool enough to handle, remove the garlic from the foil and squeeze the now-soft garlic flesh out of it, then stir it into the other vegetables.

5. While the vegetables are roasting, make the cheese sauce. Combine the milk, butter, flour and mustard powder in a saucepan, set it over a medium heat and whisk frequently until the butter has melted and the flour is all incorporated. Bring the mixture to the boil and cook, whisking regularly, until the sauce has thickened enough to coat the back of a spoon.

6. Remove the sauce from the heat, then whisk in the grated Cheddar and half the grated vegetarian Parmesan-style cheese. Taste, then season with salt and black pepper.

RICOTTA CAVATELLI WITH AUBERGINE AND TOMATO SAUCE

Make it Vegan

Cavatelli, from southern Italy, are formed by hollowing out short lengths of dough using your fingertips. This type is made with ricotta, which makes it a bit softer, almost like a cross between gnocchi and pasta. It has a pleasing bite to it, but it's tender at the same time. The shaping does seem fiddly at first, but once you get the hang of it you can make them quite quickly. *Peta*

SERVES 4

300g ricotta

210g plain flour plus extra for dusting

a pinch of salt

grated vegetarian Parmesan-style cheese to serve

FOR THE AUBERGINE AND TOMATO SAUCE

2–3 tbsp vegetable oil

1 small aubergine, diced

3 garlic cloves, finely chopped

1 tsp tomato purée

1 x 400g tin chopped tomatoes

10g unsalted butter

a small handful of basil leaves, torn

salt and black pepper to season

1. To make the sauce, heat the oil in a saucepan over a medium-high heat, then add the aubergine and garlic and cook, stirring frequently, until the aubergine is starting to soften and brown. Add the tomato purée, tinned tomatoes, the butter and 60ml hot water, then bring to the boil. Reduce the heat and simmer for a further 20 minutes. Season with salt and black pepper and stir in the basil, then remove from the heat.

2. Combine the ricotta, flour and salt in a mixing bowl and mix it to form a dough. Knead it for a few minutes, until it is smooth and elastic.

3. Take a small piece of dough and roll it into a rope, approximately 1cm (½in) in diameter. Cut the rope into 1cm (½in) lengths, then push two fingers into each piece of dough and drag it towards you across the work surface, so that it sticks on the surface a little and curls up around your fingertips. Do not be afraid to dust the dough with flour if it sticks. Put the cavatelli onto a flour-dusted tray and continue to shape cavatelli using the rest of the dough, leaving space between each one.

4. Bring a large pan of salted water to the boil, then add the cavatelli and stir with a slotted spoon. Return the water to the boil, and when the cavatelli float to the surface, they are done. Be careful not to overcook them.

5. Put the warm sauce into a serving bowl, then, using a slotted spoon, lift the cavatelli out of the water and add them into the bowl. A little of the cooking water will cling to them, but this is fine. Toss with the sauce, then serve immediately, with grated vegetarian Parmesan-style cheese on the side.

Tip

A dried pasta like rigatoni is a delicious vegan option. Omit the cheese.

FREGOLA 'RISOTTO'

Make it Vegan

Fregola is a Sardinian pasta, which is very similar to giant couscous. It's becoming more widely available in supermarkets and you can buy it online. It's delicious when cooked in the style of a risotto as it absorbs the flavour of the stock and tomatoes, while retaining its lovely nutty texture. *Peta*

SERVES 4

2 tbsp vegetable oil

1 onion, diced

2 garlic cloves, finely chopped

2 tsp tomato purée

220g baby plum tomatoes or cherry tomatoes

120g fregola

60ml dry white wine

1 litre hot vegetable stock

30g unsalted butter

60g vegetarian Parmesan-style cheese, grated, plus extra to serve

a good bunch of basil, leaves finely chopped

salt and black pepper to season

basil leaves to garnish

1. Heat the vegetable oil in a large frying pan over a medium heat, add the onion and garlic and cook for 3–4 minutes until softened. Add the tomato purée and tomatoes and cook, stirring frequently, for 10–12 minutes until the tomatoes have broken down.

2. Add the fregola to the pan, cook over a medium heat for a minute or two, then add the wine and let it boil for a minute.

3. The stock should be added in stages: begin by adding a ladleful and stirring frequently, cook until the stock has been absorbed, then add the next ladleful of stock. Continue in this way until the fregola is just cooked (it should taste cooked but still have a bit of bite). You may not have used up all of the stock, depending on what fregola you are using, or you may need to add a touch more stock (or water, if you've used up your stock).

4. Turn off the heat once the fregola is cooked, stir in the butter and vegetarian Parmesan-style cheese, then season with salt and black pepper and add the basil. Serve immediately, with extra grated Parmesan-style cheese and basil leaves on top.

Tips

The size and shape of fregola available in the UK varies. If you can't find it, feel free to substitute giant couscous, which is available in most supermarkets. Both will work, but you will need to keep a close eye on the cooking time and add the stock very gradually towards the end.

To make it vegan, you could omit the butter and cheese, and in their place stir in a drizzle of olive oil, and nutritional yeast flakes to taste.

LINGUINE WITH PORCINI, CRÈME FRAÎCHE AND TRUFFLE OIL

This is a quick dish that's exciting to make in the all-too-short autumn porcini season, but because fresh porcini are available so briefly and are expensive, we have used dried ones so that you can cook it all year round. *Prue*

SERVES 4

100ml whole milk

10g dried porcini mushrooms

150g crème fraîche

400g dried linguine

2 tbsp vegetable oil

2 banana shallots, finely diced

2 garlic cloves, finely chopped

280g button mushrooms, roughly diced

a small handful of flat-leaf parsley, finely chopped

good-quality truffle oil for drizzling

vegetarian Parmesan-style cheese for grating

salt and black pepper to season

1. Bring the milk to the boil in a small saucepan, then remove from the heat, add the dried porcini and leave them to soak for 30 minutes. Using a stick blender or liquidizer, blend the milk and porcini until you have a smooth paste. Mix in the crème fraîche and set it aside.

2. Bring a large pan of salted water to the boil and add the linguine to it, stirring frequently to stop it from sticking. Cook for 10 minutes or until al dente according to packet instructions.

3. Meanwhile, heat the vegetable oil in a large sauté pan over a medium heat, add the shallots, garlic and mushrooms and fry for about 5 minutes until softened.

4. Take 4 tablespoons of the water that the pasta is cooking in and add it to the mushrooms, then add the crème fraîche and porcini mixture. Continue to heat and stir the mushroom sauce until it has started to simmer and looks well combined.

5. Remove the pan from the heat and add the parsley then taste and season the sauce: it may not need much salt as the pasta water is salted, but a good few twists of the peppermill will be good.

6. Drain the pasta when it is al dente, then add it to the sauce in the sauté pan with a generous drizzle of truffle oil and gently turn it all together.

7. Serve immediately, topped with grated Parmesan-style cheese.

Tip

Any flavourful mushroom works well in this dish. If I see fresh chanterelle, morels or shiitake, I'll grab them. They all have different and delicious flavours.

hearty and homely

RED DRAGON PIE

Make it Vegan

Red dragon pie is something my mother always made when I was a child — it was like a vegetarian version of shepherd's pie, really comforting when we came home from school. When I worked at the Ivy we put it onto the vegetarian menu, topped with goat's cheese mash (as here), which proved really popular. Red adzuki beans can be hard to find, but the larger supermarkets usually have them and you can buy them online. Serve with lightly cooked buttered vegetables, or a salad. *Peta*

SERVES 4

200g dried red adzuki beans, soaked overnight in cold water, then drained

1 sprig of thyme

1 bay leaf

2 tbsp vegetable oil

1 brown onion, diced

1 carrot, diced

2 celery sticks, diced

a pinch of dried chilli flakes

1 large red pepper, deseeded and diced

3 garlic cloves, finely chopped

1 tbsp tomato purée

1 tbsp dark soy sauce

a good bunch of flat-leaf parsley, chopped

650g potatoes (Maris Piper or King Edwards), peeled and cut into chunks

25g unsalted butter

80g soft goat's cheese

salt and black pepper to season

1. Put the beans in a large saucepan and cover with cold water. Add the thyme and bay leaf, bring to the boil, then reduce the heat and simmer for about 1 hour, or until the beans are tender. Drain, reserving the cooking liquid. Discard the bay leaf and thyme stalk.

2. Heat the oil in a large pan, add the onion, carrot, celery and chilli flakes and sauté until the onions have started to soften, then add the pepper and garlic, and continue to cook for 8–10 minutes until everything is softened.

3. Measure out 300ml of the bean cooking liquid (you can discard the rest) and add the tomato purée and soy sauce to that. Add the cooked beans to the pan with the vegetables, then pour over the bean liquid. Bring to the boil, then reduce the heat and simmer for 30 minutes, until reduced a little, and thickened. Season well with salt and black pepper, then add the chopped parsley. Transfer the mixture to an ovenproof dish (about 30 x 20cm/12 x 8in and 10cm/4in deep).

4. Heat the oven to 200°C/fan 180°C/gas mark 6. Put the potatoes in a large pan, cover with water, add ½ teaspoon of salt and bring to the boil. Reduce the heat and simmer until tender, then drain and mash them with the butter and goat's cheese. Season with salt and black pepper, then spread it evenly over the top of the bean mixture.

5. Bake in the oven for 40 minutes, by which point the top should be starting to brown and the centre should be piping hot. Remove from the oven and serve.

 Tip

To make this vegan, simply mash the potatoes with good-quality olive oil instead of the butter and goat's cheese.

CREAMY POLENTA WITH SWEETCORN, FETA AND CAPONATA

Make it Vegan

For me, this dish ticks all the boxes – the polenta provides a creamy sweetness, which is punctuated by the salty capers, olives and feta. It's warming, nutritious, and packed with flavour. Capers are an acquired taste (one that I have only recently learned to appreciate!) so do feel free to omit them if you don't like them. *Peta*

Polenta aficionados will tell you it is a crime to use instant or 'quick-cook' polenta, but I don't agree. Maybe polenta stirred lovingly for 45 minutes, or (as I observed in a Tuscan courtyard during a festival) all morning, can be perfection, but if a factory will pre-cook the cornmeal (polenta is just cornmeal until it's in the pot, just as mash is simply potato in its uncooked state) I'm grateful. For me, the trick with polenta is to season it well: with salt, obviously, but olive oil, cream, cheese and butter also all work wonders. The best polenta should still taste delicately of corn, just as the best mash, however much garlic, mustard or what-have-you you add to it, should still taste of potato. *Prue*

SERVES 4

FOR THE CAPONATA

2 tbsp olive oil

1 aubergine, cut into large dice

1 red onion, diced

2 garlic cloves, finely chopped

3 celery sticks, diced

2 sprigs of oregano, leaves picked

1 tbsp tomato paste or purée

6 large tomatoes, roughly chopped

1 tbsp capers, rinsed

10 green olives, pitted and halved

a small bunch of flat-leaf parsley, finely chopped

salt and black pepper to season

FOR THE SWEETCORN

splash of vegetable oil

100g tinned sweetcorn, drained, or frozen sweetcorn, thawed

FOR THE POLENTA

300ml whole milk

125g quick-cook polenta

10g vegetarian Parmesan-style cheese, grated

2 tbsp olive oil

100g feta, crumbled

1. To make the pastry, put the butter, flour and salt in a large mixing bowl and rub the butter into the flour lightly using your fingertips. Stop when there are still pea-sized pieces of butter visible (do not rub it all the way to breadcrumb consistency).

2. Add the water and use a butter knife to mix it to a shaggy dough. Handling it as little as possible, just push it together into a disc and wrap it in cling film. Chill it in the fridge for at least 1 hour, until firm.

3. Meanwhile, make the filling. Heat the oven to 200°C/fan 180°C/gas mark 6. Combine the peppers, aubergine, onions, garlic and vegetable oil in a roasting tin, and season with salt and black pepper. Roast in the middle of the oven for 40 minutes, then add the tomatoes and courgette, stir everything around, and roast for a further 20 minutes. Remove from the oven, stir in the chopped parsley, and set it aside.

4. Grease a deep 20cm (8in) loose-bottomed flan tin with butter. Unwrap the pastry and roll it out on a floured surface into a round, about 2–3mm thick. Line the greased flan tin with it, ensuring there are no holes and that it is the same thickness all over. Leave extra overhanging the sides and return it to the fridge to chill for 30 minutes. After 30 minutes, neatly trim away the edges of the pastry.

5. Line the pastry shell with baking parchment and fill it right to the top with baking beans or dry rice, then blind-bake it in the oven for 25–30 minutes until light golden and cooked through. Remove it from the oven, remove the baking parchment and beans or rice and return to the oven for 2–3 minutes to crisp up the base.

6. To make the custard, whisk the flour and the eggs together until smooth, then add the cream and milk and pass through a fine sieve. Season with salt and black pepper.

7. Fill the cooked pastry case with the roasted vegetables, then pour over the custard. Return it to the oven and bake it for 30–40 minutes, until the custard is completely set and the top is golden. Remove from the oven and allow it to cool in the tin for 15 minutes before turning it out onto a serving plate. Serve immediately.

Tip

This is delicious hot or cold, but if you want to reheat it, do it in a warm oven – a microwave will make the pastry soggy.

PANEER CURRY

For years I had been reluctant to try paneer, as descriptions often liken it to cottage cheese, which immediately puts me off. However, that description is so wildly inaccurate – it's far more like a halloumi, and since discovering it, I cook with it all the time. The curry below is one of my favourite ways to use it. *Peta*

SERVES 4

4 tbsp vegetable oil

1 onion, diced

2 garlic cloves, finely chopped

1 mild red chilli, finely chopped (with seeds)

2.5cm (1in) piece of ginger, peeled and finely chopped

1 tbsp tomato purée

1 tsp ground cumin

1 tsp garam masala

1 tsp hot curry powder

1 x 400g tin chopped tomatoes

100ml double cream

salt and black pepper to season

100g baby leaf spinach

250g paneer, cut into bite-sized cubes

100g frozen petits pois

a pinch of caster sugar

squeeze of lemon juice

rice and/or naan bread to serve

1. Heat 2 tablespoons of the vegetable oil in a large saucepan over a medium heat, then add the onion, garlic, chilli and ginger and sauté for 3–4 minutes until the onion is soft and translucent, then add the tomato purée, cumin, garam masala and curry powder. Cook for 30 seconds, then add the tinned tomatoes and the double cream.

2. Season well with salt and black pepper, bring the mixture to the boil, then reduce the heat and simmer for 10 minutes. Rinse the spinach leaves.

3. Meanwhile, heat the remaining vegetable oil in a frying pan over a medium–high heat. Add the paneer and fry it, turning it frequently, until golden brown and crisp all over. Add the paneer to the curry.

4. Return the curry to the boil, then reduce the heat and simmer for a further 10–15 minutes. Add the frozen petits pois and spinach, return to the boil, and simmer for just a few minutes until the peas are cooked and the spinach has wilted.

5. Add the sugar and a small squeeze of lemon juice, check the seasoning, and serve with rice or naan bread.

BLACK BEAN CHILLI
WITH CORN AND LIME SALSA

This is a really hearty, warming chilli, perfect for a cold night. As a vegetarian, I usually stir a handful of grated Cheddar cheese and a dollop of yoghurt or sour cream into my bowl of chilli, but the fresh, zingy corn salsa here is so delicious, it makes that entirely unnecessary. I always think it's a very good sign of a vegan dish when a non-vegan wouldn't want to add anything. This is definitely one of those dishes. *Peta*

SERVES 4–6

1 onion

3 garlic cloves

1–2 green chillies

2 tbsp olive oil plus 2 tsp

1 red pepper, deseeded and finely chopped

1 carrot, peeled and diced

2 celery sticks, finely diced

1 tsp chipotle paste

1 tsp smoked paprika

1 tsp ground cumin

2 tsp tomato purée

2 x 400g tins black beans

1 x 400g tin chopped tomatoes

500ml vegetable stock

salt and black pepper to season

100g drained tinned sweetcorn

juice of ½ lime

½ red chilli, deseeded and finely chopped

a small handful of coriander, finely chopped

1. Finely chop the onion, garlic cloves and green chillies.

2. Heat 2 tablespoons of oil in a large saucepan over a medium heat, add the onion, garlic and green chillies and sauté for 3–4 minutes until the onion is soft and translucent, then add the red pepper, carrot and celery. Sweat for a few minutes more, then add the chipotle paste, smoked paprika, cumin and tomato purée.

3. Stir to coat the vegetables evenly, then add the drained black beans, tinned tomatoes and vegetable stock. Season with salt and black pepper, bring to the boil, then reduce the heat and simmer for 30 minutes, stirring occasionally.

4. Remove from the heat and season to taste.

5. To make the salsa, mix together the sweetcorn with the lime juice, red chilli and coriander. Stir through 2 teaspoons olive oil. Serve the chilli piping hot, with the salsa on top.

PESTO AND GOAT'S CHEESE BREAD PUDDING

One doesn't often see savoury bread puddings, and you may be hesitant to try one, but please do. It's really flavoursome thanks to the quantity of cheese and the mix of fresh herbs in it, rich and warming, and it's a great way to use up bread that is past its best. Baguette is ideal. *Prue*

SERVES 4

2 large plum tomatoes, roughly chopped

4 garlic cloves, roughly chopped

1 onion, roughly chopped

3 tbsp vegetable oil

3 large eggs

180ml double cream

100ml whole milk

1 tsp finely chopped mint leaves

1 tsp finely chopped flat-leaf parsley

1 tsp finely chopped chives

250g bread, thickly sliced

3–4 tbsp shop-bought basil pesto

100g goat's cheese, roughly chopped

unsalted butter for greasing

salt and black pepper to season

1. Heat the oven to 200°C/fan 180°C/gas mark 6.

2. Put the tomatoes, garlic and onion in a roasting tin. Pour over the vegetable oil, then season with salt and black pepper and toss it all together so that the oil coats everything evenly. Roast in the middle of the oven for 30–40 minutes, until soft and jam-like, then remove the roasting tin and set aside, but keep the oven on.

3. In a large jug, whisk the eggs with the cream and milk, then add the chopped herbs and season with salt and black pepper.

4. Grease a 20cm (8in) ovenproof dish with butter. Spread each slice of bread generously with pesto. Layer the slices in the dish, distributing the roasted vegetables and cheese evenly between them.

5. Pour the egg and cream mixture all over the dish. It will seem like a lot, but don't worry, the bread will absorb a great deal of it. Bake it in the middle of the oven for 25 minutes, by which point it should have puffed up and turned golden brown and the custard should be set. Remove the dish from the oven and allow to cool slightly before serving.

 Tip

This is delicious served alongside a green salad with a sharp vinaigrette, to cut through the richness of the cheese and pesto.

CHICKPEA AND CAULIFLOWER TAGINE

This is a really great mid-week supper, as it's very quick to make, filling and nutritious. The leftovers will keep very well, and I find that kids love it, so what I tend to do is freeze any leftovers in small portions for my daughter, which is so useful to be able to pull out of the freezer and defrost when we're in a hurry, or if I need to pack her a last-minute lunch for nursery. *Peta*

SERVES 6

a handful of flaked almonds

2 tbsp vegetable oil

1 onion, diced

1 carrot, peeled and diced

3 garlic cloves, finely chopped

1 red pepper, deseeded and diced

2 tsp harissa paste

¼ tsp ground cinnamon

1½ tsp ground cumin

1½ tsp ground coriander

1 small cauliflower, cut into bite-sized pieces

1 x 400g tin chopped tomatoes

500ml vegetable stock

1 x 400g tin chickpeas, drained

½ tsp agave syrup

6 dried apricots, chopped

salt and black pepper to season

a handful of coriander, finely chopped, to serve

1. Heat the oven to 180ºC/fan 160ºC/gas mark 4.

2. Spread the flaked almonds over a baking sheet and toast in the oven for 3–4 minutes until golden brown. Remove from the oven and set aside to cool.

3. Heat the vegetable oil in a large saucepan over a medium heat. Add the onion, carrot, garlic and red pepper and sauté for 3–4 minutes until the onion is soft and turning translucent, then add the harissa, cinnamon, cumin and ground coriander. Mix well.

4. Add the cauliflower, followed by the tinned tomatoes, vegetable stock, chickpeas, agave syrup and apricots. Season with salt and black pepper, then stir to combine everything.

5. Bring the mixture to the boil, then reduce the heat and simmer, stirring occasionally, for 20 minutes, or until the cauliflower is tender. Remove from the heat and check the seasoning.

6. Serve the tagine piping hot, with couscous, and the chopped coriander and toasted almonds scattered over the top.

MINI SPINACH, RICOTTA AND EGG PIES

This is a fantastic pastry as it's beautifully tender and requires no blind baking. The pies are equally delicious served hot, straight from the oven, or cold the next day, which makes them ideal for picnics. *Peta*

MAKES 4 INDIVIDUAL PIES

225g plain flour, plus extra for dusting

a pinch of salt

115g cold unsalted butter, cut into cubes, plus soft butter for greasing the flan cases

200g crème fraîche

FOR THE FILLING

500g spinach, washed

200g ricotta

40g vegetarian Parmesan-style cheese, grated

a pinch of grated nutmeg

4 large eggs, soft boiled

salt and black pepper to season

1. To make the pastry, put the flour, salt and butter in a mixing bowl and, using your fingertips, rub the butter into the flour until it resembles breadcrumbs. Add the crème fraîche, then bring it together with a butter knife to form a dough, trying not to work it more than necessary. Wrap it in cling film and chill in the fridge for at least 1 hour, until it is firm.

2. Place the washed spinach leaves in a large pan, cover and place over a medium heat for a few minutes, shaking the pan occasionally, until wilted. Drain, squeezing the excess water out of the spinach, then chop it roughly.

3. Combine the chopped spinach in a bowl with the ricotta, vegetarian Parmesan-style cheese, nutmeg and some salt and black pepper. Cover and chill in the fridge while you roll out the pastry.

4. Heat the oven to 200°C/fan 180°C/gas mark 6. Grease four 10cm (4in) loose-bottomed mini flan cases.

5. Take two thirds of the pastry and roll it out on a floured surface to a thickness of 2–3mm, then cut out four 15cm (6in) rounds and use them to line each of the flan cases. Return the cases to the fridge for 10 minutes, to firm up before filling.

6. Divide the filling between the cases, placing a peeled soft-boiled egg in the centre of each. Roll out the remaining pastry and use it to make lids for the pies. Place the lids over the filling, then press all around the edges in order to seal the filling inside. Trim away the excess pastry with a sharp knife, then pierce the lid in order to create a steam vent.

7. Bake the pies on the middle shelf in the oven for 25–30 minutes, until the pastry is a deep golden colour. Remove from the oven and allow to cool in the tins for 10 minutes, before removing the tins and serving.

MUSHROOM AND HAZELNUT PITHIVIER

Make it Vegan

The one thing I've learnt from having vegetarians in the family is that, if the meal is a help-yourself buffet, it's better to make the same vegetarian meal for everyone rather than do a separate dish for the veggies. The carnivores will always help themselves to the vegetarian option and if the veggies are not quick off the mark they end up going hungry. This pithivier goes well with a selection of green veg and/or roast potatoes and looks festive enough for a celebration. For a summer lunch you could serve it with a couple of salads. *Prue*

SERVES 4

7g dried porcini mushrooms

30g hazelnuts

2 tbsp vegetable oil

2 garlic cloves, finely chopped

180g chestnut mushrooms, roughly chopped

2 tsp light soy sauce

15g breadcrumbs

2 banana shallots, finely chopped

a good bunch of flat-leaf parsley, leaves picked and finely chopped

300g all-butter puff pastry

1 large egg, beaten with a splash of milk

salt and black pepper to season

1. Heat the oven to 200°C/fan 180°C/gas mark 6. Line a baking sheet with baking parchment.

2. Pour 100ml boiling water over the dried porcini in a heatproof bowl and set aside to soak.

3. Spread the hazelnuts over the baking sheet and toast them in the oven for 2–3 minutes, or until beginning to brown. Check them often as they burn very quickly. Remove from the oven and leave to cool completely.

4. Turn the oven up to 210°C/fan 190°C/gas mark 6–7.

5. Heat 1 tablespoon of the vegetable oil in a large frying pan over a medium heat, add the garlic and half the chestnut mushrooms and fry until completely softened. Add the soy sauce and cook for a further minute, until the soy sauce has almost evaporated.

6. Put the cooled hazelnuts in a food processor and blitz to a coarse powder. Add the contents of the pan, the breadcrumbs and the porcini mushrooms with the water they soaked in and blitz everything until smooth. The mixture should be soft, but just about hold its shape. Add a few more breadcrumbs if it is too wet.

7. Add the remaining vegetable oil to the pan over a medium heat. Add the shallots and the remaining chestnut mushrooms and sauté until the shallots are really soft and translucent. Season with salt and black pepper, then remove from the heat and stir in the chopped parsley. Add to the porcini mix and stir it in by hand.

SLOW-ROASTED TOMATO AND GOAT'S CURD GALETTE

I can't get enough of slow-roasting tomatoes: tossed with garlic, olive oil, salt and black pepper, even the most average tomato becomes sweet and intensely flavoured.

Here, tomatoes are partnered with buttery, crunchy pastry and fresh, tangy goat's curd – it's delicious. If you can't find goat's curd, a soft goat's cheese would work just as well, as indeed, would any soft creamy one, including a blue. *Prue*

SERVES 4

400g cherry tomatoes or baby plum tomatoes

3 garlic cloves, finely chopped

4 sprigs of oregano, leaves picked

3 tbsp olive oil

250g goat's curd, or very soft goat's cheese

salt and black pepper to season

FOR THE PASTRY

140g cold unsalted butter, cut into cubes

225g plain flour, plus extra for dusting

a pinch of salt

90–100ml iced water

1. Heat the oven to 160°C/fan 140°C/gas mark 3. Line a baking tray with baking parchment.

2. Cut the tomatoes in half and toss them in a bowl with the chopped garlic, oregano leaves and olive oil, and season with salt and black pepper. Spread them out on the lined baking tray and arrange them all so they are cut side up.

3. Bake in the middle of the oven for 2 hours, by which point they should be softened and slightly shrunken. Remove from the oven and set aside.

4. Meanwhile, make the pastry. Put the butter, flour and salt in a large mixing bowl and rub the butter into the flour lightly using your fingertips. Stop when there are still pea-sized pieces of butter visible. Add the water and use a butter knife to mix it to a very shaggy dough – do not knead it at all. Simply push it together into a disc, and wrap it in cling film. Put it in the fridge to chill for 1 hour, or until firm.

5. Increase the oven temperature to 210°C/fan 190°C/gas mark 6–7. Line another baking sheet with baking parchment.

6. Unwrap the pastry and roll it out on a floured surface into a round, about 2–3mm thick. Spread the goat's curd evenly over the pastry, leaving a border of 5cm (2in) all around it. Arrange the tomatoes, cut side up, on the goat's curd, packed in tightly next to each other, so the goat's curd is all covered. Lift up the pastry around the edges and fold it over the top, to create a crust that will hold the tomatoes in place.

7. Season with salt and black pepper, then bake the galette in the middle of the oven for 35–40 minutes, covering it with foil after 20 minutes to prevent it over-browning. Serve while crisp and warm.

light and refreshing

PEA, MINT AND GOAT'S CHEESE FRITTERS

I used to think only of sweetcorn when I thought of fritters, but over the past year, I've realized how adaptable they are, and what a great vehicle they are for getting vegetables into picky toddlers! These ones are popular with kids and adults alike, and they make a great vegetarian main course, served with mashed potatoes and hot veg, or just with a selection of salads. *Peta*

SERVES 2 OR 4 AS A STARTER

150g frozen petits pois

1 large egg

50g self-raising flour

40ml whole milk

2 tbsp finely chopped fresh mint

50g goat's cheese log, crumbled

vegetable oil for frying

salt and black pepper to season

1. Bring a small pan of salted water to the boil and add the petits pois. Wait for the water to return to the boil, then drain the peas and set aside.

2. In a mixing bowl, whisk the egg with the flour, then add the milk and whisk to form a smooth batter. Add the cooled peas, chopped mint, goat's cheese and some salt and black pepper, then stir to combine everything.

3. Heat a generous glug of vegetable oil in a large non-stick frying pan over a medium–high heat.

4. When the oil is hot, use a serving spoon to carefully add spoonfuls of the batter into the pan. Use the back of the spoon or a spatula to lightly press down and flatten the dollop of batter once it is in the pan. Leave a decent space between each fritter as they will spread a little when they cook – you may need to cook them in batches.

5. Cook each fritter for 2–3 minutes on each side, until both sides are golden and cooked through. (If you are unsure, press a butter knife into one of them and check that no wet batter comes out.)

6. Transfer the cooked fritters to a plate lined with a piece of kitchen paper, in order to soak up any excess oil. Serve at once.

Tip

The cooked and cooled fritters freeze excellently and defrost very quickly. To serve after defrosting, simply wrap them in foil and put them in a hot oven for 10 minutes, to warm them through.

SHAKSHUKA WITH BAKED EGGS

Both my husbands have adored aubergine, so it has featured heavily in my repertoire for years. But this now-very-fashionable Turkish dish is probably my favourite. It doesn't always have eggs baked in it – take them out if you want this to be vegan – but it's delicious this way, and makes a great brunch item. *Prue*

SERVES 4

4 tbsp vegetable oil

1 large aubergine, cut into bite-sized pieces

4 plum tomatoes, deseeded and diced

2 red peppers, deseeded and diced

6 garlic cloves, crushed

2 tbsp tomato purée

a good bunch of flat-leaf parsley, finely chopped

4 large eggs

salt and black pepper to season

TO SERVE

crusty bread

green salad

1. Heat the oven to 220°C/fan 200°C/gas mark 7.

2. Heat the oil in a large pan over a high heat, add the aubergine and cook, stirring frequently, until the aubergine is soft. Add the tomatoes, peppers, garlic and tomato purée, then cook for around 12–15 minutes until the tomatoes have broken down and the peppers are soft. Depending on how juicy your tomatoes are, you may have to add a splash of hot water if it looks dry – it should be very moist.

3. Remove it from the heat and stir in the chopped parsley. Transfer to an ovenproof shallow dish, spread the shakshuka mix out evenly, then, using the back of a spoon, make four indents in it.

4. Crack an egg into each of the hollows, add a good twist of black pepper over it all, and bake in the oven for about 10–15 minutes, until the egg whites are cooked through.

5. Remove from the oven and serve immediately with crusty bread and a green salad.

Tip

You could make this vegan by serving up at after stirring in the parsley in step 3 instead of breaking in the eggs.

CRUSTLESS QUICHE WITH SWEETCORN, LEEK AND WENSLEYDALE

This is a great dish for weeknight meals when you haven't time to make pastry. The flavours in this just taste like summer to me, and the citrusy tang of the Wensleydale cheese works brilliantly with the sweetness of the corn. *Peta*

SERVES 4

10g butter for greasing

30g dry breadcrumbs

FOR THE FILLING

20g unsalted butter

a splash of vegetable oil

2 large leeks, trimmed, washed and finely chopped

1 tsp fresh thyme leaves

165g sweetcorn (frozen or tinned)

80g Wensleydale cheese, grated

1½ tbsp plain flour

2 large eggs

125ml double cream

90ml whole milk

salt and black pepper to season

1. Heat the oven to 200°C/fan 180°C/gas mark 6.

2. Smear the butter all over the inside of a 20cm (8in) ovenproof frying pan (or ovenproof dish), then scatter the breadcrumbs over the butter, turning the pan in order to get a good coating of breadcrumbs stuck all over.

3. Melt the butter with a splash of vegetable oil in a saucepan or large frying pan over a medium heat, add the chopped leeks and thyme leaves and cook until the leeks are softened. Add the sweetcorn, cook for a few minutes further, then remove from the heat. Stir in the Wensleydale, then taste and season with salt and black pepper.

4. To make the custard, whisk the flour and the eggs together until smooth, then add the cream and milk and pass through a fine sieve. Season with salt and black pepper.

5. Once the oven is hot, fill the ovenproof pan or dish with the leek and sweetcorn mixture, spreading it evenly. Gently pour the custard on top of the mixture. Bake in the oven for 25–30 minutes, until puffed up, golden and set. Stick a knife into it to check no liquid custard runs out. Remove it from the oven, and allow it to cool for 20–30 minutes before serving.

SLIGHTLY ASIAN RICE SALAD

This is a really light and zingy salad, packed full of fresh, vibrant flavours. Candying the cashew nuts does require a bit of extra work, but it's very quick to do and they're delicious. They make great nibbles to enjoy with a pre-dinner drink, too. If you don't have time to make them, substitute a handful of roasted salted peanuts. (Image on pages 120–21.) *Peta*

SERVES 2 OR 4 AS A MAIN

1 tbsp caster sugar

a pinch of dried chilli flakes

1 tsp rice wine vinegar

50g cashew nuts, roasted

100g brown rice (dry weight)

1 tsp peeled and finely chopped ginger

1 tsp finely chopped red chilli

juice of ½ lime, plus wedges

1 tsp sesame oil

2 tsp mirin

1 tsp dark soy sauce

1 tsp agave nectar

25g sugar snap peas, thinly sliced at an angle

40g carrot, cut into julienne

25g cucumber, cored and cut into julienne

2 large pak choi leaves, sliced

1 spring onion, trimmed and thinly sliced

a handful of coriander

salt

1. Oil a plate which you will need later for the candied nuts.

2. To make the candied cashews, put the sugar, a pinch of salt, the chilli flakes and vinegar in a small heavy-based saucepan and add enough water to wet the sugar. Heat the sugar gently until it dissolves and turns into a syrup, then swirl over the heat until it starts to colour. Now tip in the nuts and stir briskly as the sugar coats them. Stir over the heat until the pan seems dry and the sugar is toffee coloured, then tip the nuts onto the oiled plate or silicone sheet. As they cool you will be able to use your hands to separate them. Do this before the caramel sets into a solid block.

3. Simmer the rice in a pan of plenty of salted boiling water for 20–25 minutes or until it is just al dente. Drain, and cool it immediately by running cold water over it in a sieve.

4. In a jug, make the dressing by whisking together the ginger, chilli, lime juice, sesame oil, mirin, soy sauce and agave.

5. In a mixing bowl, combine the rice with the sugar snaps, carrot, cucumber, pak choi and spring onion. Finely chop the coriander (leaving a few leaves whole to garnish the salad with, if you like) and add to the bowl. Pour the dressing over the salad and mix to combine.

6. Garnish with a handful of the candied cashews and coriander. You should have more nuts than you need, but if you are anything like me you'll probably have already eaten half of them! Serve with the lime wedges.

 Tip

To roast the cashews, bake them on a tray in an oven (heated to 180°C/fan 160°C/gas 4) for 4–5 minutes, shaking them every so often until golden.

SLOW-ROASTED TOMATO, CHICKPEA, HALLOUMI AND FRENCH BEAN SALAD

This is one of my favourite salads of recent years. I made it as part of a big spread for my daughter's first birthday party last year, and this salad (along with the cheese straws on page 162) vanished in the blink of an eye, with everyone asking for the recipe! *Peta*

SERVES 4

250g baby plum tomatoes or cherry tomatoes

1 garlic clove, finely chopped

1 tbsp olive oil

120g French beans, topped and tailed

a splash of vegetable oil

250g halloumi, cut into cubes

1 x 400g tin chickpeas, drained and well rinsed

4 tbsp extra virgin olive oil

1 tbsp pomegranate molasses

salt and black pepper to season

1. Heat the oven to 160°C/fan 140°C/gas mark 3. Line a baking tray with baking parchment.

2. Cut the tomatoes in half and place them cut side up on the lined baking tray. Scatter the chopped garlic over them, season with salt and black pepper, and drizzle with the olive oil. Bake in the oven for 2 hours, until softened and jammy.

3. Cook the French beans in a large pan of salted water for 4–5 minutes until just tender. Drain and allow to cool.

4. Heat a splash of vegetable oil in a frying pan over a medium–high heat, add the halloumi cubes and fry, turning them frequently, until they are golden brown all over.

5. In a serving bowl, combine the chickpeas with the beans, fried halloumi and roasted tomatoes. Pour over the olive oil and pomegranate molasses, then season with salt and black pepper and toss well. Serve immediately.

PUY LENTIL AND SWEET POTATO SALAD

This salad is really simple, but the flavours all marry together perfectly, and the Puy lentils offer a lovely, nutty texture. If you can't find Puy lentils, green or brown lentils cooked very al dente would be a good substitute, but it really is worth finding Puy if you can. *Peta*

SERVES 4

350–400g sweet potato, peeled and cut into 2–2.5cm (¾–1in) pieces

1½ tbsp vegetable oil

150g Puy lentils

FOR THE DRESSING

3 spring onions, trimmed, and pale green and white part thinly sliced

1 tbsp clear honey

4 tbsp extra virgin olive oil

2½ tbsp white wine vinegar

a small bunch of chives, finely chopped

salt and black pepper

1. Heat the oven to 200°C/fan 180°C/gas mark 6.

2. Make the dressing by whisking all the ingredients together and seasoning to taste with salt and black pepper.

3. Put the sweet potato pieces in a roasting tin with the oil and season with salt and black pepper. Turn to coat them evenly, then roast in the oven for 35–40 minutes, until they are tender and a little charred at the edges.

4. Meanwhile, put the lentils in a saucepan, cover with cold water, bring to the boil, then reduce the heat and simmer for 20–25 minutes until just cooked but still al dente. Drain.

5. Combine the lentils and sweet potatoes in a bowl and toss in the dressing. Serve at room temperature.

Tips

The dish keeps very well in the fridge for a couple of days; just allow it to come back to room temperature before serving.

The dressing will keep for 3 days in the fridge and is delicious on a green salad, or with tomatoes, so it's worth making extra for other meals.

To make it vegan, substitute the honey for half the amount of agave nectar.

QUICK-PICKLED SUMMER VEGETABLE SALAD

Pickles are often thought of as vinegary, but this very fashionable, modern method means the vegetables are pickled so briefly that they retain all their crunch and vibrancy, picking up a mild little zing from the pickling liquor. It's good as a starter with a little crumbled feta or goat's cheese on top. *Prue*

SERVES 4 AS SIDE OR STARTER

55ml vegan white wine vinegar

1 tsp caster sugar

¼ tsp black mustard seeds

slice of ginger

¼ tsp black peppercorns

5 radishes

¼ large cucumber

1 small carrot

1 small courgette

½ red onion

a good bunch of fresh mint, leaves finely chopped

1. In a small pan, combine 40ml water with the vinegar, caster sugar, mustard seeds, ginger and peppercorns. Bring to the boil, then remove from the heat and allow to cool a little. Strain the liquid once cooled and discard the flavourings.

2. On a mandoline, or using a vegetable peeler, thinly slice the vegetables into rounds (for the radishes), long ribbons, or rings (in the case of the onion). Combine all the shaved vegetables in a bowl and pour over the warm pickling liquor. Allow to sit at room temperature for at least 30 minutes, turning the vegetables over from time to time.

3. To serve, drain off the excess pickling liquor (you can reserve this and use it again) and toss the fresh mint through the vegetables.

Tips

This can be adapted endlessly, and you can add any spices to the pickling liquor or herbs to the salad that you like, so do experiment.

It works really well as part of a selection of salads.

MIXED GRAIN SALAD WITH ROASTED PEPPERS AND HARISSA DRESSING

The less obvious ancient wheats like bulgur, spelt, kamut and buckwheat, and grains like barley, millet, quinoa and amaranth have become foodies' favourites. Most of them are now available in supermarkets and all of them can be bought online. I've been experimenting a bit with them, and there is no doubt that mixed grains make a great alternative to plain rice, are good in a risotto and make an interesting salad. This recipe requires cooked grains; here we have used bulgur wheat and quinoa, but you could use any mixture you like. If you're using several kinds, boil or steam them separately if they require different cooking times. Alternatively, for an even easier salad, use the pre-cooked mixed grains in ambient pouches that you can buy in the supermarket. *Prue*

SERVES 4

75g bulgur wheat (raw weight)

75g quinoa (raw weight)

2 red peppers, deseeded and cut into strips

10 baby plum tomatoes or cherry tomatoes, halved

2 garlic cloves, finely chopped

2 tbsp vegetable oil

2½ tbsp extra virgin olive oil

4 tsp harissa paste

1 tsp pomegranate molasses

8 green olives, pitted and halved

60g feta, crumbled

a small handful of flat-leaf parsley, finely chopped

juice of ¼ lemon (2–3 tsp)

salt and black pepper to season

1. Heat the oven to 200°C/fan 180°C/gas mark 6.

2. Cook the bulgur wheat in plenty of boiling water for 10–15 minutes, or until just tender. Drain and set aside.

3. Cook the quinoa in a pan of salted boiling water for 15 minutes, or until the grains start to pop their shells and you see little transparent rings appearing. Drain.

4. In a roasting tin combine the pepper strips with the tomatoes, garlic and vegetable oil, and season with salt and black pepper. Roast in the oven for 25–30 minutes, until the peppers are soft and just starting to char. Remove from the oven and allow to cool a little.

5. In a small bowl, whisk together the olive oil, harissa paste and pomegranate molasses.

6. In a large serving bowl, combine the cooked grains, roasted peppers and tomatoes, olives, feta, parsley, and the dressing. Season with salt and black pepper, squeeze the lemon juice over, and toss well to ensure the dressing coats everything. Serve immediately.

Tip

To make this vegan, use cubed avocado instead of feta.

TABBOULEH-MUJADARA HYBRID SALAD

This salad came about because I had half a bowl of each of my two favourite Middle Eastern salads (tabbouleh and mujadara) left over. I mixed them together and the combination was better than either dish alone. *Prue*

SERVES 4 AS A SIDE

100g bulgur wheat
(raw weight)

80g green lentils

40ml vegetable oil

4 large onions, thinly sliced

½ tsp ground cumin

½ tsp ground coriander

¼ tsp ground cinnamon

2 tbsp extra virgin olive oil

30g bunch of flat-leaf parsley, leaves picked and finely chopped

4–5 sprigs of mint, leaves picked and finely chopped

juice of ½ lemon

salt and black pepper
to season

1. Cook the bulgur wheat in plenty of boiling water for 10–15 minutes, or until just tender. Drain and set aside.

2. Put the lentils in a small saucepan with enough water to cover them, bring to the boil, then reduce the heat and simmer for 12–15 minutes until just tender but still retaining a little bite. Drain.

3. Heat the vegetable oil in a large frying pan over a medium heat, add the onions and cook until soft and starting to colour, then add the spices and cook for 5 minutes more, stirring to brown the onions evenly.

4. Mix the bulgur wheat, lentils, spiced onions, olive oil, herbs and lemon juice together in a bowl. Taste and season with salt and black pepper, then tip into a serving bowl. Serve at room temperature.

CHARRED CORN SALAD WITH HALLOUMI

This is one of my favourite summer salads – it's filling, fragrant, colourful and brightly flavoured; everything I want for lunch on a hot day. Ensure you serve it straight away once it is made, as the halloumi toughens as it cools. *Peta*

SERVES 4 AS A SIDE OR 2 GENEROUSLY AS A MAIN

1 tbsp vegetable oil

200g sweetcorn (tinned or frozen)

200g halloumi, cut into bite-sized pieces

2 small gem lettuces

6 baby plum tomatoes, quartered

1 celery stick, thinly sliced

1 ripe avocado, halved, stoned, peeled and cut into bite-sized pieces

a small handful of flat-leaf parsley, roughly chopped

a small handful of mint, leaves chopped

2 tbsp extra virgin olive oil

2 tsp good-quality balsamic vinegar

salt and black pepper to season

1. Heat the vegetable oil in a large frying pan over a high heat, then add the sweetcorn and cook for 5–6 minutes until it starts to colour. Turn it occasionally, but not too frequently, and don't remove it from the heat until it is really well coloured. Transfer the corn to a mixing bowl.

2. In the same pan, fry the halloumi, turning it frequently, until it is deep brown on all sides. Add this to the bowl with the corn.

3. Leave the small lettuce leaves whole and tear any large ones in half. Mix them and all the remaining ingredients together with the corn and halloumi. Taste and adjust the seasoning.

RED LENTIL AND LEMON KOFTE

A Turkish chef I once worked with used to bring these in for us whenever he had his mother visiting, as she used to make them. They make perfect picnic food, or would be a great vegan addition to a salad table at a barbecue. You can shape them as large or small as you like, but I think they're delicious eaten with crunchy baby gem lettuce, so I make mine to fit inside a baby gem leaf. Serve them with extra wedges of lemon for your guests to squeeze over before eating them. And if you happen to have made the pickled cabbage from the Harissa Falafel Wrap on page 41, they are HEAVEN with these – a happy discovery I made when testing both on the same day! *Peta*

SERVES 8

150g red lentils

75g bulgur wheat

1 tbsp vegetable oil

1 onion, finely diced

½ tsp ground cumin

2 tsp harissa paste

2 tsp tomato purée

a handful of flat-leaf parsley, finely chopped

juice of ½ lemon plus wedges to serve

16 baby gem lettuce leaves, washed

salt and black pepper to season

1. Put the red lentils in a medium saucepan with 240ml water and bring to the boil. Reduce the heat and simmer gently for 15–20 minutes or until the lentils are well cooked and the water has boiled off.

2. In a separate pan, cook the bulgur wheat in plenty of boiling water for 10–15 minutes, or until tender. Drain it well, then mix the bulgur wheat with the lentils in a mixing bowl.

3. Heat the vegetable oil in a frying pan over a medium heat, add the onion, cumin, harissa and tomato purée and sauté until the onion is soft and well cooked, then add it to the lentils and bulgur wheat in the mixing bowl.

4. Add the chopped parsley and lemon juice, and season well with salt and black pepper. Mix it together so everything is evenly mixed, then put the mixture in the fridge for 1 hour, until well chilled.

5. Take a serving plate and arrange the lettuce leaves on it. Using clean hands, take small pieces of the mixture and squeeze them into sausage shapes in the palm of your hand. Place each one into a lettuce leaf and continue until the mixture is all used – there should be enough for sixteen kofte.

6. Add lemon wedges to the plate so that your guests can squeeze extra lemon juice over them themselves. Allow them to sit at room temperature for 30 minutes before serving, so that they aren't fridge-cold.

breads

MALTED WHOLEMEAL SODA BREAD

My husband John is forever bemoaning the lack of soda bread in our house. Once, he bought a postcard from the famous Ballymaloe hotel and cookery school in Ireland, with a cartoon of a woman holding a soda bread and this legend, a quote from Ballymaloe's doyenne, Myrtle Allen: 'I was many years married before I triumphantly put a really good brown soda loaf on the tea table. Of course, this brought me no praise. Only a few disillusioned grunts about the pity it was that I had taken so long to learn the art.'

The trick to handle the dough as though it were hot coals, mixing it by cutting through it with a round bladed knife, using dry hands and barely touching it. And then, I promise, it's foolproof. Or almost foolproof. When testing this recipe I forgot it was in the oven and left for the Bake Off location. There was pleasure in John's voice when he rang my mobile and said, 'I smell burning. Did you forget something in the oven?' Even that loaf had disappeared by the time I got home; just one (tasty, if a bit tough) crust left. *Prue*

MAKES 1 LOAF (SERVES 4–5)

400g malted wheat flour (often labelled as 'country grain flour' or 'granary')

200g plain white flour plus extra for dusting

1 tsp table salt

1 tsp bicarbonate of soda

300g buttermilk

125ml whole milk

1. Heat the oven to 240°C/fan 220°C/gas mark 9. Line a baking tray with baking parchment.

2. Combine all the dry ingredients in a large mixing bowl. Combine the buttermilk and milk together in a jug, then pour into the dry ingredients and mix together very lightly, just to form a wet dough – do not knead it.

3. Turn the mixture out onto a floured surface and then, using clean, dry hands, lightly pat it into a round. Transfer this onto the lined baking sheet.

4. Use a sharp knife to cut across the dough, as though to split it in two, but only go halfway down to the baking sheet. Repeat at right angle to the first cut to get a deep cross.

5. Bake the bread in the middle of the oven for 20 minutes, then reduce the heat to 220°C/fan 200°C/gas mark 7 and bake for another 15 minutes. It should sound hollow when tapped on the base. Remove from the oven and allow it to cool completely before cutting or breaking it apart.

Tip

This freezes well. Defrost it at room temperature, then to serve, wrap it in foil and put it in a hot oven for 10 minutes.

WHOLEMEAL SEEDED BREAD

This is such a satisfactory loaf to make. It's healthy, delicious and makes the best cheese sandwiches! As with most breads, kneading should be vigorous. Don't 'play' with the dough: give it a good bashing, repeatedly pushing it against the work surface with the heel of your hand to stretch and then fold it. *Prue*

MAKES 1 SMALL LOAF

120g mixed seeds (sunflower, pumpkin, millet, flax, poppy, sesame etc.)

95g strong white flour plus extra for dusting

155g strong wholemeal flour

1 tsp clear honey

½ tsp table salt

1 tsp fast action dried yeast

oil for greasing

1. Combine 70g of the mixed seeds in a heatproof mixing bowl with 80ml boiling water and leave them to soak for 10 minutes.

2. Add the flours, 135ml tepid water, honey, salt and yeast to the bowl with the soaked seeds, and mix to form a dough. Either by hand, or using a stand mixer fitted with a dough hook, knead the dough vigorously for 5 minutes (10 minutes if kneading by hand) until it is smooth and elastic.

3. Transfer the dough to a very lightly oiled bowl and cover it with a clean tea towel. Leave somewhere free from draughts at room temperature for 1 hour. After 1 hour, give the dough a very brief knead, just to deflate it, then put it back under the towel and leave it for another hour.

4. Grease the two long sides of a 450g (1lb) loaf tin and line the bottom and short sides with a single long strip of baking parchment.

5. Lightly dust a clean work surface with flour, turn the dough out onto it, then shape it into a loaf. Brush the loaf lightly with a little water, then roll it gently in the remaining mixed seeds, so that they stick to the outside of it. Transfer the loaf to the lined tin, seam side down.

6. Cover it with a clean tea towel and leave at room temperature, free from draughts, for 1 hour, or until a finger pressed lightly into the top of the loaf leaves an indent which springs back slowly. Heat the oven to 240°C/fan 220°C/gas mark 9.

7. Bake in the middle of the oven for 20 minutes, then without opening the door, reduce the heat to 200°C/fan 180°C/gas mark 6 and bake for a further 10 minutes. Check it is ready by carefully turning it out and tapping on the base of the loaf – it should sound hollow.

8. Remove from the oven and turn the bread out onto a wire rack. Leave to cool completely before slicing. It's very important not to cut into it while it's still warm, as it will cause the texture to be gummy and unpleasant.

TOMATO AND BASIL FOCACCIA

This focaccia does require some hand-holding and needs tending to frequently, but the results really are worth the time spent. And, once you get the hang of it, the half-hourly turns won't take you more than a minute. The success of this bread relies a lot on the heat of your oven, so make sure you only open the door briefly to put the bread in, so that you don't lose too much heat. If you don't want to use the flavourings, you could keep it plain by omitting the basil and tomatoes, and just top it with fresh rosemary and sea salt, as is traditional for focaccia. *Peta*

MAKES 1 SMALL LOAF

250g strong white flour

1 scant tsp table salt

½ tsp fast action dried yeast

a bunch of fresh basil, leaves finely chopped

40ml extra virgin olive oil plus extra for shaping and greasing

12 whole cherry tomatoes or baby plum tomatoes, tossed in olive oil

1 tsp flaky sea salt (such as Maldon)

1. Combine the flour, 200ml tepid water, salt, yeast, basil leaves and 2 teaspoons of the olive oil in a large mixing bowl. Mix the ingredients together by hand to form a wet, sticky dough. Cover the bowl with a clean tea towel and set it aside somewhere free from draughts at room temperature.

2. Every half hour, add another teaspoon of olive oil to the dough and give it 30 'folds'. ('Folding' means sliding your hand underneath the mass of dough and lifting/stretching one half of it up and away from the rest, then folding it over the top.) Give the bowl a half turn, then repeat until you have folded it 30 times. Replace the tea towel over the bowl and set aside for another half hour, before repeating this. In total, you should do this 6 times, adding a teaspoon of olive oil each time. A sample schedule might look like this:

8am: Mix the dough
8.30am: Add 1 tsp olive oil and fold the dough 30 times
9am: Add 1 tsp olive oil and fold the dough 30 times
9.30am: Add 1 tsp olive oil and fold the dough 30 times
10am: Add 1 tsp olive oil and fold the dough 30 times
10.30am: Add 1 tsp olive oil and fold the dough 30 times
11am: Add 1 tsp olive oil and fold the dough 30 times

3. Heat the oven to 240°C/fan 220°C/gas mark 9. Lightly grease a 20cm (8in) square or round tin with olive oil.

4. Around 30 minutes after the final fold, turn the dough into the tin and gently press and stretch it out into the tin. Use the tips of your fingers to dimple the dough all over and lightly rub a drizzle of extra virgin olive oil over the surface of it. Try not to deflate the dough too much as you shape it.

5. Press the tomatoes into the dough in whatever pattern or order you prefer, but try to distribute them evenly so that each slice will contain one. Finally, scatter the sea salt generously over the top of it. Set aside somewhere warm, uncovered, for 20–30 minutes, to prove.

6. Bake the focaccia in the middle of the oven for 18–20 minutes, by which point it should be well risen, golden brown, and sound hollow when tapped on the underside.

7. Remove from the oven, transfer it to a wire rack and allow it to cool completely before serving.

Tip ———————————————————

Focaccia is unbeatable, but it doesn't keep well. Try to eat it on the day it is baked. This won't be hard, as it's pretty well irresistible. If you do have leftovers, use them the next day for bruschetta (see page 38) or grilled cheese on toast.

BRIOCHE

Freshly made, brioche is one of the best breads in the world. I defy you not to eat the majority of it as soon as it's cool. Traditionally a breakfast bread, it also makes excellent burger buns, though you may want to reduce the sugar if you're using them for a savoury purpose. *Prue*

MAKES 8 BUNS OR 1 SMALL LOAF

250g strong white flour plus extra for dusting

25ml milk

1 tsp table salt

30g caster sugar

1 large egg

1 tsp fast action dried yeast

80g unsalted butter, at room temperature, plus extra for greasing

1 egg, beaten with a splash of milk

1. Combine the flour, 60ml tepid water, milk, salt, sugar and egg with the yeast in a large mixing bowl, or the bowl of a stand mixer fitted with a dough hook. Mix it to form a dough, then knead it vigorously for a few minutes until the dough is nice and elastic.

2. Gradually add the butter, a tablespoon or so at a time, kneading to incorporate it fully between additions. Once all the butter is in, transfer the dough to a lightly greased mixing bowl, cover it with a clean tea towel, and leave it to prove at room temperature for 1½ hours. Knock it back, cover it directly with cling film, and then transfer it to the fridge for 4 hours, or overnight if you prefer.

3. Heat the oven to 200°C/fan 180°C/gas mark 6. Grease a 20cm (8in) round cake tin or a 450g (1lb) loaf tin with butter. Line the bottom with baking parchment.

4. Turn the dough out onto a lightly floured surface and divide it into eight equal pieces. Shape each piece into a round bun, then arrange them in the lined cake tin, evenly spaced, with seven around the edges and one in the centre. Alternatively, shape it into a loaf and put it into the lined loaf tin. Cover with cling film and leave at room temperature for 1 hour. It is ready to bake when it has doubled in size, and a fingertip pressed into the top of it leaves a dent that springs back slowly.

5. Brush it lightly with the beaten egg and milk, then bake in the middle of the oven for 30–35 minutes. To check it is ready, turn it out and tap the underside of it – it should sound hollow. Remove from the oven and leave it to cool completely before slicing, or pulling apart the buns.

Tip

Because this is an enriched bread (i.e. has eggs and butter in it) it keeps for a good few days if stored in an airtight container. It also freezes perfectly.

EVERYDAY OAT BREAD

This is a fantastic bread for beginners. It's very easy and quick to make, and ideal for toast and sandwiches, so it's really useful as an everyday loaf. It also freezes excellently, so I always make a big batch and freeze it, sliced, ready to pull out and toast. *Peta*

MAKES 2 SMALL LOAVES

85g rolled or porridge oats

55ml whole milk

300g strong white flour plus extra for dusting

200g plain wholemeal flour

20g clear honey

40ml vegetable oil plus extra for greasing

1½ tsp table salt

1 tsp fast action dried yeast

1. Combine the oats with the milk and 310ml water in a mixing bowl. Leave to stand for 10 minutes, then add the remaining ingredients. Using a stand mixer fitted with a dough hook (or a wooden spoon if you are making it by hand) mix the ingredients together to form a dough. Once everything is incorporated, increase the speed to medium-high and mix it for 5 minutes, or knead it vigorously by hand until the dough is smooth and elastic, and no longer sticky.

2. Transfer the dough to a very lightly oiled bowl and cover it with a clean tea towel. Leave it somewhere free from draughts at room temperature for 1 hour. After 1 hour, give the dough a very brief knead, just to deflate it, then put it back under the towel and leave it for another hour in the same place.

3. Grease the two long sides of 2 x 450g (1lb) loaf tins and line the bottom and short sides of each tin with a single long strip of baking parchment.

4. Lightly dust a clean work surface with flour, then turn the dough out onto it. Divide the dough in two, then shape each piece into loaves and put them into the lined tins, seam-side down. Cover them with a clean tea towel and leave at room temperature, free from draughts, for 1 hour, or until a finger pressed lightly into the top of the dough leaves an indent which springs back slowly. Heat the oven to 240°C/fan 220°C/gas mark 9.

5. Bake the loaves in the middle of the oven for 20 minutes, then (without opening the door) reduce the heat to 210°C/fan 190°C/gas mark 6 and bake for a further 10 minutes. Check that the loaves are ready by carefully turning one out and tapping on the base of the loaf – it should sound hollow.

6. Remove from the oven and turn the loaves onto a wire rack. Leave to cool completely before slicing. It's very important not to cut into them while they are still warm, as it will cause the texture to be gummy and unpleasant.

Tip

If you are going to freeze a loaf, slice it as soon as it is cool, and freeze in a sandwich bag straight away. If you don't want to freeze it, it will keep well in a bread bin for 2–3 days but will be better used for toast after the first 2 days.

FRUIT BREAD

This is a bit like a tea cake but in loaf form – it's absolutely delicious when toasted and buttered, and I warn you, one slice is never enough! It freezes brilliantly, so it's perfect to keep sliced in the freezer, ready to toast whenever the urge takes you. Children love it too. *Prue*

MAKES 1 SMALL LOAF

180g dried fruit (any combination of raisins, sultanas, cranberries, cherries, apricots, prunes, figs, or candied peel)

180g strong white flour

120g whole wheat flour

1 sachet (7g) fast action dried yeast

20g caster sugar

1 tsp table salt

1 large egg, beaten

80ml tepid whole milk

1. Roughly chop the dried fruit so that every piece of fruit is roughly the size of a raisin. Put the fruit into a heatproof bowl and pour boiling water over it. Leave it to soak for 20 minutes, then drain it well.

2. Combine all the ingredients, including the soaked fruit, in a mixing bowl. Add 50ml tepid water. Mix it to form a dough, then knead it vigorously by hand for 5–10 minutes, until it is smooth and elastic, and the fruit is well distributed through the dough.

3. Cover the bowl with a clean tea towel and leave it at room temperature for 2 hours, giving it a quick knead just to deflate it after the first hour.

4. Grease the two long sides of a 450g (1lb) loaf tin and line the bottom and short sides with a single long strip of baking parchment.

5. Shape the dough into a loaf and put it into the lined loaf tin, seam-side down. Cover with a clean tea towel and leave at room temperature for 35–45 minutes, until it has puffed up and a finger gently poked into the top of it leaves a dent that springs back slowly. Heat the oven to 210°C/fan 190°C/gas mark 6.

6. Bake the loaf in the oven on the middle shelf for 15 minutes, then without opening the door, reduce the heat to 190°C/fan 170°C/gas mark 5 and bake it for a further 25 minutes. It should then be puffed up and golden. Remove it from the tin and tap the bottom. It should sound hollow when tapped on the base.

7. Remove from the oven and allow it to cool completely on a wire rack before serving or freezing.

biscuits and scones

BLUE CHEESE AND RAISIN SCONES

These savoury scones make a fantastic accompaniment to a creamy soup (like our Really Easy Cauliflower Soup, see page 26) as an alternative to bread or crackers. In this recipe they're cut smaller than a usual scone, as they are quite rich. If you don't have a small cutter, cut similar-sized square scones with a knife. Do use Roquefort cheese if you can – it is pungent enough for the blue cheese flavour to come through in the baked scone. *Peta*

MAKES 12–14 SMALL SCONES

80g raisins

1 large egg

135ml cold whole milk plus an extra splash

225g self-raising flour plus extra for dusting

½ tsp baking powder

a pinch of table salt

55g cold unsalted butter, cut into rough cubes

90g Roquefort cheese, cut into chunks

1. Heat the oven to 200°C/fan 180°C/gas mark 6. Line a baking sheet with baking parchment. Put the raisins in a heatproof bowl and cover with boiling water. Allow to sit for 10–15 minutes, then drain and squeeze out any excess water. They should be cold by the time you add them to the mix, so either do this in advance or soak them then put them into the fridge until required.

2. Whisk the egg with the splash of milk and set aside.

3. Put the flour, baking powder and salt in a mixing bowl, then add the cold butter and 60g of the Roquefort. Using your fingertips, lightly rub the butter and cheese into the flour, until the mixture resembles breadcrumbs. Add the raisins, tossing to distribute them evenly in the mixture, then pour in the remaining milk. Using a butter knife, bring the mixture together to form a shaggy dough.

4. Turn the dough out onto a lightly floured surface and push it together gently to form a rectangular block, being careful not to work the dough too much. Leave it to rest for 10 minutes, covered with an upturned bowl or piece of cling film.

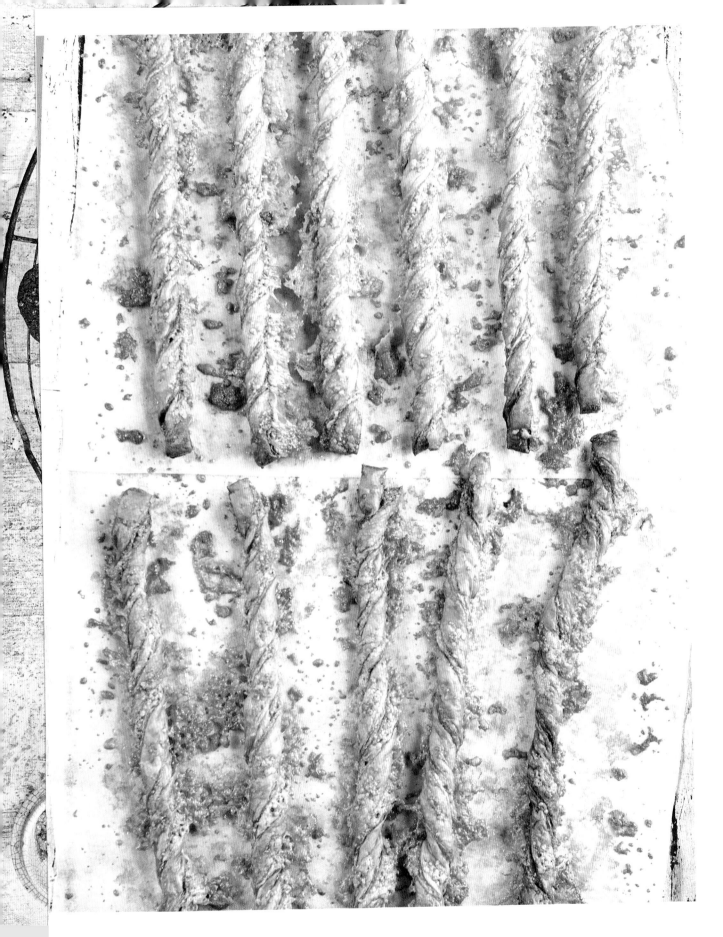

RICCIARELLI WITH CANDIED PEEL

This recipe was given to me by my great friend and colleague Liza, the head pastry chef at The Ivy, who has taught me an enormous amount. She sent me the recipe for these ricciarelli with a note saying they were so simple even my toddler daughter, Luna, could make them. Well, I tried and failed, again and again, wracking my brains as to why they weren't working, and reluctant to admit my failings to her. Eventually I 'fessed up and together we worked it out – I had substituted the granulated sugar for caster sugar, thinking it wouldn't make the slightest bit of difference in this type of biscuit. How wrong I was. The lesson here is always to read your ingredient list properly and use the correct ones! I have added candied peel here, but you could keep them plain, or as Liza does, encase a preserved cherry in each one – heaven! *Peta*

MAKES 12

125g granulated sugar

100g ground almonds

1 large egg white

a pinch of table salt

30g mixed candied peel, finely chopped

icing sugar for rolling

1. Heat the oven to 200°C/fan 180°C/gas mark 6. Line a baking sheet with baking parchment.

2. Whisk the sugar and ground almonds together in a bowl, to ensure they are well combined and there are no lumps.

3. In a clean bowl, whisk the egg white with the salt until it forms soft peaks. Fold the almonds and sugar into the egg white, then stir in the candied peel and mix to distribute it evenly.

4. Use your hands to divide the mixture into twelve evenly-sized balls. Put some icing sugar into a shallow dish, then roll each ball in it until it is coated.

5. Arrange the balls of dough on the baking sheet, evenly spaced, and press down very lightly on each one, just to flatten the top a little.

6. Bake in the middle of the oven for about 10 minutes, until the tops are cracked and the bottoms are just golden. Remove from the oven, transfer to a wire rack and allow to cool completely.

Tip

As with most biscuits these are best eaten fresh, but they will keep happily in an airtight container for up to 1 week.

puddings

SUMMER FRUIT AND AMARETTI GALETTE

This is a delicious, quick-to-put-together fruit tart. The fruit you use is up to you. Just remember that a variety of fruits make it look appealing and taste great, too. We've used nectarines and cherries, but apples and blackberries would be good, as would apricots and prunes. *Prue*

SERVES 4–6

3 nectarines, halved, pitted and sliced

6 cherries, pitted and halved

2 tbsp jam sugar

8 amaretti biscuits, crushed

ice cream, clotted cream or pouring cream to serve

FOR THE PASTRY

110g plain flour, plus extra for dusting

a pinch of salt

a pinch of caster sugar, plus extra for sprinkling

70g cold unsalted butter, cut into cubes

45ml iced water

1 egg white for glazing

1. To make the pastry, combine the flour, salt and pinch of sugar in a mixing bowl, and using your fingertips, rub the butter into the flour until the lumps of butter are roughly the size of petits pois. Add the iced water, then use a butter knife to bring the mixture together to form a very raggedy, ropey-looking dough – do not bring it into a ball of dough. Press it gently together, then wrap in cling film and chill in the fridge for at least 1 hour, until it is firm.

2. Heat the oven to 210°C/fan 190°C/gas mark 6–7. Line a baking sheet with baking parchment. Combine the fruit with the jam sugar in a mixing bowl, mix well, and leave it to sit while you roll out the pastry.

3. Unwrap the pastry and roll it out on a floured surface into a round, about 2–3mm thick. Cut it into a perfect round about 30cm (12in) across, using a pan lid or plate. Lift it onto the lined baking sheet. Scatter the crushed biscuits evenly over the centre of the pastry, leaving a border of 5cm (2in) all around. Pile the fruit on top, then bring the edges of the pastry up, pinching pleats into it as you go to keep it in place.

4. Brush the pastry with the egg white, then sprinkle caster sugar generously over. Bake the tart in the middle of the oven for 30 minutes, or until the pastry is golden brown and cooked through. Check the underside of it with a palette knife to ensure the pastry is cooked underneath.

5. Remove from the oven and serve it hot, ideally with pouring cream.

Tip

Jam sugar contains pectin which thickens the juices and prevents the galette from becoming soggy from the juice. The amaretti biscuits help to absorb some of the juice. All the same, eat this on the day it's made. The leftovers will taste great the next day, but the pastry might be a bit limp.

GRAPEFRUIT TREACLE TART

I adore treacle tart. At lunch before my wedding, I had 24 oysters followed by a bowl of treacle tart and custard. Bliss. But I do recognize that most treacle tarts are too sweet, so I devised this variation in which grapefruit cuts through the sweetness of the syrup. Serve it with ice cream, cream, or good old-fashioned custard, homemade or shop-bought. *Prue*

SERVES 12

3 pink grapefruit

3 large eggs

450g golden syrup

50ml double cream

100g coarse fresh white breadcrumbs

2 tbsp caster sugar

FOR THE PASTRY

140g cold unsalted butter, cut into cubes

250g plain flour, plus extra for dusting

a pinch of salt

2 large egg yolks

2–3 tbsp iced water

1. To make the pastry, put the butter, flour and salt in a large mixing bowl and rub the butter into the flour lightly using your fingertips until the mixture resembles fine breadcrumbs. Use a butter knife to mix in the egg yolks and enough water to bring it together to a crumbly dough – it should only just hold together. Wrap the dough in cling film, and chill it in the fridge for at least 1 hour, until firm.

2. Finely grate the zest of one grapefruit. Cut the fruit in half and extract the juice. Put the grapefruit juice into a saucepan and bring to the boil. Boil rapidly until the juice has reduced by about two thirds and has become syrupy. Peel and segment the other two grapefruit, removing all pith.

3. To make the filling, whisk the eggs in a medium bowl until yolks and whites are smoothly combined, then add the golden syrup, cream, reduced grapefruit juice and zest, and the breadcrumbs. Stir vigorously to combine.

4. Heat the oven to 190°C/fan 170°C/gas mark 5. Place a baking sheet in the oven to heat up. Grease a 24cm (9½in) loose-bottomed flan tin.

5. Unwrap the pastry and roll it out as thinly as you can on a dusted surface, ideally to a thickness of only 1mm. Line the greased tin with the pastry, then put it in the freezer for 20 minutes to chill.

6. Trim the excess pastry from the top of the pastry case, then fill it with the treacle mixture. Put it directly onto the pre-heated baking sheet in the oven. Bake in the middle of the oven for 40–50 minutes, covering it with foil towards the end of cooking if it is browning too much on top.

5. To make the chocolate glaze, place the chocolate in a heatproof bowl. Bring the cream to the boil in a pan, then pour it over the chocolate and whisk until smooth. Add the butter and stir until smooth. Allow to cool to almost room temperature – it needs to be just runny enough to coat the top of the éclairs. If it cools too much, and it's too stiff to spoon over the éclairs, simply warm it very gently over a bain marie, or give it a couple of seconds in a microwave to loosen it.

6. Once the éclairs are completely cool, take the piping bag of cream filling and, using the tip of the nozzle, make a couple more holes in the bottom of each éclair to make filling the length of the éclair easier. Insert the pastry bag nozzle and fill each éclair with the caramel cream.

7. To top the éclairs, hold each one at a 45-degree angle over the bowl of chocolate glaze and spoon it over the top, angling it so that it runs down the length of the éclair, coating the top in chocolate. Alternatively, just dip the top side of each éclair into the bowl of ganache and allow the excess to run off before setting it back on a tray. Allow them to sit at room temperature until the chocolate ganache has set solid, then serve.

Tip

While these would keep for a day in an airtight container in the fridge, they are so much better fresh, so it would be a shame not to eat them all on the day they are made.

DELUXE BREAD AND BUTTER PUDDING

This is a far cry from the bread and butter pudding you remember from school. Absurdly indulgent though it sounds, this really is best served with a generous glug of Jersey cream on the side. It's a wonderful second life for stale pain au chocolat. And if it's stale plain croissants you are trying to use up, add a sprinkling of chopped chocolate before pouring on the custard. *Peta*

SERVES 6

butter for greasing

220ml whole milk

220ml double cream

grated zest of 2 oranges

2 large eggs plus 2 egg yolks

100g caster sugar

6 pain au chocolat

thick cream (preferably Jersey) to serve

1. Heat the oven to 160°C/fan 140°C/gas mark 3. Grease an ovenproof pie dish, roughly 12 x 22cm (5 x 8½in) and 10cm (4in) deep.

2. Put the milk, cream and orange zest in a pan and bring to the boil. Whisk the eggs with the egg yolks and sugar in a heatproof bowl, then pour the boiling cream over them and whisk to combine.

3. Tear the pain au chocolat into pieces and put them into the greased pie dish. Pour the hot custard over the top and use the back of a spoon to push the pieces down, to soak and submerge them.

4. Bake in the middle of the oven for 35–40 minutes, by which point there should be no liquid pooling when you press down on the surface with a knife.

5. Serve immediately, with thick cream on the side.

If you prefer a non-chocolatey bread and butter pudding, use plain croissants, and perhaps add some pre-soaked raisins. Equally, if you don't like orange, you could flavour the custard with ground cinnamon or vanilla.

GOOSEBERRY AND ELDERFLOWER FOOL

There's something really appealing about a fool – it's such a quintessentially English dessert, and almost ethereal in its lightness. Traditionally, fools were made with sieved fruit purées so were silky smooth and seed-free, and with custard and/or double cream. This fool is a healthier modern adaptation for cooks with no time for sieving and who like to retain the texture of the fruit.

You can make fool from any number of fruits, but for me gooseberry has the perfect tartness to cut through the rich cream. And elderflower, as everybody knows, is a gooseberry's best friend. *Peta*

SERVES 6

450g gooseberries, topped and tailed

2 tbsp elderflower cordial

40g jam sugar

60g caster sugar

300ml double cream

150g natural yoghurt

1. Combine roughly three quarters of the gooseberries in a saucepan with the elderflower cordial, jam sugar, caster sugar and a splash of water. Set over a low-medium heat and cook, stirring occasionally, for about 10–15 minutes until the gooseberries have completely broken down and the whole mixture has come to the boil.

2. Add the remaining gooseberries, then return to the boil for 2–3 minutes, by which point the last addition of gooseberries will be soft, but retaining their shape. Turn off the heat and leave the compote to cool completely.

3. Once the compote is cold, whisk the double cream and yoghurt together in a bowl until it holds firm peaks. Very gently fold all but 100g of the compote through the whipped cream. Spoon it into either a large serving dish or individual bowls, then spoon the remaining compote over the top. Serve immediately, or cover and chill until you are ready to eat it.

Tips

This is delicious with a crunchy biscuit like the shortbread on page 200.

Rhubarb is a brilliant substitute for gooseberries. Simply combine 560g pink rhubarb (chopped) with 80g caster sugar, and the grated zest and juice of 1 orange in a roasting dish. Roast at 180°C/fan 160°C/gas mark 4 for 12–15 minutes, checking frequently towards the end of cooking. The rhubarb should be soft but holding its shape. Remove from the oven and leave to cool, then proceed from step 3 above.

PRUE'S PATENT-IMPROVED ETON MESS

Eton mess is generally simply strawberries and whipped cream muddled up with broken meringue, and pretty damn good it is too. But, by way of a change, here is something slightly more sophisticated and every bit as delicious. *Prue*

SERVES 6

FOR THE MERINGUE

1 large egg white

60g soft dark brown sugar

FOR THE COMPOTE

300g raspberries

50ml dark, spiced rum

½ cinnamon stick

1½ tbsp caster sugar

FOR THE CREAM

300ml double cream

1½ tbsp caster sugar

450g natural yoghurt

1. Heat the oven to 120°C/fan 100°C/gas mark ½. Line a baking tray with baking parchment.

2. To make the meringue, whisk the egg white with the brown sugar in a bowl with an electric whisk at high speed until stiff and glossy. Spoon the mixture onto the baking sheet in 5–6 evenly-sized dollops. Bake in the middle of the oven for about 1 hour, until firm and dry to the touch, and easy to lift off the parchment. Remove from the oven and allow to cool at room temperature.

3. To make the compote, put two thirds of the raspberries into a saucepan with the rum, cinnamon and sugar and set over a low heat. Bring to the boil and simmer, stirring, for a few minutes until syrupy, then remove from the heat and allow to cool completely. Remove the cinnamon stick.

4. Whisk the double cream in a large mixing bowl until it just holds its shape. Mix the sugar into the yoghurt then add it to the cream in the bowl. Fold it in gently.

5. Lightly crush the meringues. Keep aside a few pieces back for decoration, then add the rest to the bowl, along with the cooled compote, and most of the fresh raspberries (again, keep a few back for the top). Use a serving spoon and a very light touch to fold everything together, but not too much – it should remain streaky. Transfer the mixture to a glass serving bowl or individual serving bowls and garnish with the remaining bits of meringue and raspberries.

Tip

A great way to use up your egg yolks is to make pasta. Use 100g of pasta flour (type 00) per yolk, with a pinch of salt and a tiny splash of olive oil. Mix to a stiff dough, then knead it vigorously until it's very smooth and elastic. Wrap it in cling film and rest it at room temperature for at least two hours before rolling and cutting it.

MONSTER MERINGUES

My first husband, growing up before the second world war in suburban Johannesburg, used to get a penny for his Saturday pocket money and almost invariably spent it, after a mile-and-a-half walk, on a single meringue. He used to complain of the smallness and lack of whipped cream that his penny bought, but nevertheless, he could not resist. So here is a monster meringue with attitude. It's even better, of course, with cream. *Prue*

I have used two of my favourite flavour combinations here, but you could put any fresh berries, or passion fruit, apricot or mango pulp into the meringue in place of the raspberries, and scatter any kind of nut or freeze-dried fruit over the top. *Peta*

MAKES 8 LARGE MERINGUES

6 large egg whites (see Tip on page 196 for using the yolks)

480g caster sugar

1 tsp white wine vinegar

75g fresh raspberries, lightly crushed

45g chopped pistachios, toasted

75g dark chocolate, chopped

45g flaked almonds, toasted

cocoa powder for dusting

300ml double cream, softly whipped

1. Heat the oven to 120°C/fan 100°C/gas mark ½. Line two baking sheets with baking parchment.

2. Ensure that the bowl of your stand mixer is spotlessly clean and dry. Combine the egg whites and caster sugar in the bowl, then whisk on high speed until the meringue is glossy and stands in stiff peaks when the whisk is lifted out of it. Add the white wine vinegar and whisk again briefly to ensure it is completely mixed in. (You can also do this using an electric whisk.)

3. Divide the meringue mixture in two, putting half of it into a clean mixing bowl. Into one half, fold the raspberries, then using a large metal spoon, spoon out four large dollops onto one of the lined baking sheets, ensuring that the raspberries are divided evenly between them. Sprinkle the chopped pistachios over the top of them, then set aside.

4. Melt the chocolate in short bursts in the microwave, or in a heatproof bowl placed over a pan of simmering water. Fold the melted chocolate into the remaining meringue mixture, very lightly – the aim is for the chocolate to ripple through the meringue, rather than be completely mixed in. Using a large metal spoon as before, spoon out four large dollops onto the other lined baking sheet. Scatter the flaked almonds over the top of them and dust them lightly with cocoa powder.

5. Bake both trays simultaneously in the oven for 2 hours, by which point the meringues should be hard and lift off the baking parchment with ease.

6. Remove from the oven and allow to cool on the baking sheets before serving with whipped cream.

PEPPERMINT ICE WITH CHOCOLATE SAUCE

This ice is made without an ice-cream maker or the need to re-mix when half frozen. It's quick and easy to make and is creamy, crunchy and refreshing all at once. I can't get enough of it! There are so many ways in which you could serve it – simply sliced, as here, with hot chocolate sauce poured over, or scooped like ice cream and served in a cone. You could sandwich it between two chocolate cookies (I recommend the chocolate fudge cookies on page 168) or set it in a round cake tin and sandwich it between two layers of sponge to make an ice-cream cake fit for a celebration. If you're not a fan of mint, you could use orange zest or coffee flavouring in its place. *Peta*

SERVES 8

4 large eggs, separated

120g caster sugar

a pinch of salt

400ml double cream

peppermint oil to taste

120g dark chocolate, finely chopped

FOR THE CHOCOLATE SAUCE

100g dark chocolate, chopped

1½ tbsp milk

100ml double cream

1. Line 2 x 450g (1lb) loaf tins or 1 x 900g (2lb) loaf tin with 2–3 layers of cling film and place in the freezer to chill.

2. Whisk the yolks with the caster sugar in a large mixing bowl until the mixture has doubled in volume, is a very pale yellow, and forms a ribbon-like trail when the whisk is lifted.

3. In a spotlessly clean bowl, whisk the whites with the pinch of salt until they form stiff peaks when the whisk is lifted.

4. Whisk the double cream in a third bowl until it forms a ribbon trail when you lift the whisk – it should be thickened but not stiff. Fold the yolks into the whipped cream, then gently fold in the whites, taking care not to knock out too much air. Add peppermint oil, starting with 2–3 drops. Taste, then add a drop at a time until you're happy with it. Fold in the dark chocolate.

5. Turn the mixture into the chilled loaf tin(s), cover with cling film and freeze overnight.

6. To make the chocolate sauce, put the dark chocolate into a heatproof bowl. Bring the milk and double cream to the boil in a pan, then pour it over the chocolate and whisk until smooth.

7. To serve, turn the peppermint ice out of the tin(s), remove the cling film and use a sharp knife to cut it into eight slices. Pour over hot dark chocolate sauce.

BLACKBERRY AND LEMON PAVLOVA

I often find myself in a Pavlova rut during the summer months when fruit is cheap and plentiful. Pavlovas are so easy to make and I've yet to meet anyone who doesn't like them. This one's for late summer, when the raspberries and strawberries give way to blackberries. It's so good that it will fend off any end-of-summer blues. It is a little more complicated than the usual simple filling of fresh fruit and whipped cream but it's worth making the lemon curd, the boozy cream and the compote for a special occasion. *Peta*

I first had Pavlova in South Africa made with banana and mango. Delicious. The original Pavlova is said to have been invented to honour the Russian ballerina Anna Pavlova in New Zealand or Australia (both countries claim the honour) and contained pineapple and passion fruit. Certainly, any fruit at all works. *Prue*

SERVES 6

FOR THE MERINGUE

3 large egg whites (see Tip on page 196 for using the yolks)

240g caster sugar

10g cornflour

1½ tsp white wine vinegar

FOR THE LEMON CURD

1 large egg

juice of 1 lemon

40g caster sugar

35g unsalted butter, at room temperature

FOR THE BLACKBERRY COMPOTE

500g blackberries

3 tbsp caster sugar

FOR THE CREAM LAYER

400ml double cream

about 2 tbsp Limoncello

TO GARNISH (OPTIONAL)

candied peel of 1 lemon (see page 184)

1. Heat the oven to 120°C/fan 100°C/gas mark ½. Line a baking tray with baking parchment.

2. Start by making the meringue. Put the egg whites, caster sugar and cornflour in a clean bowl and whisk with an electric mixer on medium speed. Meanwhile, bring 2 tablespoons of water and the white wine vinegar to the boil in the smallest pan you have. Tip the boiling liquid onto the mixing whites, then increase the speed and whisk for 10–15 minutes, until the meringue is thick and glossy and forms stiff peaks when the whisk is lifted.

3. Tip the meringue onto the lined baking sheet and use the back of a spoon to spread it out into a circle roughly 23cm (9in) across, thinner in the middle, and thicker around the rim. Bake in the middle of the oven for 1 hour, until it feels set and dry. Remove from the oven and allow to cool completely on the sheet.

4. To make the lemon curd, break the egg into a small saucepan and whisk until the yolk and white are evenly combined, then add all the other ingredients and set over a medium heat. Stir briskly as the butter melts and the curd comes to the boil, then immediately remove from the heat. By this time it will be thickened. Pass through a fine sieve.

5. To make the blackberry compote, put a third of the blackberries and all the sugar in a small saucepan with just a tiny splash of water. Use a fork to mash the berries, then set it over a medium heat and, stirring frequently, bring it to the boil, then reduce the heat and simmer until the compote is syrupy and the blackberries have broken down completely. Remove from the heat and leave to cool.

6. Whisk the double cream in a bowl until it is just thickened enough to hold its shape – be careful not to over-whip it. Add the Limoncello to taste: you may prefer more than 2 tablespoons, or less.

7. Spread a layer of the curd over the pavlova, then pile the whipped cream on top of it. Toss the fresh blackberries in the blackberry compote, then spoon them all over the cream. Finally, garnish with the thin strips of candied lemon peel (if using). Serve immediately.

Tip

You could use lemon curd from a jar if you are pressed for time.

POMEGRANATE AND MINT GRANITA

Granita is a fantastically refreshing summer dessert, for hot days when you don't want anything substantial after a meal. Being, essentially, shards of flavoured ice, it melts very quickly, so if you are making this for a dinner party, be sure to serve it in frozen bowls, and get it out of the freezer only when your guests are seated and ready to eat it. I'd serve this with just a handful of raspberries and pomegranate seeds. (Image on page 213.) *Peta*

SERVES 4–6

100g caster sugar

a small handful of mint leaves, crushed

300ml unsweetened pomegranate juice

100ml lemonade

1. To make the sugar syrup, combine the sugar and mint with 100ml water in a saucepan and bring to the boil. Once boiled, remove from the heat, then allow to cool at room temperature before straining the mixture through a fine sieve to remove the mint.

2. Mix together the pomegranate juice, sugar syrup and lemonade in a lidded freezerproof container and freeze. After 45 minutes, take a fork and scrape down the sides of the container, dragging it through the mixture to prevent big ice blocks forming – the idea is to end up with something that looks like snow. Return it to the freezer for another 2–3 hours, dragging your fork through it as before once or twice during that time.

3. Before serving, place the bowls you wish to serve it in into the freezer. Granita melts very quickly, so if you serve it in frozen bowls you will have more time to eat it before it melts.

MANGO SORBET

We used to make the most delicious sorbets when I worked at The Ivy, and one of my favourite guilty pleasures at the end of a long shift was to take a small cup with a scoop of mango sorbet and a scoop of lime sorbet down to the changing room to eat while I changed to go home. So refreshing, and just the sugar hit I needed to fuel my journey home! Here, I've rolled those two sorbets into one, and it couldn't be easier to make, whether you have an ice cream machine or not. *Peta*

SERVES 10

350g caster sugar

grated zest and juice of 3 limes

850g tin mango pulp (see Tip) or fresh mango, blitzed to a pulp

1. Combine the sugar and lime zest with 425ml water in a saucepan. Bring to the boil, then remove it from the heat and pass through a fine sieve into a bowl, to remove the lime zest. Combine it with the mango pulp and lime juice in a large lidded freezerproof container, then put it into the fridge to get completely cold.

2. If you have an ice-cream machine, you can now churn it according to your machine's instructions.

3. If you do not have an ice-cream machine, freeze the mixture overnight. Once it is completely frozen, scoop it out and blitz it (in batches) in a high-powered blender – a smoothie maker is ideal. Once it is blended and smooth, return it to the freezer to firm up again before serving.

Tip

Tinned mango pulp is available in the world-foods aisle of most supermarkets.

cakes

MADEIRA CAKE FOR EVERY OCCASION

A good Madeira cake is such a useful thing to have in your baking repertoire. It's plain, but not boring – the lemon and orange zest gives it a lovely, subtle flavour which allows it to pair well with any kind of icing, or fruit. You can eat it plain with a cup of tea, serve it as a dessert with a fruit compote and whipped cream, use it in a trifle, or decorate it for a celebration. It's firm enough that it can withstand stacking, or carving into novelty shapes too. *Prue*

SERVES 8–10

125g unsalted butter, at room temperature, plus extra for greasing

125g caster sugar

grated zest of 1 lemon

grated zest of 1 orange

2 large eggs

1 tsp baking powder

140g plain flour

2 tbsp whole milk

1. Heat the oven to 190°C/fan 170°C/gas mark 5. Grease the two long sides of a 450g (1lb) loaf tin and line the bottom and short sides with a single long strip of baking parchment. Alternatively, grease and line a 20cm (8in) square brownie tin with baking parchment.

2. Cream the butter, sugar and citrus zests in a mixing bowl until pale and fluffy, scraping down the sides of the bowl frequently. Gradually beat in the eggs, one by one. In a separate bowl, combine the baking powder and flour, then stir it into the mixture and pour in the milk. Mix well, then transfer the batter to the lined loaf tin or brownie tin.

3. Bake in the middle of the oven for 20 minutes if you are using a square brownie tin, or 40 minutes if you are baking it in a loaf tin, until well risen and golden. A skewer inserted into the centre should come out clean. If it doesn't, give the cake another 5–10 minutes in the oven.

4. Remove the cake from the oven and leave it to cool in the tin for 20 minutes, then remove and transfer to a wire rack. Once cool, it can be iced, served plain, or carved to form the base of a novelty cake.

Tip

This cake will keep in an airtight container for up to 1 week.

PRUE'S STICKY DATE CAKE

Make it Vegan

This is an old recipe of Prue's, which I first made intending to drizzle it with caramel sauce, imagining it would be redolent of a rustic sticky toffee pudding. I couldn't have been more wrong – when I tried the cake I immediately wanted to spread it thickly with cold salted butter, straight from the fridge. It's a bit like malt loaf and is utterly delicious.
Peta

SERVES 8–10

90g prunes, stoned and chopped

110g dates, stoned and chopped

55g raisins

55g sultanas

200g condensed milk

140g unsalted butter plus extra for greasing

150g plain flour, sifted

½ tsp bicarbonate of soda

1 tbsp marmalade

1. Heat the oven to 190°C/fan 170°C/gas mark 5. Grease the two long sides of a 450g (1lb) loaf tin and line the bottom and short sides with a single long strip of baking parchment.

2. In a large saucepan, combine the prunes, dates, raisins, sultanas, condensed milk, butter and 140ml water. Set it over a medium heat, stirring frequently, and bring it to the boil. Once it boils, let it simmer for 3 minutes, then remove from the heat.

3. Transfer the dried fruit mixture to a large heatproof mixing bowl and set aside to cool for 30 minutes.

4. Combine the flour and bicarbonate of soda in a separate bowl. Using a wooden spoon, beat the sifted flour and bicarbonate of soda into the slightly-cooled fruit mixture, then add the marmalade and beat until everything is incorporated and there are no streaks of flour.

5. Transfer the mixture to the lined loaf tin, then cover it with foil and bake it in the middle of the oven for 45 minutes. Remove the foil, then bake for a further 15 minutes, until a skewer inserted into the centre of the cake comes out clean.

6. Remove from the oven and allow the cake to cool in the tin for 15 minutes, then transfer it to a wire rack and allow to cool completely.

Tips

This will keep very well in an airtight container for up to 2 weeks.

To make it vegan, substitute the butter for Stork baking block, and the condensed milk for coconut condensed milk, which can be bought online.

BING CHERRY AND ALMOND CAKE

In my first season on The Great British Bake Off, one of the contestants in a Christmas Special was Val Stones, a great character and altogether lovely woman. She introduced me to dried Bing cherries from Oregon. Bing cherries are particularly sweet and full-flavoured but are too juicy to be used fresh – they'd make the sponge soggy – so I buy the dried ones online. (Image on page 220.) *Prue*

SERVES 12

150g dried cherries, preferably Bing

40g ground almonds

270g plain flour

2 tsp baking powder

115g unsalted butter, at room temperature, plus extra for greasing

210g caster sugar

3 medium eggs

½ tsp almond extract

190ml whole milk

120g chilled marzipan, coarsely grated

30g flaked almonds

1. Heat the oven to 190°C/fan 170°C/gas mark 5. Grease the sides of a deep 20cm (8in) round cake tin and line the bottom with baking parchment.

2. Put the cherries in a heatproof bowl, cover with boiling water, set aside and leave to soak.

3. Spread the ground almonds out on a baking tray and toast them in the oven for 3–4 minutes, or until just starting to colour. Be careful! They burn in a flash. Remove from the oven and set aside to cool.

4. Sift the flour and baking powder together, then add the toasted ground almonds.

5. In a large mixing bowl or stand mixer, cream the butter and sugar together until pale and fluffy, scraping down the sides of the bowl frequently.

6. Beat in the eggs, one at a time, followed by the almond extract.

7. Beat in half the flour and almond mixture, followed by half the milk. Add the remaining flour mixture, then the remaining milk. Beat only until everything is incorporated and there are no streaks of flour remaining.

8. Drain the water off the cherries, then squeeze and pat them dry. Cut the cherries up until they are the size of currants.

9. Add the chopped cherries to the cake batter along with the grated marzipan and stir to distribute them evenly. Transfer the mixture to the lined cake tin, then sprinkle the flaked almonds over the top of it.

10. Bake in the middle of the oven for 60–70 minutes. Check it after 40 minutes, and if the top is browning too quickly, cover the cake loosely with foil for the remaining cooking time. When it is ready, it should be well risen and golden, and a skewer inserted into the middle should come out clean. If it doesn't, give it another 5 minutes in the oven.

11. Remove from the oven and allow the cake to cool in the tin for 20 minutes, then turn it out onto a wire rack to cool completely.

Tips

This cake will keep well in an airtight container for up to 1 week. It also freezes perfectly.

It's good served with a blob of crème fraîche, mascarpone or Greek yoghurt streaked with cherry jam.

LEMON AND BERGAMOT DRIZZLE CAKE

Everyone loves a lemon drizzle cake, but bergamot makes the cake more grown-up and unusual. It's the oil from the bergamot rind that gives Earl Grey tea its distinctive flavour so if you don't like that, you might want to omit the bergamot and stick to lemon, lime or regular oranges. Bergamot oranges are seasonal and often hard to find, but you can usually buy them online in the winter. (Image on page 224.) *Prue*

SERVES 8–10

130g unsalted butter, at room temperature, plus extra for greasing

grated zest and juice of 1 bergamot orange

130g caster sugar

2 large eggs

20ml whole milk

130g self-raising flour

a pinch of table salt

FOR THE DRIZZLE

juice of 1 lemon

juice of 1 bergamot orange

75g caster sugar

1. Heat the oven to 200°C/fan 180°C/gas mark 6. Grease the two long sides of a 450g (1lb) loaf tin and line the bottom and short sides with a single long strip of baking parchment.

2. Cream the butter, bergamot zest and sugar together in a bowl or a stand mixer until light and fluffy, scraping down the sides of the bowl frequently. Add the eggs one at a time, incorporating the first before adding the second. Mix the bergamot juice into the milk. Add half the flour to the mixing bowl, combine gently, and once incorporated, stir in the salt, milk and juice. Add the remaining flour, then stir to combine. Don't beat any further at this stage.

3. Transfer the mixture to the lined loaf tin and bake in the middle of the oven for 40 minutes. To check if it is done, insert a skewer into the cake – it should come out clean. If there is still wet cake batter clinging to the skewer, give it another 5–10 minutes in the oven.

4. Remove from the oven and allow the cake to cool in the tin while you prepare the drizzle. Combine the lemon and bergamot juices in a small saucepan with the caster sugar and bring to the boil over a gentle heat. Remove from the heat and set aside.

5. Using a fine skewer or toothpick, pierce the cake all over the top, pushing the skewer right the way down to the bottom of the cake – this is to allow the drizzle to penetrate the whole cake. Once you have pierced it all over, use a pastry brush to liberally brush the hot syrup all over the cake – don't be shy with it, you really want to drench it.

6. When it seems as though the cake won't take any more syrup, leave it for 20 minutes, then come back and try again – it should take the remaining drizzle at that point.

7. Leave to cool completely in the loaf tin, then turn it out.

Tip

This cake, being moist, will keep very well in an airtight container for up to 3–4 days.

ORANGE POUND CAKE WITH YUZU GLAZE

Orange cakes can be disappointingly bland but here the orange flavour is intensified by reducing the juice, and the increased quantity of zest results in a deeply flavoured sponge. Yuzu is a sour Asian citrus fruit, the juice of which is bottled and sold in most supermarkets. It provides a really bright, zingy lift to the cake, so it's worth using if you can find it. If you can't, just replace it with more lemon juice. *Prue*

SERVES 8–10

zest of 4 oranges and juice of 2

200g unsalted butter, at room temperature, plus extra for greasing

180g caster sugar

4 large eggs, separated

200g self-raising flour

½ tsp baking powder

a pinch of table salt

FOR THE ICING

100g icing sugar

20ml yuzu juice

1. Heat the oven to 195°C/fan 175°C/gas mark 5. Grease the two long sides of a 900g (2lb) loaf tin and line the bottom and short sides with a single long strip of baking parchment.

2. Reserving just under a tablespoon of the orange juice for the icing, put the rest in a saucepan over a medium heat, and boil it down to 2 tablespoons. Towards the end, watch carefully to prevent it boiling dry.

3. Cream the butter and half the sugar with the orange zest in a mixing bowl until light and fluffy, scraping down the sides of the bowl frequently. Add the egg yolks one at a time, incorporating each before the next addition. Beat in the flour, baking powder and reduced orange juice.

4. Whisk the egg whites with the pinch of salt and the remaining sugar in a clean bowl until it forms soft peaks. Fold the whites into the cake batter, starting with one third of the whites to loosen it, and then gently folding in the remaining whites, keeping as much air in the mixture as you can.

5. Transfer the mixture to the lined loaf tin and bake in the middle of the oven for 50–60 minutes, covering it with foil towards the end if the cake is browning too quickly. It is ready when it is well risen, golden brown, and a skewer inserted into the centre comes out clean.

6. Remove from the oven, allow it to cool in the tin for 20 minutes, then turn it onto a wire rack to cool completely before icing.

7. Sift the icing sugar, then whisk it into the reserved tablespoon of orange juice and the yuzu juice. Spoon this over the cold cake, allowing it to drip down the sides a little. Leave the icing to set at room temperature.

Tip

This will keep well in an airtight container for up to 1 week.

BEST BANANA-CHOC BREAD

This loaf, served warm with custard, is childish heaven. But it's good as a not-too-sweet tea-time cake too. Useful for using up over-ripe bananas – the riper they are the more sweet and delicious your cake will be! *Prue*

SERVES 8

100g soft dark brown sugar, free from hard lumps

70ml vegetable oil plus extra for greasing

1 large egg

125g ripe banana (peeled weight), mashed

55g buttermilk

80g self-raising flour

¼ tsp bicarbonate of soda

¼ tsp table salt

¼ tsp ground cinnamon

40g dark chocolate, finely chopped

2 tsp cocoa nibs

2 tsp demerara sugar

1. Heat the oven to 200°C/fan 180°C/gas mark 6. Grease the two long sides of a 1lb (450g) loaf tin and line the bottom and short sides with a single long strip of baking parchment.

2. Whisk the brown sugar, vegetable oil and egg together in a mixing bowl. Add the mashed banana and the buttermilk and beat to combine.

3. Sift the flour, bicarbonate of soda, salt and cinnamon together, then add this to the mixing bowl and whisk just until smooth. Finally, stir in the chopped chocolate.

4. Transfer the mixture to the lined loaf tin, then sprinkle the cocoa nibs and demerara sugar evenly over the top. Bake in the middle of the oven for 50 minutes, by which point the loaf should be well risen, and a skewer inserted into the loaf should come out clean. If it doesn't, give the loaf another 5 minutes in the oven.

5. Remove from the oven and leave to cool in the tin for 30 minutes, then transfer to a wire rack and allow to cool completely, before serving or storing in an airtight container.

Tip

This cake will stay moist and fresh in an airtight container for up to 3 days.

GINGER CAKE

I love ginger in any form: dried, crystallized, preserved in syrup (stem ginger) or fresh. It's important to know that fresh ginger becomes milder with cooking and powdered ginger does not. In my twenties I wrote a recipe for the Daily Mail and failed to specify stem ginger when I called for an 'ounce of ginger' to go at the bottom of two little ramekins of crème brulée. Dozens of readers used an ounce of ground ginger (which is a whole mini-carton). Unfortunately, one of them was the editor's wife, who said it blew her husband's head off. Happily he didn't fire me, and I learnt a lesson about careful recipe-writing. *Prue*

SERVES 12–14

225ml Guinness

225g black treacle

½ tsp bicarbonate of soda

60g piece of root ginger, peeled and finely minced

3 large eggs

200g soft dark brown sugar

180g caster sugar

175ml vegetable oil, plus extra for greasing

255g plain flour

1½ tsp baking powder

2 tsp ground ginger

1 tsp ground cinnamon

¼ tsp ground cloves

¼ tsp mixed spice

6 good twists of black pepper

1. Heat the oven to 180°C/fan 160°C/gas mark 4. Grease and line the base and sides of a 20cm (8in) springform cake tin with baking parchment.

2. Heat the Guinness and black treacle in a large saucepan over a medium heat until the mixture starts to boil, then remove from the heat. Whisk in the bicarbonate of soda, then the minced ginger. Leave it to cool to room temperature.

3. Whisk the eggs with the brown sugar and caster sugar in a bowl until it is free of lumps, then whisk in the oil. Combine the dry ingredients in a separate bowl. Stir the now-cool Guinness mixture into the eggs, then mix in the dry ingredients, ensuring they are fully incorporated.

4. Pour the batter into the lined cake tin, then bake it in the middle of the oven for 1 hour 15 minutes, checking it after 1 hour and covering it with foil if necessary to prevent it browning too quickly. Test it is done by inserting a skewer into the centre – it should come out clean.

5. Remove from the oven and allow it to cool in the tin for 5 minutes, then turn it out onto a wire rack to cool completely before serving.

Tip

This cake keeps brilliantly, and even improves after a day or two, if kept tightly wrapped in an airtight container.

DORSET APPLE CAKE

In my handwritten notebook full of recipes, this is titled 'Jack's apple cake'. I adapted it from a cake my sister-in-law's mother made for her and my brother Alex after the birth of their first child. Our youngest brother Jack went to visit the baby, and ended up eating about nine-tenths of it. It was an enormous cake, obviously designed to sustain the new parents through their first week of sleepless nights, but Jack was so enamoured with it that I don't think he even noticed the baby. Since then, I make it for his birthday most years. *Peta*

SERVES 12–14

340g caster sugar

3 large eggs

225g unsalted butter, melted, plus extra for greasing

340g self-raising flour

1½ tsp baking powder

1 tsp ground cinnamon

100ml whole milk

550g Bramley apples, peeled, cored and diced (start with 3 large apples)

30g chopped hazelnuts

1 tbsp demerara sugar

1. Heat the oven to 180°C/fan 160°C/gas mark 4. Grease and line the base and sides of a deep 20cm (8in) round cake tin with baking parchment.

2. Whisk together the sugar and eggs in a mixing bowl by hand until combined, then whisk in the melted butter. Combine the flour, baking powder and cinnamon in a separate bowl, then beat into the wet ingredients and whisk in the milk to loosen the batter. Finally, fold in the diced apple.

3. Tip the mixture into the lined cake tin, then level it with a spatula and sprinkle the chopped hazelnuts and demerara sugar over the top.

4. Bake the cake in the middle of the oven for 1½ hours, covering it with foil after the first hour. It is ready when a skewer inserted into the centre comes out clean.

5. Remove from the oven and allow it to cool in the tin for 30 minutes, then turn it out onto a wire rack and let it cool completely before cutting.

Tips

This makes a brilliant dessert cake, delicious served with hot custard, or ice cream.

The cake lasts very well. It is excellent for up to 3 days and OK for a few more. Store it in an airtight container.

BROWN BUTTER, RHUBARB AND ALMOND TRAY BAKE

This is such a versatile cake – it's a doddle to make, keeps well, freezes well and is easy to transport for picnics and school bake sales. For a perfect pudding, serve it warm with crème fraîche or custard and extra poached rhubarb. *Prue*

SERVES 8–10

360g rhubarb, trimmed

225g caster sugar

2 drops of vanilla paste or extract

FOR THE SPONGE

115g unsalted butter

3 medium eggs

115g caster sugar

100g plain flour

¾ tsp baking powder

60g ground almonds

1½ tbsp whole milk

4 tbsp flaked almonds

1. Heat the oven to 190°C/fan 170°C/gas mark 5. Grease and line the base and sides of a 20cm (8in) square baking tin with baking parchment.

2. Start by preparing the rhubarb. Cut the rhubarb stems into 1cm (½in) pieces. If your rhubarb stems are thick, cut them in half lengthways beforehand so that the pieces are not too large. In a medium saucepan, bring the caster sugar, vanilla and 225ml water to the boil. Once the syrup is boiling, add the rhubarb and return to the boil. Remove from the heat as soon as it boils, then drain it, saving the juice for another recipe (see Tip on page 234). Set the rhubarb aside while you prepare the sponge.

3. Melt the butter in a pan over a medium heat until it foams, then turns brown and has a nutty aroma. Take it off the heat at once and pass it through a sieve into a jug to catch any burnt bits.

4. Whisk the eggs and sugar together by hand in a large mixing bowl until combined. Add the melted butter and whisk until combined. Combine the flour, baking powder and ground almonds in a separate bowl, then add to the wet ingredients and pour in the milk, whisking to make a smooth batter.

SEA SALT AND CARAMELIZED NUT CHOCOLATE BROWNIES

I love brownies, but I don't like that the nuts inside tend to go soft and waxy. In this version, I caramelize the nuts before adding them to the batter, which gives them a crunchy shell and prevents them from going waxy. I also like to sprinkle cocoa nibs on top, for added crunch and cocoa flavour, but they could easily be omitted if you prefer. *Peta*

SERVES 16

oil for greasing

300g dark chocolate (55% cocoa solids), broken into pieces

150g unsalted butter

3 large eggs

50g caster sugar

150g soft light brown sugar

100g plain flour

½ tsp baking powder

½ tsp flaky sea salt

2 tbsp cocoa nibs to serve (optional)

FOR THE CARAMELIZED NUTS

50g whole almonds, skin on

50g whole hazelnuts, skin on

75g caster sugar

5g butter

1. Heat the oven to 200°C/fan 180°C/gas mark 6. Grease a 20cm (8in) square brownie tin with oil and line it with baking parchment, and line a baking tray with baking parchment.

2. To make the caramelized nuts, roast the nuts on the baking tray for 5–6 minutes, until they are golden and aromatic. Remove from the oven. Put the caster sugar in a large saucepan with enough water just to wet it (about 25ml), and set over a medium heat. Once the sugar dissolves and the mixture comes to the boil, continue to heat, swirling the syrup around the pan gently, until it turns a deep golden colour. Remove the pan from the heat, then stir in the nuts. Stir in the butter, then turn the nuts out onto the lined baking tray, so they are not touching each other.

3. For the brownies, melt the chocolate and butter together in a heatproof bowl set over (but not in) a pan of simmering water. Don't let it get too hot.

4. Whisk the eggs with the caster sugar and brown sugar in a bowl until the mixture is thick and doubled in size.

5. Combine the flour, baking powder and salt in a separate bowl. Whisk the melted chocolate and butter into the eggs, then beat in the dried ingredients. Finally, tip the caramelized nuts into the batter and stir well.

6. Tip the batter into the lined brownie tin and scatter the cocoa nibs over the top (if using). Bake in the middle of the oven for 20 minutes, or until the cake has risen, has a shiny crust on top, but is still slightly wobbly in the centre. Remove from the oven and leave it to cool completely in the tin before turning out and slicing.

Tip

These keep for up to 1 week if wrapped tightly in cling film, and they also freeze well. Just allow them to thaw at room temperature.

CARROT CAKE

This is adapted from a brilliant recipe devised by Liza, the pastry chef at The Ivy. We used to make it for vegan guests celebrating birthdays in the private dining room, and it was always a popular choice. Often vegan cakes can be disappointing, either crumbly and dry, or flavourless – this cake is neither of those things, and most people I make it for don't even realise it's vegan. I tend to serve it plain, as a teatime cake, but if you wanted to dress it up, simply whip cold coconut cream with a little sugar until it thickens enough to spread over it. *Peta*

SERVES 6

50g walnut halves

105ml vegetable oil plus extra for greasing

65ml orange juice

160g caster sugar

170g strong plain white flour

2 tsp baking powder

1 tsp ground cinnamon

a pinch of mixed spice

105g ground almonds

80g sultanas

200g grated carrot (about 2–3 medium carrots, but do weigh them)

1. Heat the oven to 180ºC/fan 160ºC/gas mark 4. Grease and line the base and sides of a 20cm (8in) loose-bottomed round cake tin with baking parchment.

2. Toast the walnuts on a baking tray in the oven for 2–3 minutes, then remove them from the oven and set aside to cool.

3. In a mixing bowl, whisk the vegetable oil and orange juice together, then beat in the sugar, flour, baking powder, cinnamon, mixed spice and ground almonds.

4. Add the sultanas, toasted walnuts and grated carrot and mix them into the batter. The batter will seem very stiff at first, but the carrots contain a lot of moisture, so the batter will loosen once they are mixed in.

5. Transfer the mixture to the lined cake tin and bake in the middle of the oven for 45 minutes, or until a skewer inserted into the centre comes out clean.

6. Remove from the oven and leave to cool slightly in the tin, then turn out and place on a wire rack to cool completely.

Tip

This will keep well in an airtight container for up to 1 week.

thank you

First of all, I'd like to thank my co-author Peta who has probably done the lion's share of the hard graft, and who has been an absolute pleasure to work with. And thanks too to everyone at Bluebird, especially the ever-patient food editor Martha Burley, to David Loftus for his delicious photographs, to Pip Spence home economist extraordinaire, Superfantastic for inspired design and Jane Turnbull (my agent and Peta's) for endless hand holding. And, as ever, Francisca Sankson, for proofreading and much else. Yes, I know you were all just doing your job, but 'over and above the call of duty' does spring to mind. *Prue*

With thanks to my husband, Rich, without whom I would never have made it through my first few months at the Ivy; his support and words of encouragement back when I would come home crying after every shift were the only thing which stopped me packing it in after a few days. Huge thanks also to my parents, James and Penny, both of whom instilled a love of good food and cooking in me from a young age, and have supported me through thick and thin. Thanks also to Liza Mustafa, a great friend, and culinary mentor, who has taught me an enormous amount, and without whom I doubt I would have been in a position to write this. Thanks to Jane Turnbull for being so instrumental in this, and to everybody at Bluebird who have made this book such a pleasure to work on, and who have produced it so beautifully. And last but definitely not least, thanks to Prue, an absolute inspiration to me, and to us all I think it's safe to say. Thank you for all that you've taught me, and most of all, for giving me the opportunity to write this with you. *Peta*

index

Note: page numbers in **bold** refer to illustrations.

a

almond 98, 173–4, 198, 202, 235, 237–40
   apricot and almond tarte Normande 180–1
   Bing cherry and almond cake 218–19, **220–1**
   brown butter, rhubarb and almond tray bake
      232, 233–4
amaretti biscuits, summer fruit and amaretti galette
    178, **179**
apple, Dorset apple cake 228, **229**
apricot 98
   apricot and almond tarte Normande 180–1
aquafaba 15
artichoke, sunblush tomato and mozzarella bruschetta
   39, 40
asparagus
   asparagus galette with mascarpone 105
   pea gnudi with asparagus and garlic butter 66, **67**
aubergine 70–2, 84–8, 116
   ricotta cavatelli with aubergine and tomato sauce
      74, **75**
avocado 41–3, 133
   twice-baked potatoes with chilli, garlic and
      avocado 37

b

banana, best banana-choc bread 226
bean(s) 32, 82
   black bean chilli with corn and lime salsa 94, **95**
   butter bean and sweet potato stew 90
   homemade baked beans 91
   slow-roasted tomato, chickpea, halloumi and French
      bean salad 122, **123**
biscuits
   black pepper oat biscuits 159
   cinnamon shortbread bites 164
   coconut macaroons 174, **175**
   lemon posset with shortbread 200–1
   odds and ends cheese biscuits 158
   ricciarelli with candied peel **172**, 173
   see also cookies
bitter after dinner bites 166, **167**
black bean chilli with corn and lime salsa 94, **95**
black pepper oat biscuits 159
blackberry
   blackberry compote 208–10, **209**
   blackberry and lemon pavlova 208–10, **209**
blue cheese and raisin scones 152–4, **153**
borek, spinach and feta borek **52**, 53
bread 137–48
   best banana-choc bread 226
   brioche 145
   bruschetta two ways 38–40, **39**
   courgette, pea and mint soup with goat's cheese toasts
      28, **29**
   everyday oat bread 146–7
   fruit bread 148, **149**
   malted wholemeal soda bread 138, **139**
   pesto and goat's cheese bread pudding 96, **97**
   tomato and basil focaccia 142–4, **143**
   wholemeal seeded bread 140–1
bread and butter pudding, deluxe 194
breadcrumbs 45–7, 62, 102–4, 118, 188–90
brioche 145
broccoli, potato gnocchi with pistachio pesto and purple
   sprouting broccoli 68–9
brownies, sea salt and caramelized nut chocolate
   brownies **236**, 237
bruschetta two ways:
   artichoke, sunblush tomato and mozzarella bruschetta
      39, 40

chocolate and orange mousse 182, **183**

chocolate and orange trifle 184–6

chocolate sauce 184–6

peppermint ice with chocolate sauce 206, **207**

salted caramel éclairs with a chocolate glaze
191–2, **193**

sea salt and caramelized nut chocolate brownies
236, 237

choux pastry, salted caramel éclairs with a chocolate glaze
191–2, **193**

cinnamon shortbread bites 164

clementines in Drambuie 199

coconut 32

coconut macaroons 174, **175**

coconut madeleines 230–1

coconut rice pudding with tropical fruit compote 205

coconut syrup 230–1

compote 196, **197**

blackberry compote 208–10, **209**

tropical fruit compote 205

cookies

chocolate chip and brown sugar cookies 170, **171**

chocolate fudge cookies 168, **169**

courgette 28, 70–2, 87–8, 128

cream 184–6, 191–2, 194–6, 198, 200–2, 206,
208–10

crème fraîche 100

linguine with porcini, crème fraîche and truffle oil 79

crumble 235

greengage crumble 204

cucumber 119, 124, 128

curry

curried pea and potato samosa 48, **49**

curried tomato sauce 108–9

lentil dhal with poached eggs and roti canai 22–4, **25**

paneer curry 92, **93**

custard, for vegetable tarts 87–8

d

dairy replacements 15

date(s)

date and walnut flapjacks 165

Prue's sticky date cake 217

dhal, lentil dhal with poached eggs and roti canai
22–4, **25**

Drambuie, clementines in Drambuie 199

dressings 126

harissa dressing 130, **131**

tahini dressing 41–3, **42**

dried fruit 148, 152–4, 217, 240

e

éclairs, salted caramel éclairs with a chocolate glaze
191–2, **193**

egg

leftover vegetable frittata 44

lentil dhal with poached eggs and roti canai 22–4, **25**

mini spinach, ricotta and egg pies 100, **101**

pasta frittata with tomato sauce 73

shakshuka with baked eggs 116, **117**

egg replacements 15

elderflower cordial, gooseberry and elderflower fool 195

Eton mess, Prue's patent-improved Eton mess 196, **197**

f

falafel, harissa falafel wraps with quick-pickled cabbage
41–3, **42**

feta 130

creamy polenta with sweetcorn, feta and caponata
84–6, **85**

spinach and feta borek **52**, 53

l

laksa, fragrant laksa with tofu puffs 32, **33**

lasagne, big roasted vegetable lasagne 70–2, **71**

leek

    crustless quiche with sweetcorn, leek and Wensleydale 118

    leek and Cheddar sausage rolls 45–6, **47**

legumes 14

    see also specific legumes

lemon

    blackberry and lemon pavlova 208–10, **209**

    lemon and bergamot drizzle cake 222–3, **224**

    lemon curd 208–10, **209**

    lemon posset with shortbread 200–1

    red lentil and lemon kofte 134, **135**

lentil(s) 132

    lentil dhal with poached eggs and roti canai 22–4, **25**

    Puy lentil and sweet potato salad 126, **127**

    red lentil and lemon kofte 134, **135**

lettuce 41–3, 124, 133, 134

lime salsa 94, **95**

linguine with porcini, crème fraîche and truffle oil 79

m

macaroni, best macaroni cheese 62, **63**

macaroons, coconut macaroons 174, **175**

Madeira cake for every occasion 216

madeleines, coconut madeleines 230–1

malted wholemeal soda bread 138, **139**

mango 205

    mango sorbet 212, **213**

Marmite and cheese soufflé 36

mascarpone with asparagus galette 105

meat 10–11

    see also specific meats

meringue 196, 208–10

    meringue drops 184–6

    monster meringues 202, **203**

milk, vegetarian 15

mint 132, 133

    courgette, pea and mint soup with goat's cheese toasts 28, **29**

    pea, mint and goat's cheese fritters 114, **115**

    peppermint ice with chocolate sauce 206, **207**

    pomegranate and mint granita 211

mousse

    chocolate mousse 184–6

    chocolate and orange mousse 182, **183**

mozzarella, artichoke, sunblush tomato and mozzarella bruschetta **39**, 40

mushroom

    linguine with porcini, crème fraîche and truffle oil 79

    mushroom and hazelnut pithivier 102–4, **103**

n

nut(s) 15

    sea salt and caramelized nut chocolate brownies **236**, 237

    see also specific nuts

o

oat(s) 165

    black pepper oat biscuits 159

    everyday oat bread 146–7

    oat milk 15

oil, walnut and parsley oil 20, **21**

olive(s) (green) 84–6, 130

onion, mixed onion tarte tatin 110–11

orange 194, 198

    caramelized blood orange and polenta upside-down cake 238–9

    chocolate and orange mousse 182, **183**

about

Prue

Prue Leith has been at the top of the British food scene for nearly sixty years. She has seen huge success not only as founder of the renowned Leith's School of Food and Wine, but also as a caterer, restaurateur, teacher, TV cook, food journalist, novelist and cookery book author. She's also been a leading figure in campaigns to improve food in schools, hospitals and in the home. Well known as a judge on *The Great British Menu*, now she is a judge on the nation's favourite TV programme, *The Great British Bake Off*. Prue was born in South Africa and lives in the UK.

Peta

Peta Leith is a professional pastry chef, food writer and menu consultant who trained at the French Culinary Institute in New York. Following a year-long apprenticeship with Claire Ptak, she went on to spend seven years as a pastry chef at The Ivy. She lives in Bedfordshire with her husband and two children. This is her first book.

First published 2020 by Bluebird
an imprint of Pan Macmillan
The Smithson, 6 Briset Street, London EC1M 5NR
Associated companies throughout the world
www.panmacmillan.com

ISBN   978-1-5098-9150-4

9 8 7 6 5 4 3 2 1

A CIP catalogue record for this book is available from the British Library.

Printed and bound in China.

Publisher Carole Tonkinson
Managing Editor Martha Burley
Editorial Assistant Zainab Dawood
Senior Production Controller Sarah Badhan
Art Direction & Design Superfantastic
Food Styling Pip Spence
Prop Styling Cynthia Blackett

Visit www.panmacmillan.com to read more about all our books and to buy them. You will
also find features, author interviews and news of any author events, and you can sign up for
e-newsletters so that you're always first to hear about our new releases.

Paper Flower Art

Paper Flower Art

Create beautifully realistic floral arrangements

JESSIE CHUI

Contents

Introduction

THE ART OF PAPER FLOWERS came to me unexpectedly. I stumbled upon it when I was planning my own wedding. But it wasn't very long before capturing nature's essence became a passion. I began as a student of the paper flower artists that came before me. Techniques from Lia Griffith, Livia Cetti, Lynn Dolan, Kate Alarcon, Jennifer Tran, Margie Keates, Susan Beech and Tiffanie Turner all influenced me in one way or another, some of which is evident in this book. My exposure to these amazing artists and their art fast-tracked me to where I am today, and I am grateful for their guidance and generosity.

In time, I've managed to find my own artistic aesthetic and colour expression, adapting techniques I've learned from others and discovering ones on my own. My breakthrough moment was when I stopped counting petals and relied on my intuition. It was then that I fell in love with the creative process as opposed to the result – the process of constructing a flower, the process of planning and executing paper flower sculptures, the process of envisioning unique colour combinations.

These are the processes that I hope to pass on to you through this book. I have included templates, petal counts and placement for each flower; however, I encourage you to leave that behind once you've gone through the book. Instead, try to cut petals freehand, evaluate the shape of the flower as you go along, and make on-the-spot decisions on where the petals should be placed, how they should be placed, and whether you need more or fewer petals. This dialogue with your work will elevate your creative process. I promise.

Jessie Chui

Tools and materials

CREPE PAPER

Crepe paper has deep grain lines that allow it to be stretched and pulled in different directions, expanding the paper significantly. It has a top side and a bottom side; with some types of crepe paper, such as the 180g weight, this can be quite noticeable. Each type of crepe paper has unique characteristics. There are several types of crepe paper available. These are the ones I use most frequently.

DOUBLE-SIDED (DOUBLETTE) ❶

Heavier than the fine crepe paper, this consists of two fine crepe papers fused together during the manufacturing process. It has a weight of 90g per square metre, reasonable stretch, and holds its shape well over time. It comes in a variety of colour combinations, with one side a different colour from the other. It is lightfast and will bleed when wet, so it dyes and bleaches easily. I use this for paper flowers because its grain is so fine and it has a very smooth texture. It comes in bright colours and is also comparatively the most expensive type of crepe paper available. Each fold measures 10 x 49in (25 x 124cm). Manufactured by Werola in Germany.

EXTRA-FINE ❷

To me, this crepe paper feels heavier and thicker than fine crepe paper (although not as thick as double-sided crepe paper), and stretches more effectively. It is

> **NOTE**
>
> Throughout this book, when referring to Italian crepe paper, I've used the colour references used by Carte Fini (a distributor of this type of paper), followed by that used by Cartotecnica Rossi, if applicable.

lightfast and bleeds when wet, but does not soak up liquids evenly or effectively. The paper reacts similarly to 60g Italian crepe paper (see below) with respect to liquids such as water, bleach and dyes. Unfortunately, this is quite difficult to obtain if you live outside the US. Manufactured by Werola in Germany.

60G ITALIAN ❸

Similar to fine crepe paper, lightweight crepe is thin and available at 60g per square metre. It is more robust than fine crepe paper, with a coarser grain, and holds its shape better in the long run. It is also lightfast and will bleed when wet. It does not soak up liquids as well as fine or double-sided crepe paper, so it does not dye or bleach evenly. Each roll measures $19^{1}/_{2}$ x $98^{1}/_{2}$in (49.5 x 250cm), and the colours are identified by numbers. Manufactured by Cartotecnica Rossi in Italy.

FINE (SINGLE-SIDED) ❹

This is the thinnest and lightest of all the crepe papers available, at only 32g per square metre. It comes in a rainbow of colours, including metallics. It has a fine grain and a reasonable stretch, but over time it tends to lose its shape faster than other types. It will fade over time if it is not stored in an opaque box. It will bleed when wet, so it dyes and bleaches beautifully. Be careful when you are applying glue to it; if you apply too much, it will soak through the paper and the paper will not stick. I tend to avoid using it for flowers in a bouquet, although I might use it for petals in the centre of the flower, mix it with heavier-weight crepe paper, fuse two pieces to create my own double-sided crepe paper, or use it for petal-dense flowers such as ranunculus. Each fold measures 20 x 90in (50.5 x 228cm). Manufactured by Dennison in the USA.

180G ITALIAN ❺

This crepe paper is often called 'florist crepe' because it was originally used by florists to wrap bouquets. It is heavy and sturdy, weighing 180g per square metre, with deep grain lines and machine lines. Its stretch is excellent and it holds its shape well. It comes in a multitude of solid colours, ombré colours and metallics. I use this for vibrant-coloured flowers. It is lightfast, although some colours fade quicker than others. It will bleed when wet, but does not soak up liquids as well as fine or double-sided crepe paper, so does not dye or bleach evenly. It is perfect for larger flowers, as it can be quite stiff. My preference is to stretch this paper before using. Each roll measures $19^{1}/_{2}$ x $98^{1}/_{2}$in (49.5 x 250cm), and the colours are identified by numbers. Manufactured by Cartotecnica Rossi in Italy.

100G AND 180G CHINESE ❻

These come in a lighter and a heavier weight. Their grain lines are deeper than the fine, double-sided and lightweight, but shallower than the florist crepe. They come in muted colours and have a loose stretch. They do not hold their shape well, so I only use them stretched and treat them like fine crepe paper. They are lightfast, but do not fade as quickly as the other types of crepe paper. They bleed when wet but, they don't soak up liquids evenly. They don't dye or bleach well unless the liquid is applied with a brush. Each roll measures $19^{1}/_{2}$ x $98^{1}/_{2}$in (49.5 x 250cm). Made in China.

LEFT

The Koko Loko rose (see page 76) uses 180g Italian crepe as the stiffness suits large petals.

5

6
(180g Chinese)

6
(100g Chinese)

BASIC TOOLS

WIRE ❶

I use stem wires as support for the flower structures. They come in various gauges and finishes. The higher the gauge number, the thinner the wire. I use 18 and 16 gauges for flowers stems and 20, 22, 24 and 26 gauges for branches and leaf stems. For fine details, I like to use 30 and 33 gauges. Generally, if I want a flower or stem to look more delicate, I use a thinner stem. If a flower has a heavy head or if it will be used in a tall arrangement, I use a heavier 8-gauge metal stick.

The wires can be unfinished, painted in green or white, or covered with paper or cloth. I prefer paper-covered wires, because the wire is fine and delicate, as opposed to cloth-covered stem wires, which are heavily covered. Beware of thin-gauge stem wire purchased in discount stores; they tend to be made from inferior materials and the stem wire will be too soft. I prefer Japanese-made stem wires.

TACKY GLUE ❷

Tacky glue is thicker than white glue and dries faster, so is ideal for paper crafts. You only need a dot of it to glue a petal base to the stem wire. Keep in mind that if you apply too much glue to fine crepe paper it will not stick, so use lightly. I generally use it in a squeeze bottle placed upside-down in a small glass mason jar to keep the glue ready for use. When I am priming my stamen fringes, I squeeze some onto a dish or scrap paper.

GLUE STICK ❸

These are efficient for laminating smaller crepe paper sections.

FLORAL TAPE ❹

This is a self-adhesive tape that comes in a variety of colours. I mainly use green, brown and white floral tapes to make the centre of the flower, finish stems, attach leaves and assemble the flower stem. I even use it to attach petals to the flower, as it can change the way your petals fall open. I specifically use floral tape if I know that the flower stem will be placed in water or used with fresh flowers.

PENCIL ❺

I use this to mark off where to cut on the crepe paper.

RULER ❻

This is my best friend, next to my scissors, when I am cutting freehand. I use a ruler to measure crepe paper strips and determine the size of petals.

WIRE CUTTERS/PLIERS ❼

I use these to cut or bend stem wires. In addition to a light-weight set of pliers, I also have a heavy-duty pair that can easily cut through multiple stems and thick metal rods.

HOT GLUE GUN AND HOT GLUE ❽

I like using hot glue when I am making a petal-heavy flower with 180g florist crepe, large flowers or dahlias, or using a Styrofoam ball base. My favourite hot glue gun has a micro-tip that is perfect for more intricate work.

SKEWER AND PENCIL CRAYON ❾

When I want to create a narrow petal base or a funnel in a flower, I use the tip of a skewer or pencil crayon in the petal colour.

SCISSORS ❿

I use three types of scissors. I use a big pair of heavy-duty scissors to cut my heavy crepe paper, cut through multiple folds and cut multiple petals. I use a pair of small sharp scissors to cut petals and details. For fringing, I use a pair of spring-loaded scissors.

SHORT 18- AND 16-GAUGE STEM WIRE AND TOOTHPICK ⓫

I use 16-gauge stem wire as a curling tool because I often have short lengths of it cut from different flower projects. To make tighter curls, I use a toothpick or an 18-gauge stem wire.

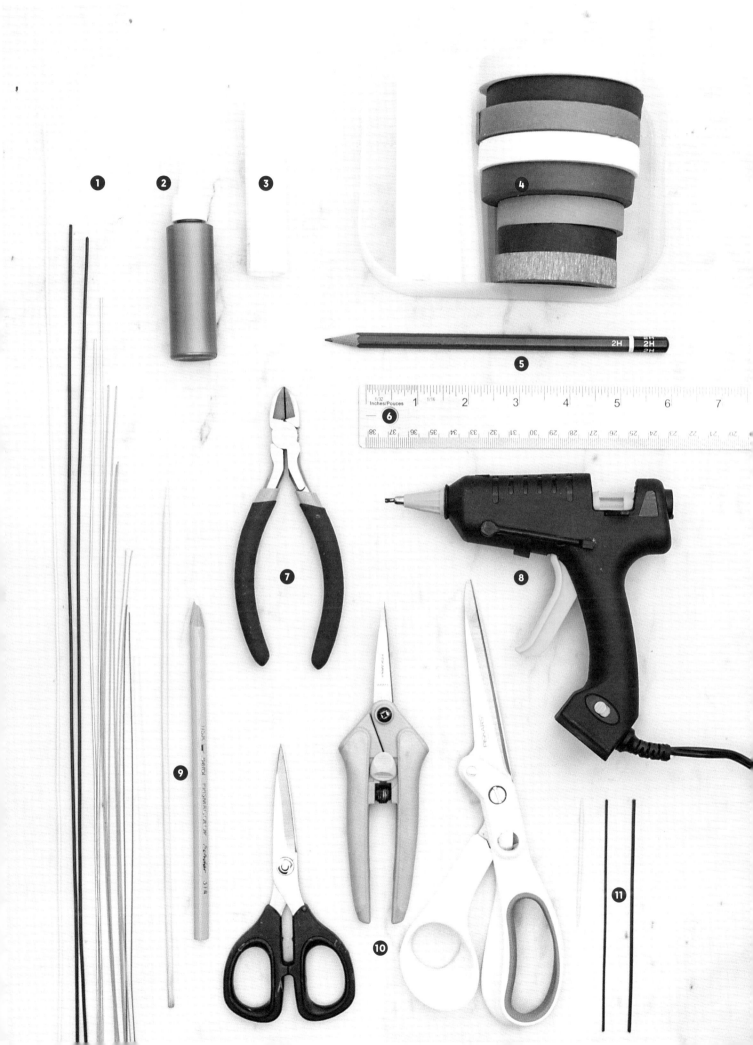

SPECIFIC TOOLS AND MATERIALS

CINNAMON AND PASTEL-OATMEAL POLLEN

I use cinnamon as pollen on fringes and also make a combination of shaved pastel and ground oatmeal to create a pollen-like mixture (see page 23).

SAFETY SWABS, COTTON WOOL BALLS, TOILET PAPER AND PAPER TOWEL ❷

I use these items to create the underlying foundations of flowers or to thicken flower stems. I use safety swabs for some flower centres, such rosebuds. I cut the ends of the safety swab from the middle tube and insert the end of a stem wire into the end tube and glue it. Another way of creating a centre is by using whatever paper you have, including toilet paper or paper towels. A section of this can be cut into smaller strips that can be used, with glue, to wrap around a stem wire or Styrofoam ball to create a different shape. For branches and ranunculus buds, I like to use kitchen paper towel, which is less fluffy, while for rosebuds I prefer to use toilet paper. Finally, I use cotton wool balls to create a spherical centre.

AIR-DRY CLAY ❸

I like Crayola Magic clay, an air-dry clay that is considerably lighter than most polymer clays. It is also non-toxic, fairly easy to clean up, does not leave a residue on hands, and is easy to work with on simple botanical parts. You can also dye it with liquid or gel food colouring (also non-toxic), although if you add liquid food colouring you will have to let it air dry before working with it or else it becomes too sticky. Once dry, you can paint over it with pastels or acrylic paint.

STYROFOAM BALLS ❹

Styrofoam balls are soft foam balls, which I use to form the underlying structure of a flower. They are usually available at art stores and come in various sizes. I most often use the ³/₄in (19mm) and 1in (25mm).

FUSIBLE WEBBING ❺

I use this to fuse two pieces of crepe paper together. There are various types; some come with paper backing and some without. I find paper-backed fusing easier to

cut to size for narrow strips and to fuse. I like Heat n' Bond LITE Iron-on Adhesive, which comes in a roll 17in x 5yd (43cm x 4.8m). Pellon also has a paper-backed fusing called Wonder-Under (#805).

PARCHMENT (BAKING) PAPER ❻

I use this to protect the work surface and iron from the fusible webbing.

IRON ❼

I use an old iron specifically for my crafts.

CLEAR TUBING ❽

I use clear tubing to thicken flower stems. This comes in various thickness and diameters. I buy ³/₁₆in (5mm) diameter clear tubing from an aquarium store, or ¹/₄in (6mm) diameter from a hardware store. I thread it over the stem wire and secure it at the flower base with hot glue. If I am using the flower for an arrangement where I will be using a pin frog (see page 222), I cut the clear tubing 1–2in (2.5–5cm) shorter than the stem wire so that the clear tubing is not inserted into the pin frog.

COLOUR SPRAYS ❾ *(shown on page 16)*

I use sprays when colouring a large quantity of paper; when I want to create an ombré gradient of colours or just a layer of colour over an existing colour; and when I want to protect my work. The Design Master brand (distributed under Smithers-Oasis) is my favourite. Their lacquer-based paint comes out of the can in a fine mist and it is very fast-drying. You can also layer the colours on top of each other, creating different combination of colours or intensity. I generally use the Colortool line, but use TintIt (also known as Just for Flowers) when I want to layer in transparent dye colours. I find the sprays protect the paper from fading.

ALCOHOL INKS ❿ *(shown on page 16)*

Alcohol-based inks are also transparent dyes. Due to their alcohol content, they are fast-drying. They are also highly pigmented. To extend the colour, you can use an alcohol ink blender or 91% (or higher) isopropyl alcohol, also known as rubbing alcohol. I use these inks sparingly,

as the fumes from the alcohol can be irritating. They are perfect for creating painterly colours on petals and leaves. That said, I find it quite challenging to control the intensity of the colour, and even its hue. The ink and alcohol come in 0.5oz (15ml) bottles and can be applied with a sponge or a regular paintbrush. The two most popular brands are Ranger Adirondack Alcohol Inks by Tim Holtz and Jacquard Piñata Alcohol Inks. I also use Copic Marker Ink refills, which are tubes of ink that are meant to refill Copic alcohol markers. These colours are much more predictable than other alcohol inks.

RUBBING ALCOHOL ⑪

I use this to dilute alcohol inks. I pour a small quantity into a squeeze bottle with a fine tip so I can have greater control over the amount that is mixed with the ink.

WATER-BASED INKS AND FOOD COLOURING ⑫

There is a variety of water-based inks, including drawing ink, watercolour ink, calligraphy ink and acrylic ink. I prefer watercolour and drawing inks. They are transparent dyes so the dye bleeds through crepe paper and the colour can be seen on both sides. I use Ecoline liquid watercolours, Winsor & Newton and Indian drawing ink, and Tim Holtz Distress Inks. I also use non-toxic food colouring to dye my papers or colour my clay.

PAINTBRUSHES ⑬

Over the years I have accumulated a variety of synthetic bristle and natural bristle brushes. I try to use specific brushes for alcohol inks.

PAINT PALETTES ⑭

I use a metal paint palette and a glass butter dish for my paints and glue. For alcohol inks, I re-use mason jars and plastic egg or food containers with small wells/cups so I can dispose of them easily.

MOD PODGE ⑮

Often used for decoupage, I like to use this all-in-one glue, sealer and finisher to create a shine on a part of the paper flower, such as the centre or the leaves. It comes in matte and gloss, and can be applied using a sponge applicator or brush.

ACRYLIC PAINT ⑯

I use two types of acrylic paint. For most of my work, I use inexpensive craft paint that comes in a bottle: it comes in a variety of pre-mixed colours and is quite fluid. When I want a specific colour or a thick viscosity for particular botanicals and flowers, I prefer a heavier artist's paint that comes in a tube.

ALCOHOL INK MARKERS ⑰

I love alcohol-ink based markers for detail work because you can blend the colours together and also blend them into the paper. I like Copic markers, although some art stores may carry cheaper own-brand versions. Their formulas are similar to alcohol-based inks in bottles, except the applicator tool is the sponged tip of the marker. Copic sells refill tubes, which carry the ink alone.

PERMANENT BLACK MARKER ⑱

I sometimes use a thick black marker for colour.

WATER, BLEACH AND TEA ⑲

I use these to change the colour of the crepe paper.

SOFT PASTELS ⑳

Pastels are a favourite of any paper florist because they come in a wide array of colours, they apply colour to crepe paper easily, and they are generally inexpensive. I mainly use soft pastels, in the traditional stick form which I scrape with a knife, and a pastel that sits in a pan; I like the brand PanPastel.

PASTEL SPONGE WEDGE AND BRUSHES ㉑

I use this to apply pastels to crepe paper. PanPastel sells sponge bars and covers in various sizes and shapes. I use inexpensive make-up sponge wedges, and a set of travel make-up brushes.

FINISHING (not shown)

At the end of a project, I will spray a finishing that protects the paper from fading, such as an archival spray or Krylon UV-Resistant Clear Coating in matte or gloss. Be aware that these sprays may slightly change the colour of your work. I also use a workable fixative spray on top of pastel to set it or to enhance the staying power of the pastel powder on paper.

General techniques

USING TEMPLATES

When reading the templates, there are specific marks to pay attention to:

Double-ended arrow line Indicates the direction of the grain line on the petal or leaf. When cutting out the petal or leaf using the template, align the grain line on the template with the grain on the crepe paper.

Place on fold Indicates where you should place the template and also that you should place that side of the template on a fold in the crepe paper. Usually this mark appears on leaves or petals where only half of the leaf or petal is shown on the template, because the crepe paper has been folded in half with the expectation that, when you cut the template, you cut both layers the same.

Dotted line Indicates where to fold or crease on the petal or leaf or, in some cases, where to make a cut.

Once you become familiar with the shapes of the petals and leaves, try cutting freehand using the templates just as visual guides.

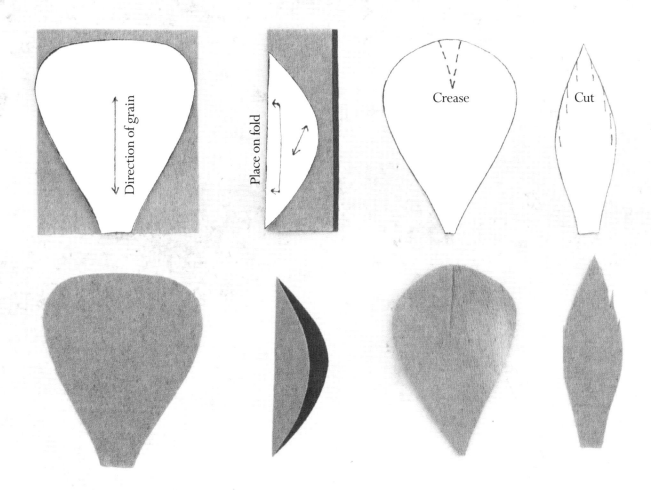

PREPARING PAPER FOR CUTTING

I like to prepare my crepe paper by cutting it into strips so that I can cut my petals as efficiently as possible. Once the paper has been cut into strips, I can then cut the petals freehand or with a template. I also colour my crepe paper after it has been cut into strips.

For fine or double-sided crepe paper, I cut across the entire fold of the paper, across the grain, to get a long strip (see right). I cut the height of the petals I will be cutting or the template. Once cut, I fold the strip along the grain, the width of the petal or template. I continue to fold the strip accordion-style until I have five to six layers stacked on top of each other. Then I place the template on the very top and cut through the five or six layers, or cut freehand.

For crepe paper that come in rolls, like the 60g or 180g, I cut a large section about 10–12in (25–30cm) into the roll from its end, and then cut strips across the grain that are the height of the petals (see below).

LAMINATING CREPE PAPER

I sometimes create my own double-layer crepe paper by gluing two to four layers of crepe paper together. I do this for several reasons: to increase the strength of the crepe paper; to maintain the shape of the paper; or to create a paper with different colours on each side. This is called laminating.

There are a few ways to create your own double-layered (or triple- or quadruple-layered) paper. You can use a glue spray adhesive, tacky glue (or glue stick) or iron-on fusible webbing. I prefer the latter two methods, and these are the two methods shown in the tutorials.

TACKY GLUE OR GLUE STICK

I like to use tacky glue or a glue stick to secure two pieces of 180g or 100g crepe paper together when I want to toughen up my petals or stamen, or if I want to shape them in a particular way. When I am laminating the florist or heavy crepe paper, I always stretch out the grain lines first; when working with fine and double-sided crepe, I don't stretch it.

I prefer to work in strips because they are easier to manage. I apply the glue with a brush (or foam applicator) to one side of a strip of crepe paper. I then place a second strip of crepe paper on top, making sure to align the grain lines, and then press to smooth out any bubbles or kinks.

Sometimes, rather than laminating two separate pieces of crepe paper, I use one single strip, fold it midway along the grain, apply glue to one side of the fold, then fold again to laminate and to get a strip half the original width.

I like to work with the laminated strip when damp; otherwise, when dry, it hardens like papier-mâché and I cannot mould it. While the paper is damp from the glue, I cut out the petals or leaves and sculpt them into shape so they will dry to that shape. While the laminated strip is damp is also the perfect time to apply pastels, as the pastel dust adheres to the glue very well. Tacky glue dries fairly quickly, whereas glue stick has a longer drying time.

IRON-ON FUSIBLE WEBBING

I prefer this method for fine, extra-fine and 60g crepe paper. I tend to use this method after I have bleached or dyed the crepe paper and wish to strengthen it.

Before fusing, I prepare my work area by placing a large piece of parchment paper on top of my iron board to protect my work surface. Next, I cut another piece of parchment paper to be placed between the crepe paper and my iron to protect my iron from getting fusible webbing on it.

First, I iron out any wrinkles before fusing. I press down on the paper rather than using a sliding motion, as movement will stretch the paper further. Then I cut a piece of fusible webbing in the same shape/length as my crepe paper. If the fusible webbing has no paper backing, I place it on one of the strips, with the edges lined up, and then place the second strip on top.

Once the iron is hot, I place it on top and press the three layers together so that the fusible webbing melts and adheres to the crepe paper. If the fusible webbing has a paper backing, you can iron it onto one piece of crepe paper, remove the paper backing, place the second piece of crepe paper on top, and apply the iron on top to fuse the pieces together. I like to use Pellon Wonder Web (#807) (with no backing) and Heat n' Bond Lite Iron-On Adhesive (with backing).

I find it is easier to use fusing with backing when your crepe paper is small or narrow, because the paper makes it easier to cut with more precision. Pellon (with no backing) is great for laminating large pieces of crepe paper because its width is 20in (50.8cm), which is the exact width of a fold of fine crepe paper.

I have found that some fusible webbing (such as Heat n' Bond) may leave a subtle pattern on the crepe paper once fused. This doesn't bother me too much because it goes when I stretch the paper. However, it may also decrease the effectiveness of tacky glue on the paper; Heat n' Bond, in particular, seems to seep through fine crepe paper and make it a little 'plastic', so the glue cannot properly adhere to the crepe paper. In these cases, I switch to hot glue.

TIP

I sometimes find that when I stretch or cup laminated crepe paper, the layers come apart or small pockets of it 'pop' up. In this case, I take the iron and press over that section to re-fuse the pieces together.

21

FRINGING

Fringe or fringing is the effect made by repeatedly cutting into the edge of a piece of crepe paper, thereby creating long thin pieces that are still attached together on the other edge. The thinner the pieces, the finer the fringe. You can cut short or long fringes depending on the purpose of the fringe.

The most common use for a fringe is to make the centre stamen of a flower. A fringe is cut on the long edge of a strip of crepe paper, with the cuts parallel to the grain lines. To be efficient, I fold the strip of crepe paper into two or four layers, and cut through all of the layers at a time. For very fine fringes, I cut only one layer at a time. It takes practice and focus to cut finely, but try to do this, as your work will look more delicate and realistic. I use my spring-loaded micro scissors when I fringe because it gives me plenty of control over the blades and the handles spring back without my hand doing any work.

REDUCING BULK

This technique is mainly applicable to fringe strips and fringed centres. When you wrap a long strip of crepe paper around a stem wire, it creates a lot of bulk, especially if the strip is very long. To reduce the bulk and to create a smooth transition from the stem wire to the fringed strip so that it is easier to finish, I like to cut off any excess paper at the bottom of the strip. There are two ways to do this.

The first is to make a diagonal cut starting from the middle of one short edge (or just below the fringe if it is a fringed strip), to the bottom corner of the other short edge.

The second is to cut triangles or notches into the paper from the bottom long edge, with the triangle point extended up to the mid-way point (or just below the fringe if it is a fringed strip). Of course, you can also combine the two techniques.

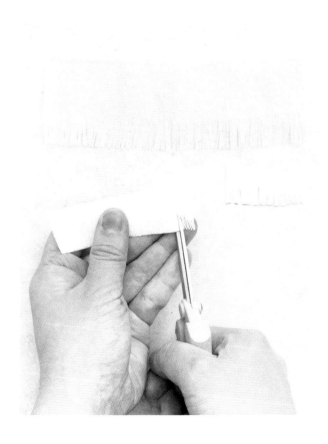

CONTINUOUS STRIP CUTTING

For certain flowers, the petals or calyx are attached together at the base along a linked strip. It is like a fringe only the long fringe strips are replaced with a petal or sepal. I often use a continuous strip for calyxes or petals where the flower is very small and delicate (such as the Chocolate Cosmos, Fruit Blossom Branch and Panicle Hydrangea) or when the type of crepe paper lends itself to this technique, like 180g Italian crepe paper.

To create a continuous strip, I fold the strip of crepe paper grain-wise accordion-style a number of times, then cut the petal or sepal shape with the base of the petal or sepal one-quarter to one-third of the way up from the bottom edge of the crepe paper. This way, when you open up the strip, the petals and sepals are linked together via the bottom edge of the crepe paper.

MAKING POLLEN

There are a number of ways to create pollen on the filament. The easiest is to use a marker in yellow-orange to paint on the colour to mimic pollen. Another way is to use spices such as cinnamon or turmeric: dip the stamen fringe into tacky glue and then into the spice and shake off the excess. These spices are easily purchased in bulk and are inexpensive, so this is what I use for workshops. However, not everyone likes the smell of spices (and turmeric can stain), so I don't use them on work for clients.

My preferred method is to use ground pastel in dark yellow-orange or goldenrod (for the colour) and mix it with finely ground oatmeal (for the thickener).

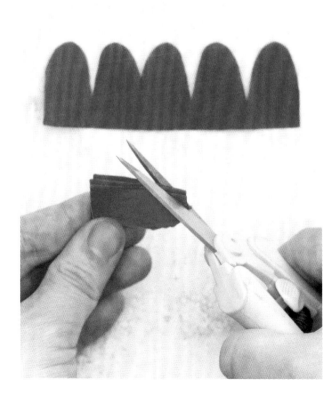

WORKING WITH FLORAL TAPE

Floral tape makes assembly very efficient. It is also waterproof, so it is perfect to use with paper flowers where the stems will go into water.

In order to use floral tape properly, you must stretch it to activate the glue; the tape will then stick to itself when wrapped. I like to roll the stem wire clockwise between the thumb and index finger of my right hand while using my left hand to hold the tape taut, on a slight diagonal, and guide its placement as the stem wire rolls over the floral tape and the tape wraps down on an angle towards the bottom of the stem wire.

If I run out of floral tape while wrapping, I just cut another piece of tape, place it over where my first strip ended, and continue wrapping from there.

I cut floral tape into half-widths when using it on thinner gauges or doing delicate work. To do this, I cut a length of floral tape from the roll, fold the length until it is about 2in (5cm) long, then cut it in half lengthwise.

24

WORKING WITH CREPE TAPE

As an alternative to floral tape, I use a thin strip of crepe paper to finish my stems. I usually use crepe tape when I want to match the colour of the calyx with the stem and I do not have floral tape that matches. I also use it when I am working with very delicate and thin stems (such as sweet peas) and do not want to add bulk to the stems. The general rule regarding the width of the strip is the thinner the stem wire, the narrower the strip of crepe tape to use. I cut thin strips between $\frac{1}{8}$in (3mm) and $\frac{1}{4}$in (6mm).

I cut across the grain for a thin strip. I usually cut the strip from the top or bottom edge of the crepe paper fold, roll or piece. If using 180g Italian or Chinese crepe paper or 100g Chinese crepe paper, I stretch the crepe tape so it is smooth, then dot it with white tacky glue as I wrap down the stem wire on an angle. I use the same technique to wrap it as for floral tape (see left). If you are using fine or extra-fine crepe paper, don't stretch it before applying glue. I find the paper too delicate to handle both the pulling while you wrap and the wet glue. Simply dot it with glue and stretch the fine crepe paper strip as you wrap around the stem wire.

One word of warning: as you are dotting the crepe paper, try to spread the glue across the entire width and length. If the glue sits only in the middle of the strip, it will not attach directly to the stem wire, or may become loose along the stem. When you bend the stem wire, or start attaching other stems to the stem wire, the crepe paper will come apart from the wire, or spin around the wire, or tear off the wire.

ATTACHING STEMS TOGETHER

At times, I like to attach bud stems or leaf stems to the main flower stem, or attach two or three flowers together. I also attach stems together when I attach leaves to the main leaf stem.

To do this, I start by wrapping floral tape or crepe tape on the main flower stem or main leaf stem. I wrap down about 1in (2.5cm), then pause and place the stem I want to attach beside the main stem. I then wrap the floral tape or crepe tape around both stems and continue to go down the main stem on an angle until the stems are covered.

Colouring techniques

I am a colour lover. I am obsessed with getting the exact hue or tint that I envisioned. I either want to replicate the precise colour of a real flower or create a specific colour that I have in mind.

COLOUR THEORY

It is important to understand colour theory and the principles of colour mixing. According to traditional colour theory, red, blue and yellow are the primary colours. The secondary colours, purple, green and orange, are formed when we mix red and blue, blue and green, and red and yellow, respectively. These six colours make up the traditional colour wheel. Colours that sit across from each other on the colour wheel are complementary colours: red and green; blue and orange; yellow and purple.

Colours can also be cool or warm. Reds are biased towards an orange or a violet; blues towards a violet or green; and yellow towards a green or an orange. It is unlikely that you'll find anything that is red, blue or yellow like in the colour wheel or colours that are 'out of the tube'. These biases are what make a flower or an arrangement interesting and unique. Understanding these biases and how colours with the same or different colour biases interact with each other can help you successfully mix coloured pastels on coloured crepe paper; mix colour inks on coloured crepe paper; and mix different coloured crepe papers with each other.

LEFT
Understanding how colours with the same or different colour biases interact will help your creations.

APPLYING COLOUR THEORY TO COLOURING TECHNIQUE
I prefer to work with the colours that come with a specific type of crepe paper. Generally, the more muted colours come in fine and Chinese crepe paper, while the more saturated colours come in Italian crepe paper.

When I have a specific colour in mind, I will first look for it among my stock of crepe papers. If I don't have that exact colour, then I consider which colour is closest and then ask whether I need to darken it, lighten it, make it warmer or cooler, or subtract or add colour. The next step is to consider which colouring techniques work with that type of crepe paper, and whether these techniques can achieve the desired colour. If there seems to be no way to create the colour I want using the paper I have, then I consider colouring or dyeing white crepe paper to the colour I want.

There are various colouring techniques you can use for paper flowers. I have described the ones I like, but don't limit yourself. I generally use the technique that suit the type of paper I'm working with and that works with the colour of that paper.

> **TIP**
>
> If the colour doesn't turn out the way you wanted, then let it be your inspiration. It may move you towards a different colour scheme or add that touch that makes the flower uniquely you. It doesn't have to be the star of the show; it can be the supporting actor, enhancing the work through contrast, or slight variance of colour bias. I often end up using what I had initially thought were rejects because they create the visual interest that I seek.

WATER WASHING AND DIPPING

Water washing or dipping is a technique that can have different effects on different types of crepe paper.

WATER WASHING 180G ITALIAN CREPE PAPER

Water washing removes the machine lines from 180g Italian crepe paper. I cut a section of the crepe paper from the end of the roll, dip it into a water bath (I usually use my sink), let it soak for a little while, then remove to dry. Hot or warm water seems to be more effective.

I hang the piece of water-dipped crepe paper over my bathtub to dry. I place wooden dowels about 24in (60cm) long across my bathtub to use as a rack for the wet crepe paper. Some paper florists dry their paper in an oven or a microwave to quicken the drying time.

Once dry, the machine lines are less obvious and the paper is softer to work with, although some of the stretch is lost and sometimes you will see some dark and some light lines along the grain because the water bled unevenly. If I will be using the crepe paper stretched, then I pre-stretch it before dipping it in water so the colour is more even.

WATER DIPPING FINE CREPE PAPER

For fine crepe paper, I first split the prepared paper (already cut across the folds into strips) into four more manageable lengths so that it soaks up the liquid more evenly. I fold the length in half midway and roll it loosely around my index and middle fingers. With my fingers still in the roll, I dip one edge into the water for two to three seconds. Then, I carefully unroll it and hang the strip on wooden dowels over my bathtub to dry.

The colour will bleed, and the result is a very subtle lightening from the dipped edge. It can be too subtle, so I generally prefer to bleach fine crepe paper instead as the colour change is more obvious.

At times, water can be quite effective in the most unexpected ways. For example, for extra-fine crepe paper in Aubergine, the colour that appears from the bleed is a completely different colour.

28

WATER WASHING DOUBLE-SIDED CREPE PAPER

With double-sided crepe paper, water washing will bleed its colour as the two colours mix together. Like the process for fine crepe paper, I cut the paper into manageable lengths, roll it loosely, and then push it into the water and let the paper soak in the water. The colours will bleed into the water and the crepe paper will end up with a colour that falls somewhere in between the two original colours.

TEA STAINING

To create a muted or slightly browned overlay, I steep black tea and dilute it to create a tea bath. The technique is exactly the same as for water washing; simply substitute tea for water. I recommend you initially make the tea stronger, then dilute the tea with water to control how dark you want the overlay to be, or dilute it gradually to get different stain strengths and tea-stained paper. Here I have cut a strip of 180g Italian crepe paper, stretched it, and immersed it in a tea bath. Similar to water washing, fine or double-sided crepe paper will expand when wet and will lose some of its stretch.

BLEACHING

I like the interesting effects created by removing colour by bleaching; the results are unpredictable, and it is fun to be inspired by the colours of the crepe paper as I cut it. I use the paper based on whether I want the light or the dark part to show. I cherish the painterly effect you can achieve with bleach, but I use it sparingly.

The technique for bleaching is similar to water washing and tea staining. I use a solution of one part bleach to seven parts water; I measure using the cap of my small bleach bottle. I pre-cut the crepe paper into strips, cut each strip into four, and then fold them in half midway and roll it around my index and middle fingers. With my fingers still in the roll, I dip one end of the roll into the bleach solution for two to three seconds. I gently unroll it and hang the strip on wooden dowels over my bathtub. The thicker the roll, the longer the dip required to achieve the same effect for a thinner roll. The longer the dip, the more the bleach liquid absorbs and spreads along the grain. Finally, the quicker the dip, the less bleach liquid is absorbed and the more concentrated the bleach is at the edges of the strip.

Like water washing and tea staining, fine or double-sided crepe paper will expand when wet and will lose some of its stretch.

I generally bleach fine crepe paper and 60g and 180g Italian crepe papers. I do not use this technique with Chinese crepe paper because the bleach removes most if not all of the colour.

SAFETY TIP

Note that the fumes from bleaching can be harmful. I strongly recommend that you bleach in a well-ventilated space and wear a respiratory mask and gloves. I also recommend extreme caution when bleaching yellow crepe paper, as the fumes from the yellow pigment can be toxic.

BLEACHING FINE CREPE PAPER

My favourite type to bleach is fine crepe paper. The paper absorbs liquid effectively and the liquid spreads the bleach evenly. Some colours bleach better than others. You can experiment with bleaching on different sides of the crepe paper; I generally only dip along one long edge to achieve an ombré effect.

BLEACHING 60G ITALIAN AND 180G ITALIAN CREPE PAPER

60g crepe paper does not absorb and spread liquid as evenly or as effectively as fine crepe paper. When I dip it, I press the edge into the bleach liquid, and even hold part of the sides of the crepe in the bleach to give it the time it needs to soak up the liquid. I rarely achieve an ombré effect, but the section where the colour transitions from the original colour to white can be quite interesting with its unevenness and a touch of an unexpected colour. Extra-fine crepe paper bleaches similarly.

180g Italian crepe paper reacts similarly to bleach as 60g paper. It does not absorb liquid well or evenly, so you really have to hold down the spots that you want to bleach. You can bleach the paper stretched or unstretched. One interesting effect is that if you bleach without stretching, it will not bleach evenly along the grain (which is thicker), so when dry and stretched, you will see lighter lines between the grains, like stripes. Otherwise, I only bleach 180g paper to get a variegated effect, as the bleach works only on the spots that were actually put into the liquid (it does not absorb and spread).

> **TIP**
>
> Try to give up control over what your colour looks like; try dyeing or bleaching but also try to use colours that already exist. Working with what you have in front of you will push you to be more creative.

DYEING

I will sometimes dye my white crepe paper. It is not my favourite way of colouring because it takes a lot of trial and error to get an exact colour and I have rarely been successful.

I use food colouring paste because the colours are quite predictable and reliable. Also, it is safe to work with and non-toxic. Still, I suggest you wear gloves to prevent staining your fingers.

I find food colouring paste mixes better in warm water. One useful aspect is that the finished colour won't get any darker or brighter than the colour swatch on the bottle, although you can achieve a lighter tint by mixing it with more water. I always test the colour with toilet paper to see how strong the colour is before dipping my crepe paper. Since the underlying medium is water, I use the same dipping technique used in water washing, tea staining and bleaching; I simply replace the water, tea or bleach with the food colouring mixture.

To dye white fine crepe paper, dip one long edge; it will naturally create an ombré effect. If you want to colour the entire strip, you can immerse it in the liquid, but do not unroll when wet as the fine crepe paper will tear; instead let it dry and then unroll.

> **TIP**
>
> Similar to water washing, fine or double-sided crepe paper will expand during the dyeing process and will lose some of its stretch.

PASTELS

Pastels are my preferred colouring tool because I have incredible control over how they sit on the paper and how they blend together with other pastel colours and the colour of the paper. I also don't need to wait for them to dry. That said, pastels might not be as efficient when working on larger-scale projects.

I use both stick pastels and pastels in a pan from the PanPastel brand. With PanPastels, the colour pigment is already in a pan, so all you need to do is to swipe an applicator (such as a make-up foam or sponge applicator) over it to charge it or use a brush to lift the pastel from the pan. PanPastels tend to be more expensive than stick pastels, but they do last for a very long time.

When there is a specific colour I want but it is not available in PanPastels, I use a traditional stick pastel. Due to the grain in the crepe paper, applying pastel straight from a stick does not create a smooth distribution of colour. Therefore, I shave the pastel with a paring knife or scissors to create dust, and then apply the dust to the paper using a small brush or foam applicator. I have an air purifier machine beside me to filter any dust particles so I don't breathe them in.

I apply pastel at all different stages of flower assembly. Depending on the flower, I will colour my paper before cutting petals, such as when I want a base colour on my crepe paper, or when I want to create an ombré effect on the prepared crepe paper strip. For the former, I just swipe colour all over the paper as evenly

Shave stick pastels with a paring knife for smooth colour.

A base or ombré effect can be added before cutting.

as possible. For the latter, I colour the entire strip by swiping my pastel foam applicator from one long edge to the other long edge, thereby creating an ombré effect as the intensity of the pastel fades. Then I cut my petals by adjusting the location of my petal on the crepe paper strip depending on if I want more or less intensity on certain parts of the petal. Sometimes I will spray the strip with an archival spray or UV protector to set the pastel so I don't get dust all over my hands. I really like how random the placement of colour can be.

More frequently, I apply pastel after I have cut my petals and before manipulation. This provides more control. I swipe the pastel foam applicator from the petal base up to the petal lip, stopping at different points of the petal depending on the effect I want.

Grazing the petal allows you to highlight creases or the area around depressions. Running the pastel foam applicator over the edge of a petal or leaf, as if you're using the edge to scrape the foam applicator, will highlight its edges.

In both cases, it is best to protect your work surface with craft paper and place the crepe paper strip or petal on top before applying the colour.

I will also finish a flower by colouring after assembly, usually as a finishing touch to add depth or a touch of a different colour. I either apply pastel with a brush or with a foam applicator. It is like painting on colour after you have your structure, similar to what sugar flower artists do. I like to colour leaves and branches after assembly.

Adding colour after cutting petals offers more control.

Finishing touches can be added after assembly.

SPRAY PAINT

When I want to create a base colour for my paper or when the colour I want only comes in spray paint form, I use Design Master Colortool and TintIt. This can be sprayed on real flowers and is a very fine mist of colour that dries within seconds. It is the quickest way to colour a large volume of flowers or large petals. As the paint mist is so light, it is perfect for spraying fine crepe paper because it doesn't soak the paper and it can be applied in layers of the same or different colours.

The main downside is that if you want to spray a thin layer over the crepe paper, you can sometimes see the tiny dots of paint, as if the colour has been pixelated. When stretched, it becomes even more obvious. I find this is particularly obvious on 180g crepe paper and with the Colortool. TintIt is a transparent spray dye that, when sprayed, doesn't seem to show the dots as much.

Here are two ways in which I like to use the spray paint for the flowers in this book.

For some flowers, I like to work with a base colour that reflects one of the layers of colours in the flower and in the correct colour bias. If it doesn't exist in my crepe papers, then I make it. For example, for a creamy yellow dahlia, I like to create a warm off-white base and then layer a warm yellow on top. That usually means I spray twice, once in off-white and once in

warm yellow, or I spray once and then apply pastel for the other layer. More often I use the latter method because pastels give me better control for the final layer of colouring.

Another example is when I am looking for a very specific colour and/or I want to create an ombré effect where the colour goes from dark to light. I spray either before or after I cut the petals or assemble the flower. For my muted purple campanula, I wanted a very specific purple colour: a warm dark violet with a yellow tinge. I used a fine crepe in English Rose (pink) and I layered on a purple spray (Design Master Tintit in Purple) that has a little blue in it but is neutralized a bit by the pink; my last layer was a sepia spray (Design Master Tintit in Sepia) to create a muddy appearance.

SAFETY TIP

Like all spray paints, inhaling the paint fumes could be harmful. I recommend that you spray outdoors and in a well-ventilated space, covering as much of your body as possible, and wearing a respiratory mask and gloves. Place craft paper beneath your paper as you spray to protect your work surface. Let the paint dry in a well-ventilated space for as long as possible and until you cannot smell the fumes coming from the paper.

ACRYLIC PAINT

Acrylic paint is opaque, so when you paint it over crepe paper the colour sits on top of the paper. The colour should not seep through to the other side unless you dilute it heavily with water.

Generally, I only use acrylic paint when I want the colour to be on only one side of the crepe paper, like when I edge the leaves of variegated foliage or when I want one side of the petal to be burgundy and the other side to be striped, as in the Café Caramel. I also use acrylic paint to colour my clay berries and when I need to do detail work with a fine brush.

Beware of diluting acrylic paint to paint on 180g Italian crepe paper. The paint might not seep through to the back, but it may make the crepe paper bleed and change colour on the non-painted side.

ALCOHOL MARKERS

I use alcohol markers when I need to draw fine details or paint small portions of a flower. There are many types of markers but I prefer alcohol-based ones because they can be easily blended to remove harsh lines. You can find Copic markers at most art stores. They come in a wonderful array of colours and also have refill tubes of the alcohol ink. They come with a blending marker that allows you to blend the ink. Each marker has two ends: a fine point end and a wide end. The Copic Sketch line comes with an end that is similar to a brush.

Some art stores carry their own brand of alcohol-based ink markers, which may be cheaper than Copic markers.

ALCOHOL INKS

Alcohol inks are translucent, so they can be used to dye both sides of crepe paper. Sometimes, the colour I want for a flower is not available in crepe paper but may be possible to obtain with alcohol ink; that's when I will start with white crepe paper and dye it. I prefer to do this for small batches, as dyeing an entire fold of crepe paper would take a lot of ink.

The other reason why I might use alcohol inks is to layer colour on top of coloured crepe paper to add dimension or character. This can create a beautiful painterly effect. Unintended effects often occur when I have not cleaned all of the alcohol ink from my brush and I use it again with a different colour.

Alcohol ink dries quickly so it can be more efficient at dyeing than water dipping or bleaching. You can use alcohol ink blender with the inks or use 91% (or higher) isopropyl alcohol to dilute the inks. I suggest you experiment with different alcohol ink colours; the colour can change depending on how much alcohol you use to dilute it. Like most of the other colouring techniques, I first prepare the crepe paper by cutting it into strips and then manageable lengths before colouring.

Here are the three ways in which I use alcohol inks to colour my crepe paper.

DABBING METHOD

This method gives me a bit more control over the placement and intensity of the colour. I prepare the work surface by laying down newsprint or craft paper, then lay the crepe paper strip on top. I first charge my paper with rubbing alcohol. I pour some alcohol into a small container, then dip and soak a fat bristle or foam brush into it. I dab the brush with alcohol all over the crepe paper, trying to saturate the paper evenly as the alcohol ink will not spread in spots where there is no alcohol.

I use a plastic egg container to prepare my colours so I can make a few colours in one container and when I'm done I can simply dispose of it. I begin by adding rubbing alcohol into one of the small cups. I squeeze it out of a

pre-filled bottle with a fine tip. Then, I squeeze a few drops of alcohol ink into the cup. I repeat with other colours in the other cups. I mix the colour with a smaller brush (or a stem wire) and then dab the colour onto the wet crepe paper. The use of a paintbrush allows me to control the placement of the colour; for example, with pre-cut leaves or petals, I can choose to colour only the edges of leaves, or only the bottom half of flower petals.

For crepe paper strips, I dab along the bottom edge with one colour so that the alcohol ink blends up to the top, creating an ombré effect; or I dab randomly all over and let the colours blend into each other. If you deliberately dab on top of another colour, it tends to create a muddier version of the colour. You can even dip first in one colour and then another colour before dabbing onto the crepe paper. Depending on how saturated the paper is, you should be able to see the true colour in a few minutes.

DIRECT APPLICATION

When I want to achieve a vibrant and saturated colour, I will directly squeeze alcohol ink onto the crepe paper after saturating the paper with rubbing alcohol to get a really concentrated colour. Then I use a brush to spread it outwards. I do this to achieve an ombré effect.

FLICK METHOD

To achieve speckles on crepe paper, I flick alcohol ink (diluted or as is) by dipping a brush into the ink, holding the brush perpendicular to the table and crepe paper, then gently tapping the front of the brush with my finger.

> **SAFETY TIP**
>
> Inhaling isopropyl alcohol can be harmful. Make sure you work in a well-ventilated space and, if possible, open the windows and wear a respiratory mask.

NON-ALCOHOL INKS

I use water-based inks, such as watercolour inks and drawing inks, when I want to create details on a petal or on the edges of a petal. Like alcohol inks, they are translucent, and I like to use them when I want the colour to seep through the petal on both sides. These inks come in both vibrant and muted colours.

The inks come in small bottles with or without a tear dropper. To use, you can dip a brush directly into the bottle or pour a little into a separate container. You can add water to dilute the colour, or even rubbing alcohol, although I've found that the inks do not always dilute well.

I turn to inks when I want to create patterns on a petal. For example, to paint lines, I apply the ink with a fan brush as in the Café Caramel ranunculus. The fan brush naturally distributes the ink into lines. Since I apply a small amount, it only takes a few minutes to dry and should not warp the paper too much. This is my favourite way of using inks.

Paper manipulation techniques

There are endless ways to manipulate the paper into your desired shape. Ask yourself what you want the flower to look like. Do you want it to be tight and round, or blowsy? Do you like deep-cupped petals or ones that hang as if they're about to fall off?

By working backwards, you can determine how you need to manipulate the shape to achieve the look you want. In this section I have listed the techniques that you will frequently encounter in this book. Although these can be used on non-crepe paper, most of them rely on crepe paper's unique grain lines. Cupping, cup stretching, fluting and stretching all rely on the grain lines running vertically. These lines can also act as support for a petal: if you cut a petal with the grain lines going vertically from petal base to petal lip, it will hold its shape, but if the lines go horizontally from petal side to petal side, it will flop down. I recommend that you play with the paper and experiment by pulling it and stretching it and seeing what form it takes.

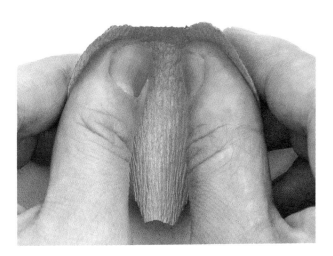

CUPPING

Cup inside or at the top of the petal by using your thumb pad and forefingers of both hands and placing them on either side of the petal with the grain lines going vertically. Push your thumbs away from you and the crepe paper will naturally create a cup-like shape due to the grain lines. To smooth the cup, slide your thumbs back towards you.

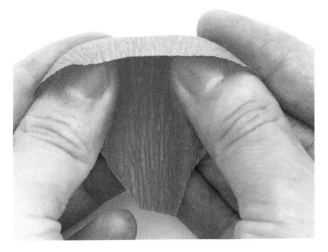

REVERSE CUPPING

Reverse cupping is the same as cupping, except that, instead of having the inside or top of the petal facing you, the outside or bottom of the petal faces you. I tend to reserve this technique for the top edge of the petal to give it a soft curl along the petal lip. The deeper your reverse cup, the stronger the curl.

38

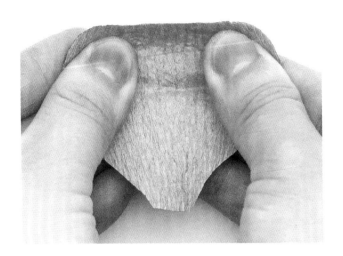

CUP STRETCHING

Stretch the crepe paper as you cup slightly. Instead of using your thumb pad to push the paper away from you, apply pressure to the outside edges of your thumbs to push the paper to opposite sides while also stretching the crepe paper by pulling your hands apart. This creates a fatter petal with a slight cup.

FLUTING

To create a ruffle on the edge of the crepe paper, hold the paper with the thumbs and forefingers of both hands. Make a tearing motion by moving your hands in opposite directions, towards and away from you, but do not tear the paper. The larger your tearing motion, the larger your ruffle. Create multiple ruffles by fluting along the edge.

CURLING

There are a few ways to curl the edges of a petal. The first is by reverse cupping; this creates a soft vast curl. The second is by using scissors and running the edge of one of the blades along the underside of a cup and up towards the petal lip. A third way is by using a narrow and thin stick with rounded edges, such as a skewer, hat pin, toothpick or pencil, and rolling the paper edge around it. You can achieve quite a tight curl with this technique. I like to use a short 16-gauge bare stem wire as my primary curling tool because I tend to have a lot of these lying around and the diameter is not too thick or too narrow. It is also a sturdy gauge that can take a lot of pulling. For tighter curls, I like to use a short 18-gauge bare stem wire. For small rosebuds, I like to use the tip of a round toothpick.

STRETCHING BEFORE CUTTING

When I am using heavier crepe paper, such as the 180g Italian crepe paper, I like to use it stretched, moulding the paper in my hands rather than relying on the grain lines to create shape. Therefore, I stretch the crepe paper before cutting my petals.

To stretch evenly, I cut a strip of the crepe paper across the grain. With the grain line running vertically, I hold the crepe paper on each end and pull in opposite directions. You can stretch a lot or a little; it depends on how much you want to rely on the grain lines.

The more you stretch, the more the grain opens up and the paper becomes smoother. I like to stretch my paper just before it becomes uncomfortable for my hands to hold; I don't want to feel as if the paper is fighting with me or that it's fighting to pull my hands together. I find at this stage there is still some give in the paper when I shape it with my fingers and hands. If you want to rely a little on the grain lines, then don't stretch it 100 per cent; stretch to a point where there is still some give.

STRETCHING AFTER CUTTING

There are times when I will cut the petal or leaf first, and then stretch it. I use this technique for my collerette dahlia calyx (see page 100). I stretch one edge of the crepe paper to create a fan that covers more space, and then I cut the fanned part into my sepals or petals. When the short edges are placed next to each other, it creates a funnel with a narrow bottom and a wider top opening. This allows for the bottom edge, which is not stretched, to wrap around the thin stem wire, while the top edge with the sepals can wrap around the flower base, or open up into small petals to be trimmed into a round shape.

GATHERING AND PLEATING

The purpose of gathering or pleating is to make a tighter and narrower bottom or base than what you started with; it may include the objective of having the top edge fan out, or it may not. Ultimately, it is similar to the shape and structure we are aiming at in stretching after cutting.

To gather, I start with the piece of crepe paper with the grain line running vertically. I hold one short edge with my holding hand, and use my other hand to push a short bit of crepe paper on the lower edge towards my holding hand, as if passing it over to my holding hand. Pushing creates a 'hill' crease. Then, I take the fingers of the holding hand and grab onto that short bit of crepe paper 'hill' and simply press down to keep it in my holding hand.

I repeat this in a controlled manner as more and more crepe paper 'hills' accumulate in my holding hand.

Pleating (below) is the same except instead of simply grabbing the crepe paper from your passing hand, you grab and create a flat crease before pressing down.

41

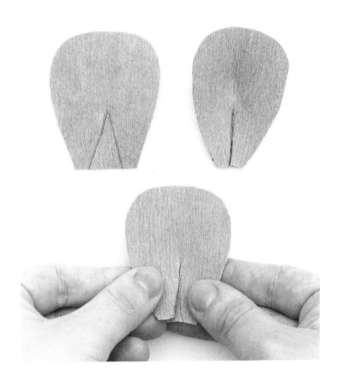

DARTING

I dart almost all of my petals and sometimes my leaves. Darting can strengthen the middle of the petal so it is useful if you find your large petals are drooping; dart the petal and the dart will function as a spine. I also dart because it can create a soft curve in the petal without jeopardizing the rigidity of the paper like stretching or cupping would. Darting can also create a deep curve or cup.

To dart, imagine a triangle with one point deep in the petal and two legs by the edge of the petal. Take one leg and move it so it touches the other leg, and then press down on the paper so that the paper lies flat at the point all the way down to where the two legs touch. To secure, apply glue between the folds of the two legs. I usually make darts that extend one-third to one-half the way up a petal. Keep in mind that the wider the two legs are apart, the deeper the cup you create.

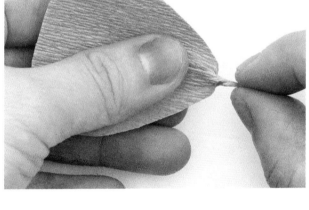

REVERSE DARTING

When you cup the top of the petal, sometimes the petal base will naturally fold back the opposite way of the cup. I apply glue to the fold to secure. I call this a reverse dart because it is secured at the back. Reverse darting can be useful when you want to create a petal with a very straight back or rigid spine.

TWISTED PETAL BASE

Twisting or squeezing the base can be an effective way of increasing the rigidity of the petal while at the same time narrowing the petal base. Simply apply a bit of glue to the petal base, and twist the base between your thumb and forefinger. The twist may extend up to the fatter part of the petal.

NOTCHING

I always cut freehand, and I find it easier to cut notches or uneven edges on a petal lip after the basic petal shape has been cut. Most if not all of the petal templates in this book do not have much detail on the petals. Instead, in the instructions, I tell you to 'notch the petals' as desired.

Once you become used to notching petal edges, you will find that notching after the basic petal has been cut gives you significant creative freedom. Here are a few types of notches that I like to use.

HEART

This can be located in the middle or on the sides; as a single notch or as a pair. It can be deep or shallow. This is mostly used for rose petals.

MITTEN

This is located on the sides. It can be deep or shallow. This is mostly used for anemones and peonies.

FEATHERS

This is usually located on the sides, but can be located in the middle. It can be deep or shallow. It is mostly used for parrot tulip petals and peony petals.

IRREGULAR

This is created by cutting perpendicular to the petal edge, turning the scissors and pulling a chunk of the paper out. It works effectively for small chunks.

SERRATED

This is made along the edges of rose leaves. You can change the character of the serrated edging to vary the type of leaf.

Heart

Mitten

Irregular

Feathers

Serrated

FINISHING

After colouring, I may finish a stem by making parts of the flower shine. I add a gloss by using a product called Mod Podge or spraying with a gloss spray. Mod Podge (which comes in gloss and matte versions) can be applied with a brush directly on crepe paper before cutting or after assembly. It applies white and dries clear. It can bind paper together just like glue and is generally used for decoupage.

The other option is to spray the crepe paper with a UV protector, such as Krylon UV-Resistant Clear Coating in Gloss. The advantage of this over Mod Podge is that you can spray a larger volume of paper. I use this method to spray a large number of berries.

You may also want to protect your flowers from fading as a result of UV rays. The UV-Resistant spray also comes in Matte, and I use this to finish all of my flowers. I apply a thin spray on my entire bouquet or arrangement; I make sure to work in a well-ventilated space like outdoors or in my garage, and wear long sleeves and a respiratory mask. Be aware that the spray may make pastel colours duller.

HOW TO USE THIS BOOK

This book is organized to reflect my creative process of planning, designing, and executing a paper floral composition in the hope that you too can elevate your paper flower artistry.

The first section consists of the techniques I use with respect to colouring and paper manipulation. It also includes the paper flower tutorials: focal flowers that are used to define and anchor an arrangement; accent flowers that highlight and enhance; texture flowers to create visual interest; flowering stems that add drama; and foliage to establish proportion and structure. The templates are at the back of the book (see pages 244–251).

The second section explains how to create five beautifully artful arrangements using all of the paper flowers taught in the first section. I guide you through the relevant fine art principles and specific arrangement techniques I use. I also describe my thought process when planning an arrangement to provide some guidance for when you go off to make your own arrangement.

Anatomy of
a paper flower

Here is a handy guide to the names of the
different parts of a flower.

Floret

Floret bud

Pistil

Stamen

Bract

Petal

Petal top

Petal bottom

Petal base

Petal lip

Flower stem

Calyx
(made up of
sepals)

Flowers

Anemone

It was only after making paper anemones that I saw real ones and appreciated their dark-coloured eyes, ruffled collar of leaves, and petals that close at night and unfurl at dawn. Anemones come in a range of colours, from white to red, purple and even blue, so experiment with colour combinations for the centre, stamens and petals. My favourites are the anemone whites with black centres, which are tinged with green before maturity, and anemone venato purples. Lamination is my preferred way of controlling the final shape of the petals and leaves.

YOU'LL NEED

- ✿ Scissors
- ✿ Ruler
- ✿ Tacky glue
- ✿ Wire cutter
- ✿ Pastel foam applicator or brush
- ✿ Paintbrush or foam applicator for glue

CENTRE
18-gauge stem wire
Fine crepe paper in Black
Cotton wool ball

STAMEN FRINGE
Fine crepe paper in Grey or Black,
    or 180g Chinese crepe paper in Brown
180g Italian crepe paper in Lilac/Light Lilla (#592)

PETALS
180g Italian or Chinese crepe paper in Bright
    White/White (#600) or Plum/Violet-Purple (#593)
Pastels in light green, light blue and blue,
    such as PanPastel Bright Yellow Green Shade,
    Ultramarine Blue Tint and Ultramarine Blue

LEAVES
180g Italian or Chinese crepe paper in green,
    such as Ivy Green/Leaf Green (#591)

1 CENTRE Cut narrow strips of 180g Italian or Chinese crepe paper in green, such as Ivy Green/Leaf Green, to make crepe tape. Cut across the grain for a strip ¼in (6mm) tall grain-wise; cut across the grain for another strip ½in (13mm) tall grain-wise. Stretch both strips. These crepe tapes will be used to wrap and finish the stems. Next, cut a 2 x 2in (5 x 5cm) square from fine crepe paper in black. Take half a large cotton wool ball and roll it between your hands to make a round ball with a diameter of ¾in (1.9cm). Place the cotton wool ball onto the centre of the black fine crepe square. Dot glue lightly on the black crepe paper and around the cotton wool ball. Place the end of an 18-gauge stem wire in the middle of the cotton wool ball. Gather the black square with the cotton wool ball around the stem wire, then squeeze the edges around the stem wire to create a black ball on the end of the stem wire.

2 Secure the ball by wrapping the thin crepe tape (dotted with glue) around the base and wrapping upwards, pushing the cotton wool ball up and into the black crepe paper to fill. The ball should feel full and should not feel loose. Repeat the crepe tape again if necessary to tighten the centre ball. The black centre does not have to be completely round, just full enough to remove most of the fold lines, if any. Continue to wrap the stem wire with the crepe tape all the way down to the end of the stem, applying glue to secure the black centre ball onto the stem wire.

3 STAMEN FRINGE Cut a strip of fine crepe paper in Black or Grey, unstretched (or 180g Chinese crepe paper in Brown, stretched), 2in (5cm) tall grain-wise, and 6in (15.3cm) long. Fold it in half, long edge to long edge, and dot with glue to secure together. Cut short fringes about ⅛in (3mm) long and ⅛in (3mm) wide along the folded edge. Reduce the bulk of the strip by cutting triangle darts into the strip, ¼in (6mm) below the fringe.

4 Apply a line of glue just below the fringe and dot the rest of the fringe strip. Wrap the fringed strip around the black ball so that a third to a half of the top of the ball is visible above the strip when viewing from the side. It should remind you of a muffin top. As you wrap, you may find that the fringe wants to slip down off the centre ball; to keep the fringed strip in place, use one hand to hold the rolled fringe where it wraps around the centre ball and guide it as you use the other hand to roll the centre ball over the strip. Do not squeeze the fringed strip base as you roll. Cut the fringe strip once it has wrapped around the centre ball three times. Hold the fringe in place as you use your rolling hand to squeeze the fringe strip base secure.

5 Cut across the grain of 180g Italian crepe paper in Lilac/Light Lilla for a strip 2in (5cm) tall grain-wise. Stretch the crepe paper, then cut a 16in (40.6cm) long piece. Using a thick black marker, draw a ¼in (6mm) line along one long edge of the strip; this will be the tip of your filaments. Lightly draw 1½in (3.8cm) short parallel lines perpendicular to and from the black edge. Repeat with the other side of the crepe paper strip to mirror. Next, cut fine fringes, about ½in (13mm) long, along the black edge. Trim the bottom of the strip diagonally to minimize bulk, and cut two to four triangle darts into the wider end of the fringe base to further reduce bulk. Curl the fringes towards you. Note: The fringed strip in this image is not to scale.

6 Apply a line of glue just below the fringe and dot the rest of the fringe strip. Place the wider end of the outer fringed strip against the inner fringed strip so that the black edge sits just above the inner fringed strip. Roll the stem over the outer fringed strip, keeping the outer fringe strip taut. As you roll, try to keep the tip of the outer fringe as even as possible. To keep the outer fringed strip from slipping down, gently squeeze the outer fringed strip around the inner fringed strip, and squeeze the triangle-darted base onto the stem wire to secure. Continue to roll the stem over the outer fringed strip. Once the outer fringed strip is completely wrapped, use one hand to hold the fringe in place while you use the other hand to squeeze the outer fringed strip base to secure.

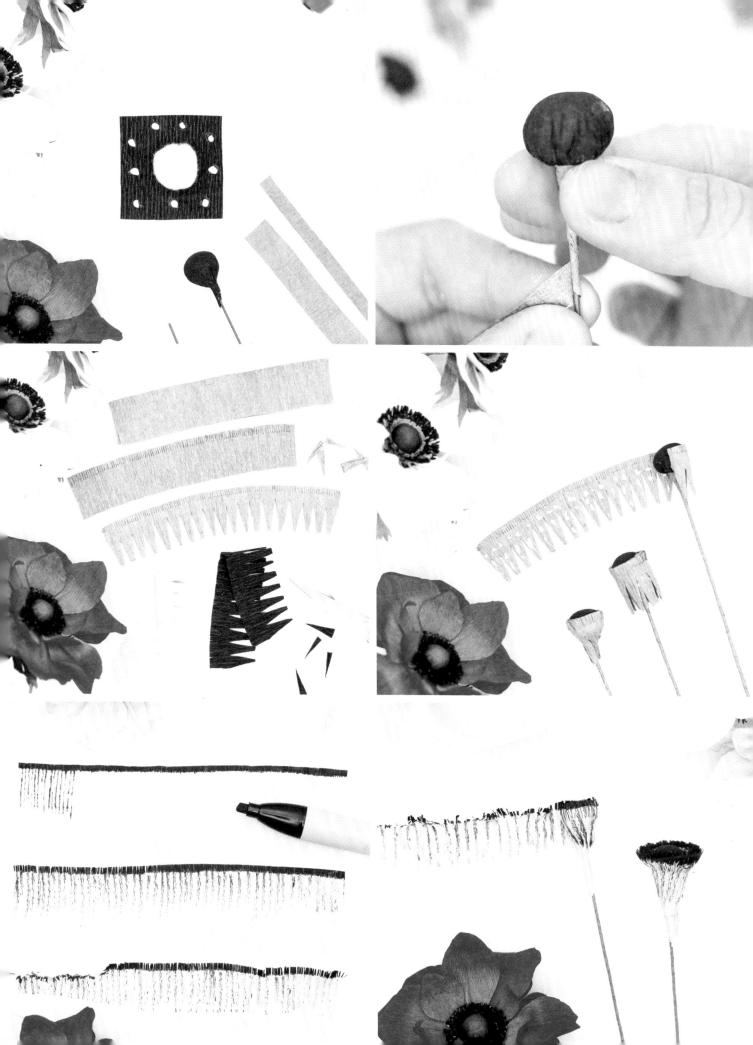

7 If necessary, trim the black fringe so it is flush. Use your fingers to gently spread the fringe open and down.

8 PETALS Cut across the grain of 180g florist crepe paper in Bright White/White (or in the colour of your choice) for strips measuring 2in (5cm) tall and 2$\frac{1}{4}$in (5.7cm) tall grain-wise. Stretch and fold the strips midway, along the grain, and apply tacky glue to laminate. From the laminated strips, cut three of template A, three of B, two of C, three of D and seven of E. Notch one or two of the petal lips in each petal size.

9 COLOURING Some anemones have a slight green, purple, blue or red/pink tinge on the petals. To colour the petals, apply pastels in your desired colour on the bottom of the petals. For the white anemone with black centres, I colour white petals with a light green pastel one-third of the way up and also two-thirds of the way up, to create two flowers at different stages of maturity. For anemone venato purples, I use a light blue and blue pastel to create the blue collar. Try to colour the petals while they are still damp with glue to get more intense colouring. Swipe some light green, purple or black pastel onto the black centre.

10 Pinch the petal base and roll it between your thumb and index finger to narrow it. Run your index or middle fingernail under the petal to create a fold in the petal, and gently pull at the petal to shape. Slightly curl the edge of the petal lips towards you or away from you or create a wave to the petal.

11 There are two layers of petals. For the first layer, distribute the A, B and C petals all around the centre. Apply glue to the petal base and place them just below the fringe, randomly spaced. As you place them, hold onto the petal base with one thumb to press and secure.

12 For the second layer of petals, start with the D petals. Apply glue to the petal bases and place them just below the fringe. The three petals should sit between and stagger the previous layer of petals, filling in any empty spaces, in no particular order. Next, glue on the E petals in the same manner, filling in any empty spaces. If all of the empty spaces have been filled, place these petals in positions that balance out the petal composition. While the bases are still damp, bend back the petals to open up the bloom.

13 FINISHING STEM Apply dots of glue on the thicker crepe tape and wrap it around the base of the stem, hiding the petal bases. Continue down the cone-shaped stem until you get to the base of the cone and the crepe tape begins to wrap upwards; cut here. To make a flower that is just starting to unfurl, simply use your hand to close the petals.

14 LEAVES Cut across the grain of 180g Italian crepe paper in green, such as Ivy Green/Green Leaf, for a strip 2$\frac{1}{2}$in (6.4cm) tall grain-wise. Stretch the strip and then laminate with glue. Cut four leaves from template L. Dart and glue the leaf bottoms. Apply glue to the leaf bases and then place them 1–1$\frac{1}{2}$in (2.5–3.8cm) below the base of the flower or at the bottom of the cone-shaped stem, spaced evenly apart. Finish by twisting or curling the petals/leaves as desired to give them shape.

ARRANGEMENT TIP

Anemones come in various sizes, so mix up the size of the flowers to create more visual interest in an arrangement. The eye is naturally drawn to anemones' dark centres, so I often use a few as focal flowers. I like to turn their heads sideways so when the viewer is looking at the arrangement, the flowers do not look as if they're staring back with their dark eyes. Anemones that are not bred as cut flowers have fairly short stems, so consider keeping them closer to the centre to make them look natural in an arrangement.

Wild rose

These wild roses were based on the yellow tea roses in my garden. As they age and mature, they lose their vibrant yellow colour and turn a pale vanilla with brown edges. Their stamens also turn a muted brown. The secret to getting the petals to dance lightly and effortlessly is to use a very narrow petal base and attach it with floral tape. As you wrap the floral tape tighter and tighter around the petal base, it forces the petal to pivot from its narrow base. The result is a flower with petals that remind me of a tutu.

YOU'LL NEED

✿ Scissors
✿ Ruler
✿ Glue stick
✿ Tacky glue
✿ Pastel foam applicator or brush
✿ Floral tape in light green or crepe tape in a green similar to the calyx colour
✿ Wire cutter
✿ Curling tool
✿ Fixative spray to set pastel (optional)

CENTRE
18-gauge stem wire
180g Italian or Chinese crepe paper in yellow, such as Lemon/Lemon Yellow (#575) or Buttercup/Carminio Yellow (#574)
180g Chinese crepe paper in Hot Pink or 180g Italian crepe paper in dark pink, such as Pink Suede/Intense Fuchsia (#570)
Cinnamon
Yellow pastel/oatmeal mix

PETALS
YOUNG YELLOW WILD ROSE
Doublette crepe paper in White/Vanilla or White/White pre-coloured with light yellow pastel
Pastels in light yellow and dark yellow, such as PanPastel in Hansa Yellow Tint and Hansa Yellow

MATURE YELLOW WILD ROSE
Doublette crepe paper in White/Vanilla or White/White pre-coloured with light yellow pastel
Pastel in light yellow, such as PanPastel in Hansa Yellow Tint
Pastel in brown, such as PanPastel Permanent Red Extra Dark

CALYX
Doublette crepe paper in Leaf/Moss or Green Tea/Moss

1 PREPARE YOUR PAPER I like to work with paper with a light base colour so I can use pastels or spray paint to build on top of that colour. The base colour I use can set the colour temperature of the flower. The Vanilla side of the White/Vanilla double-sided crepe paper is perfect for this; it is slightly yellow, so it serves as an excellent base to build deeper colours with. If you do not have White/Vanilla, you can make something similar. Cut a piece of double-sided crepe paper in White/White from the end of a fold, 4in (10.2cm) wide along the grain. Then apply a light layer of light yellow or vanilla-coloured pastel to one side of the entire piece of crepe paper to create a warm base. If desired, spray it with a fixative spray to set the pastel.

2 CENTRE Cut a piece of 180g crepe paper in hot pink, 1¼in (3.2cm) tall along the grain and 4in (10.2cm) wide. Stretch the strip. Fold midway along the grain. Laminate with a glue stick or white tacky glue. Fringe along one long edge, making cuts ¼in (6mm) down from the edge. Then cut into smaller pieces, each ½in (13mm) wide. Apply white tacky glue to the fringe base, and wrap the base around the tip of an 18-gauge stem wire with only the fringe extending over the tip. Dip the fringe lightly into white tacky glue and then dip it into cinnamon to create the filament.

3 To create a belly for the pistil, cut a long piece of half-width light green floral tape. Stretch it and wrap it around the pink centre base. Wrap around and around until you create a round belly just below the hot pink fringe, the size of a cotton bud and/or with a ¼in (6mm) diameter at its widest part. To bulk faster, fold the floral tape in half lengthwise into a double layer as you wrap. Use your fingernail to push down the floral tape around the stamen fringe to secure.

4 To create the stamen fringe centre, cut across the grain of 180g yellow crepe paper for a strip 1¾in (4.5cm) tall grain-wise. Stretch the strip. Cut the strip into a piece that is 4in (10.2cm) long. Fold the short strip midway along the grain. Laminate with a glue stick or white tacky glue. Fringe along one long edge, making cuts ⅝in (16mm) down from the edge. Roll the fringe. Dip the rolled fringe lightly into white tacky glue and then dip it into the yellow pastel and oatmeal mix for a young rose, or in cinnamon for a mature rose. Cut across the base diagonally to reduce bulk.

5 Dot the base of the stamen fringe strip with glue. Beginning on the wider end, start wrapping it around the belly pistil, with the base of the fringe sitting just below the belly. Roll the fringe so the tips of the fringe are even and flush. Open up the stamen fringe.

6 PETALS Using double-sided crepe paper in White/Vanilla, or your prepared crepe paper, cut five of template A and five of template B. Lay the petals out so that the vanilla or light yellow side faces up. Apply yellow pastel with a foam applicator on the bottom half of each petal, fading upwards, on both sides. To mimic flowers that are fading, skip the yellow pastel, and instead gently graze the petal edges with a dark brown pastel using a pastel foam applicator. Use the back of the foam applicator to smudge it and remove some of the intensity if necessary.

7 Cup-stretch the entire petal, taking care not to rip the dip/notch at the heart-shaped petal lip. Gently flute the petal lip around the dip. Curl back the top left and right edges of the 'heart'. Apply a dot of tacky glue on the petal base, pinch the base narrow, then twist it to secure.

8 Take a strip of floral tape and pull it to activate the glue. Wrap it once around the bottom of the stamen fringe. You will attach the petals one by one, working anti-clockwise in two layers. For the first layer of petals, use only the A template petals. Take the first petal so that the back side is facing you and the front side (with the colour) faces away from you and towards the centre of the flower. Place the pinched bottom on the stem/centre, just below the fringe. Secure it by wrapping once around the floral tape around the stem/centre and the pinched petal bottom. Take another petal and place it randomly across, then wrap it, along with the stem/centre, with floral tape.

9 Distribute the next three template A petals between and around the first two petals, overlapping as needed.

10 For the second layer, use only the five template B petals. Distribute them around the first layer of petals in the same manner, making sure to place the petal bases directly on top of the petal bases of the first layer. Placing the subsequent petal layers tight right under the previous petal layers will prevent the petals from gradually descending down the stem. Take any opportunity to slip the petal between the previous layer's petals. Once all of the petals are secured, continue to wrap the stem all the way down to the end with floral tape or, alternatively, with crepe tape in a similar colour to the calyx in the next step.

11 **CALYX** Cut five sepals using template CA from double-sided crepe paper in green, such as Leaf/Moss. Make three short cuts along each side of the sepal to mimic the serrated edge. Lightly apply a brown pastel colour to the edges of leaves to create dimension. Cup-stretch the entire sepal (including the bottom) and twist in your hands.

12 Apply white tacky glue to the sepal, one-quarter of the way up from the base, on the side that will be seen when looking at the rose from above. Glue the sepal to the base of the flower, covering the petal bases and the stem wire. Envision the flower base as a clock and attach the five sepals evenly around it; place the first three sepals at 12 o'clock, 5 o'clock and 7 o'clock; attach the last two sepals at 2 o'clock and 10 o'clock. To finish, wrap floral tape or crepe tape around the sepal bases to blend it into the stem wire. Pinch the tips of the sepals. Bend the rose stem slightly and tilt the flower head in one direction.

13 I like to attach two to three wild roses on the main flower stem. When I do, I attach both young and mature roses at different heights. See Rose Foliage (page 188) for instructions on how to attach a stem of rose leaves to the flower stem below the flowers.

ARRANGEMENT TIP

Since these blooms are on the small side, I like to gather multiple blooms on a single flower stem to create greater impact. With their blooms clustered together, their delicateness is preserved as opposed to being lost in a sea of flowers. When attaching the rose stems together, try to stagger the height of the blooms. When placed in an arrangement, the blooms will appear to be at different levels, which creates a sense of depth.

Juliet rose

The Juliet rose comprises six sets of folded petals in the middle, surrounded by deeply cupped petals to create the rosette. Here I have given you one structural recipe for two sizes and coloration recipes for three different colours. Juliet roses don't come naturally in magenta and white, but using them in different colours expands your garden flower palette.

YOU'LL NEED

- ✿ Scissors
- ✿ Ruler
- ✿ Tacky glue
- ✿ Hot glue gun
- ✿ Hot glue
- ✿ Wire cutter

CENTRE
180g Italian or Chinese crepe paper or fine crepe paper in Goldenrod/Yellow (#576) or a dark orange-yellow
16-gauge stem wire

FOLDED PETALS
PEACH/PINK JULIET ROSE
Fine crepe paper in a variety of pinks in warm and cool hues. For warm pinks use Whisper Pink, Pink, 60g Italian crepe paper in Salmon Pink (#200); for cool pinks, use extra-fine crepe paper in Blush or 60g in Camelia Pink (#201); and any of these fine crepe papers bleached

MAGENTA JULIET ROSE
Fine crepe paper in a warm dark pink such as Hot Pink, bleached Hot Pink and/or 60g Italian crepe paper in Bougainvillea (#212), which is a cool dark pink

CREAM/WHITE JULIET ROSE
Fine crepe paper in a warm white such as White or 60g Italian crepe paper in White Cream (#303) and/or White (#330) for a cool white

INNER AND OUTER PETALS
PEACH PINK ROSE
180g Italian crepe paper in Sweet Pea/Light Pink (#569) or Peach by Tiffanie Turner (#17A5)
Pastel in light orange, such as PanPastel in Orange Tint (optional)
Pastel foam applicator or brush

MAGENTA ROSE
180g Italian crepe paper in Marionberry (#552)

CREAM/WHITE ROSE
180g Italian crepe paper in Bright White/White (#600)

CALYX
Double-sided crepe paper in Leaf/Moss
Green floral tape or crepe tape in 180g Italian crepe paper in Olive Green by Tiffanie Turner (#17A/8) or fine crepe paper in Cypress, or 60g Italian crepe paper in Musk Green (#264)

1 **PREPARE YOUR PAPER** To make a peach/pink Juliet rose (or a magenta rose), take a fold of Whisper Pink or light pink fine crepe paper (or Hot Pink fine crepe paper), and cut a long strip across the grain, 3in (7.6cm) tall grain-wise. Cut the strip into four equal sections and bleach on one long side. Each strip should cut six to seven of the A templates. If not, gently stretch the strip before cutting.

2 **STAMENS** Cut across the grain of the 180g Italian crepe paper in Goldenrod/Yellow for a strip 1in (2.5cm) tall grain-wise. Stretch the strip. Cut off a small piece 1 x 1in (2.5 x 2.5cm) and cut stamens using the S template. Apply tacky glue to the base and wrap it around the tip of a 16-gauge stem wire, with the stem wire sitting just below the stamen fringe. Use a finger to open up the fringe. Let it dry completely.

3 **FOLDED PETALS** There are six sets of folded petals to assemble separately before combining them together around the stamens. Each set consists of eight petals. I like to mix crepe paper in various colour temperatures to create the illusion of depth or to repeat the colour temperatures that appear within an arrangement. My recommendations for this flower include both a cool and warm version of the same colour.

Cut 48 petals from the A template, then create six piles of eight petals. For a peach/pink Juliet rose, cut 24 petals in Whisper Pink fine crepe (WP); 12 petals in bleached Whisper Pink fine crepe (BWP); and 12 in Blush extra-fine crepe (B). For each set, you will have four petals in WP, two petals in BWP, and two in B. Work on each pile one at a time. Stack the petals so that every other petal is a WP petal. Each pile should look like this, from bottom to top: B, WP, BWP, WP, B, WP, BWP, WP. For a magenta Juliet rose, use your discretion when determining how many petals of each colour you need. For the cream/white Juliet rose, I suggest you work with an equal number of each type of white fine crepe, and alternate them in the pile.

As you compile each set, cup the petal before laying it on top of the pile. Dot a bit of glue between the petals, along the petal bases, to secure all the petals together; try to keep the petal bases as flush as possible. Trim the petal bases and the sides to even. Cut three triangle notches up the bottom edge of the layers, about $^3/_4$in (1.9cm) deep, to reduce bulk.

4 Dot glue along the bottom edge and between the notches of the folded petal set. Then, fold the petal set in half (along the grain), and gather the bottom together. Preferably, this should be done while the glue between the petals is still damp. Loosen the packed petals: hold the gathered bottom with one hand, and use your other hand to gently tug the petals apart. Repeat with the other five sets.

5 Glue three of the sets together at a time. Attach two petal set bases by placing their bases side by side, applying hot glue between their bases and pressing to secure. Attach a third petal set base in a similar manner. When the three sets are attached together at the bases, they should create a semicircle. Repeat with the other three folded petal sets to create two semicircles of folded petals.

6 Apply hot glue along the inside of one semi-circle, and place the stamens in the middle so that they stick out a bit and are visible from the top. Once the glue cools, apply hot glue to the stamens and press the second semi-circle to it to complete the circle. As you are positioning the semi-circles, keep in mind that the straighter the backs/outside of the folded petals, the more depth you will create in the middle. Apply hot glue between the semi-circles and the petal sets as required to secure to the rosette.

7 **INNER PETALS** There are two layers of inner petals. The purpose of the first layer of petals is to hold the shape of the flower and contain the folded petals. Cut across the grain of 180g Italian crepe paper in Sweet Pea/Light Pink or Peach, for a strip $3\frac{1}{2}$in (9cm) tall grain-wise. Cut eight to nine rectangles with the width of template B. The 180g Italian crepe paper has a top side and a bottom side. The top side shows the machine lines coming forward. The petal template is asymmetrical and shows the outside of the flower; if you want the machine lines to come out on the outside, make sure you place your template on that side. Arrange the rectangle pieces so they all face the same way with the machine lines facing you. Cut the petals using template B. Once cut, flip the petals so the machine lines face away from you and cup the middle section of the petal, leaving the petal tip and base untouched. Trim the edges as necessary for a smooth edge. Colour the inside of the petals with a light orange pastel if you want to create a peach-coloured cast over the light pink rosette.

8 You can make both a larger and a smaller version of this flower using the same folded petals and petal sizes. The trick is to squeeze the folded petals close together and then, as you glue the petals in the first layer, use one hand to hold the petal in place while using your other hand to pull the base of the petal towards the stem, creating a tighter circumference around the folded petals. With practice, you will be able to control the sizes effectively. Secure the first petal by applying hot glue in a V-shape to the inside petal base and placing it at the base of the rosette, near the stem wire. The petal should envelope two of the rosettes. To create depth, the lip of the petal should sit about $\frac{1}{4}$in (6mm) above the rosette/top of the flower. For each remaining petal, apply hot glue to the petal base and along the bottom edge, half of the way up. Then place it next to the previous petal, overlapping by a half to two-thirds, at an angle, so that the lip of the petal is not vertical but on a slant facing northwest at about a 45-degree angle. The petal bases should lie on the right of the stem wire; do not try to attach the petal bases to the stem wire. As you glue the petals, use one of your hands to create a cup or C-shape to hold the petals as the hot glue dries so they wrap around the rosette, creating a tight, round shape, while using the other hand to pull the petal and rein in the folded petals. The tighter you are able to keep these inner petals connected together, the tighter and smaller the flower.

9 You will need nine petals for this second petal layer. These petals visually define the circumference around the rosette. Using the same 180g crepe paper as in the previous steps, cut a strip $3\frac{1}{2}$in (9cm) tall along the grain, and cut seven to nine rectangles with the width of template C. Arrange the rectangle pieces so they all face the same way with the machine lines facing you. Cut the petals using template C. Once cut, flip the petals so the machine lines face away from you, cup the middle section of the petal, and slightly cup-stretch the top so that the petal has only a slight curve along the edges. These are to fit around the first layer of petals, so test how closely it cups the first layer; you want it to hug the first layer as closely as possible. Apply hot glue in a V-shape to the inside petal base and place it on top of the first layer where you ended off in the first layer. The flat lip of the petal should lie horizontally and sit flush or only a little lower than the first layer of petals. Continue gluing and placing the rest of the petals so that the subsequent petal covers the previous petal by a half or two-thirds; vary the overlap to get a more relaxed flower.

10 Take your curling tool (with a diameter of an 18-gauge wire or less and no larger) and curl some of the lips of the petals in the first and second layer away from the centre.

11 OUTER PETALS For the outer petals, place the petals in pairs to create a double layer. For a larger flower with a 3in (7.6cm) inner petal diameter and 4$\frac{1}{2}$in (11.4cm) outer diameter, cut 18 for petal pairs. For a smaller flower with a 2$\frac{1}{2}$in (6.4cm) inner petal diameter and 4in (10.2cm) outer diameter, cut 16 petals – 12 for petal pairs, and four for finishing in Step 13. In both cases, use template D. Cut the crepe paper into rectangles first, arranging them so they face the same direction (with the machine lines facing you), before cutting the petals with the template. Flip the petal over so the machine lines are facing away from you and cup-stretch the top, middle and bottom of the petal so that the petal has only a slight curve on the edges. Then, use your curling tool to curl the petal lips tightly at the corners. Pair up the 18 large petals or 16 small petals. Glue the petals at the base in pairs so that the petals are placed at an angle from each other with the base as the pivot point, and the petals overlapping by half. Glue a few with the left petal on top of the right petal and a few with the right petal on top of the left petal.

12 Apply hot glue to the petal pair in a V-shape at the base of the petal closest to the flower. Distribute the pairs so they look pleasing around and on top of the second layer of inner petals. The curled petal lips should sit about $\frac{1}{4}$in (6mm) below the petal lips of the previous layer. As you position subsequent pairs, try to slip one petal or both petals of the petal pair behind petals from previous layers.

13 FINISHING PETALS This step is optional. I like to finish the flower with two to four larger petals to balance out the shape. If making the smaller rose, you can use the four template D petals from Step 11. If making the larger rose, cut two, three or four petals from template E. Repeat the petal manipulation in Step 11 for the petals. Slip these finishing petals between the outer petal pairs or place them on top of the outer petals as you see fit. Once you have completed this step, or if you have decided not to do this step, glue down any petals that are sticking out.

14 CALYX Before gluing on the calyx, secure the flower by filling any gap between the petals and the stem wire with hot glue. Then cut five sepals using template CA from double-sided crepe paper in green, such as Leaf/Moss. Make three short cuts along each side of the sepal to mimic the serrated edge. Cup-stretch the entire sepal (including the bottom) and twist in your hands.

15 Apply tacky glue on the sepal, a quarter of the way up from the base on the side that will be seen when looking at the rose from above. Glue to the base of the flower, covering the petal bases and the stem wire. Push the sepals into any empty spaces between the petals. Envision the flower base as a clock and distribute the five sepals evenly around it: attach the first three sepals at 12 o'clock, 5 o'clock and 7 o'clock; attach the last two sepals at 2 o'clock and 10 o'clock. To finish, wrap floral tape or crepe tape from the sepal to the end of the stem wire. Pinch the tips of the sepals. Bend the rose stem slightly and tilt the flower head in one direction. If desired, you can attach two or three rose stems together. See Rose Foliage (page 188) for instructions on how to attach a stem of rose leaves to the flower stem below the flowers.

ARRANGEMENT TIP

My favourite thing about Juliet roses is the folded petal centres, and I love showing off their faces. With their deeply cupped and round rosettes, they fit perfectly with other round flowers, such as ball dahlias and ranunculus. The full-bloom ones are quite big, so they make a statement in any arrangement. The unique colouring of the peach version makes them stunning focal flowers; however, they can be tricky to pair with flowers that are not the same peach/apricot.

Small garden rose

This is my go to whenever I want a garden rose that is compact but still has petals that seem as if they could drop at any time. I have made different sizes of this rose simply by increasing or decreasing the size of the petals by ¼in (6mm). The key to getting the inner petals to swirl without squashing into each other is the thick stamen centre. This structure gives the petals space to be positioned away from each other. I had used reverse darts on my petals before, but they were never that successful with a smaller centre. With a thicker centre, they can show off their upright petals in all their glory.

YOU'LL NEED

* Scissors
* Ruler
* Tacky glue
* Hot glue gun and glue stick
* Wire cutter
* Pastel foam applicator or brush

CENTRE
180g Italian crepe paper in yellow, such as
   Goldenrod/Yellow (#576), Lemon/Lemon Yellow
   (#575) or Buttercup/Carminio Yellow (#574)
Marker in brown or cinnamon
18-gauge stem wire

PETALS
FOR A DARK PINK ROSE
Double-sided crepe paper in Pink/Berry,
   water-washed

FOR A BLUSH ROSE
Double-sided crepe paper in White/White
Design Master Colortool in Blush or Ivory
Pastel in light pink, such as PanPastel
   in Pearlescent Red or Red Iron Oxide Tint

FOR A PEACH ROSE
Double-sided crepe paper in Peach/Petal
   (or White/Peach, or Salmon/Peach)
Pastel in light pink or light peach,
   such as PanPastel in Orange Tint

CALYX
Double-sided crepe paper in green,
   such as Leaf/Moss
Green floral tape or crepe tape in fine crepe paper
   in Moss Green or 180g Italian crepe paper
   in Amazon Green (#561, 16A/8)
Pastel in dark red or maroon such as PanPastel
   in Permanent Red Extra Dark

1 PREPARE THE PAPER Cut across an entire fold of double-sided crepe paper in your colour of choice, 1¹/₂in (3.8cm) tall grain-wise. Use a Pink/Berry for a dark pink rose; a White/White for a blush rose; and a Peach/Petal (or White/Peach, Salmon/Peach) for a peach rose. For the dark pink rose, water-dip the Pink/Berry strip and hang to dry before using. For the blush rose, spray the White/White strip with a blush, light pink, or ivory paint on both sides and dry before using.

2 INNER STAMEN CENTRE To create the effect that the petals in the centre spiral naturally, we need to thicken the centre of the flower stem. Cut across the grain of 180g Italian crepe paper in yellow for a strip 1¹/₄in (3.2cm) tall grain-wise and 6in (15.3cm) long. Then cut one stamen piece from template S. You will cut across the piece of yellow crepe paper as per the dotted lines on the template to create two pieces of yellow crepe paper, each with one narrow and one wider end. You only need one of these pieces; save the other for your next rose. Apply a line of hot glue along the grain on the wider end and place the tip of an 18-gauge stem wire on the glue with the top of the stem wire flush with the top of the crepe paper. Let the hot glue cool. Apply hot glue to the crepe paper strip, about 2in (5cm) at a time as you wrap the strip around the stem wire. Keep the top of the crepe paper flush and even.

3 STAMEN FRINGE CENTRE Cut across the grain of 180g florist crepe paper in yellow for a strip 1¹/₄in (3.2cm) tall grain-wise and stretch. Cut a section 6in (15.3cm) long for your stamen strip. Using a brown marker, draw a fine line along one long edge. Cut fine fringes along the coloured edge, stopping halfway down. Trim the base diagonally to reduce bulk. An alternative to using a brown marker is to use cinnamon: cut the fringes first, then dip the fringe tip into tacky glue and then into cinnamon, and gently shake off any excess. You could also use shaved pastel.

4 Apply hot glue on the wider end of the stamen fringe strip, and place the inner stamen on top, just flush with the bottom of the fringe. Wrap the fringed strip around the inner stamen, applying hot glue every 2in (5cm) or so. Keep the top of the fringe even. Use your finger to ruffle the stamen fringe so the fringe covers the inner stamen.

5 LAYER 1 PETALS If the double-sided crepe paper has different colours on each side, like the Peach/Petal for the peach rose, decide which colour you want facing away from you (the outside of the petal) and which colour facing towards you (the inside of the petal). Keep in mind that the inner petals (first two layers of petals) keep the flower closed so it will show a different colour from the outer petals (three subsequent layers) in which the petals are open.

Cut seven rectangles, 1¹/₂in (3.8cm) tall, along the grain and 1¹/₄in (3.2cm) wide. If you are working with double-sided crepe paper with the same colour on both sides, it is not necessary to cut rectangles before cutting the petal from the template. If your paper has different colours on each side, turn all of the rectangles with the colour you want on the outside of the flower (for example, peach) facing down or away from you. Place template A on top and cut; repeat until you have seven petals in total. The petal edge should appear lower on the left side and higher on the right side. Turn the inside of the petal so it faces up.

6 For the blush or peach rose, apply a pastel in light pink or light peach, respectively, one-third of the way up from the petal base and fading into the petal. If you colour it only on one side, colour the side that is on the inside; for the Peach/Petal, colour the Petal side. This technique can be applied to any flower petals to create subtle colour and depth when the flower is assembled.

7 Cup the lip of each petal deeply, and then cup the middle section. The petal base will naturally start folding the opposite way from the cup to create a 'valley' in the back of the petal; dab a bit of hot glue in the valley and fold to create a reverse dart. Repeat with all petals.

8 As the reverse darts are perpendicular to the petal, you will be gluing the petals sideways onto the stamen fringe, and anti-clockwise. Hold the petal in front of you with the cupped side facing you. Apply a dab of hot glue on the bottom right side of the reverse dart. Slide the cupped side of the petal into the stamen fringe so that the cupped part is inside the fringed section. Press the glued bottom to the side of the stamen below the fringe. The petal should look like it is attached on sideways, with at least half of the petal submerged into the stamen fringe. Repeat with each petal, placing the next petal on the right of the previous petal (hence, anti-clockwise) to fit all seven petals.

9 Take a strip of floral tape (white if you are making a light-coloured rose; green for all other roses) and stretch it to activate the glue. Wrap it around the base of the petals, and $1/8$in (3mm) higher than the glued base so that it wraps around the petals themselves, thereby closing the swirl. I like to then gently pull a few of the petals looser so the swirl is not as tight and there is space to slip petals from the second layer.

10 **LAYER 2 PETALS** For the second layer of petals, cut five petals from template B. Notch the petal lips as desired. Apply pastel halfway up from the petal bases in the same colours as Step 5. Have the flower colour facing away from you. For petals 1 and 2, cup, dart the base, and roll the lip back; for petal 3, cup and roll back the lip; for petal 4, cup only; for petal 5, reverse cup the top lip, cup and dart.

11 Imagine the flower stamens as a clock. If necessary, draw a line on the floral tape to mark off the side that is facing you as 6 o'clock. Dot the inside base of the petals with hot glue before securing them into their positions, $1/16$in (1.5mm) above layer 1. Determine the 12 o'clock position and place petal 1 there, slipping its left side between the petals in layer 1. Place petal 2 at 6 o'clock; 3 at 4 o'clock; and 4 at 9 o'clock. At every opportunity, slide the left side of the petal between the petals of the previous layer. Place petal 5 at 7 o'clock.

12 **LAYER 3 PETALS** For Layer 3, cut four of template C. Notch the petal lips as desired. Apply pastel three-quarters of the way up from the petal bases in the same colours as Step 6. Have the flower colour facing away from you as you reverse-cup the top lip, cup normally, and dart for each petal.

13 As you glue, place the petal bases directly on top of the petal bases of layer 2. Glue one petal at 4 o'clock; glue another at 3 o'clock, with its base overlapping layer 2 petal's base; glue another at 11 o'clock; and glue the last petal at 10 o'clock, with its base overlapping the layer 2 petal's base. As you place the petals, consider placing the petals at an angle so the petal lip slopes gently down towards the bottom right.

14 **LAYER 4 PETALS** For layer 4, cut nine of template D. Notch the petal lips as desired. Apply pastel three-quarters of the way up from the petal bases in the same colours as Step 4. Have the flower colour facing away from you. Take one petal and reverse-cup, roll the lip back, and dart. Glue this one to any empty area (likely 6 o'clock).

15 Have the flower colour facing away from you as you shape the remaining eight petals. For each, reverse-cup the top edge, roll the lip back, and cup-stretch the middle section slightly. With the exception of one petal, dart the bases normally. Attach the darted petals in three pairs of two. For two of the pairs, have the right petal overlap the left; for one pair, have the left petal overlap the right; for all three pairs, line the petal bases together so that the petals pivot from their bases with their petals angled away from each other. This makes the most natural placement of petals.

16 Dot with hot glue and randomly place the pairs around the previous layer. Try to slip the petals between the petals of previous layers. Experiment with placing the petals on an angle, using the petal bases as pivot points. Fill in any gaps with the two single petals.

17 To finish, randomly pinch petal lips at their mid-point, and roll back the edges of the lips. Sometimes I like to bend, or reflex, the outer petals back and down to mimic a hybrid tea rose that is opening up its petals.

18 **CALYX** Cut five sepals using template CA from double-sided crepe paper in green, such as Leaf/Moss. Make three short cuts along each side of the sepal to mimic the serrated edges. Lightly apply a brown or burgundy pastel colour to the sepals to create dimension. Cup-stretch the entire sepal (including the bottom) and twist in your hands.

19 Apply tacky glue on the sepal, a quarter of the way up from the base, on the side that will be seen when looking at the rose from above. Glue to the base of the flower, covering the petal bases and the stem wire. Push the sepals into any empty spaces between the petals. Envision the flower base as a clock and distribute the five sepals evenly: attach the first three sepals at 12 o'clock, 5 o'clock and 7 o'clock; attach the last two sepals at 2 o'clock and 10 o'clock.

To finish, wrap floral or crepe tape from the sepal to the end of the stem wire. Pinch the tips of the sepals. Bend the rose stem slightly and tilt the flower head in one direction. If desired, you can attach two or three rose stems together. See Rose Foliage (page 188) for instructions on how to attach a stem of rose leaves to the flower stem below the flowers.

Koko Loko rose

These roses are versatile because their colours are unique: the buds are copper coral, then, as the rose blooms, its colour changes from tan beige to muted lavender. Some open to expose its stamens; some do not and instead curl their petals tightly. This version is modelled after the Koko Loko roses that bloom in my own garden.

YOU'LL NEED

- ✿ Scissors
- ✿ Ruler
- ✿ Tacky glue
- ✿ Hot glue gun and glue stick
- ✿ Curling tool
- ✿ Wire cutter
- ✿ Pastel foam applicator or brush

CENTRE
18-gauge stem wire
180g Italian crepe paper in yellow, such as Goldenrod/Yellow (#576), Lemon/Lemon Yellow (#575) or Buttercup/Carminio Yellow (#574)
Brown marker or cinnamon

PETALS
180g Italian crepe paper in Distant Drums (#17A/3) or Tanned Yellow for Peonies (#17A/4) water-washed and/or tea-stained

CALYX
Double-sided crepe paper in green, such as Leaf/Moss
Green floral tape or crepe tape in extra-fine crepe paper in Cypress or in a slightly lighter green such as 60g in Musk Green (#264), 180g Italian crepe paper in Amazon Green (#561, 16A/8) or Olive Green by Tiffanie Turner (#17A/8)
Pastel in dark red or maroon such as PanPastel in Permanent Red Extra Dark

ARRANGEMENT TIP

These medium-sized blooms are perfect colour transition pieces. Their muted colours help bring together pinks, purples and browns of various shades and tones. They can also stand on their own as focal flowers since they're medium-sized blooms and their colouring is so unique and prominent. I like to pair them up to create greater impact and let their blooms hang over the edge of the rim of a vase to create a sense of heaviness.

1 PREPARE THE CREPE PAPER You can use the crepe paper in Distant Drums straight from the roll. I prefer to create variety in the hue by water-washing or tea-staining strips of crepe paper to lighten or mute the colour, respectively. For the inner petals, cut across the grain for strips 1¹⁄₂in (3.8cm) tall grain-wise; stretch the strips and then immerse them in water. For the outer petals, cut across the grain for strips 2¹⁄₄in (5.7cm) tall grain-wise; stretch the strips, then immerse them in a tea-bath. When the petals are assembled onto the flower, this creates a natural highlight in the centre of the flower.

2 INNER STAMEN CENTRE This flower uses the same centre as the Small Garden Rose (see page 68), so the first step is to thicken the centre. Cut across the grain of 180g Italian crepe paper in yellow for a strip 1¹⁄₄in (3.2cm) tall grain-wise and 6in (15.3cm) long. Then cut one of template S. You will cut across the piece of yellow crepe paper as per the dotted lines on the template to create two pieces of yellow crepe paper, each with one narrow and one wider end. You only need one of these; save the other for your next rose. Apply a line of hot glue along the grain on the wider end and place the tip of an 18-gauge stem wire on the glue with the top of the stem wire flush with the top of the crepe paper. Let the hot glue cool. Apply hot glue to the crepe paper strip, about 2in (5cm) at a time, as you wrap the strip around the stem wire. Keep the top of the crepe paper flush and even.

3 STAMEN FRINGE CENTRE Cut across the grain of 180g florist crepe paper in yellow, for a strip 1¹⁄₄in (3.2cm) tall grain-wise and stretch. Cut a section 6in (15.3cm) long for your stamen strip. Using a brown marker, draw a fine line along one long edge. Cut fine fringes along the coloured edge, stopping halfway down. Trim the base diagonally to reduce bulk. An alternative to using a brown marker is to use cinnamon: cut the fringes first, then dip the fringe tip into tacky glue and then into cinnamon, then gently shake off any excess. You could also use shaved pastel.

4 Apply hot glue on the wider end of the stamen fringe strip and place the inner stamen on top, just flush with the bottom of the fringe. Wrap the fringed strip around the inner stamen, applying hot glue every 2in (5cm) or so. Keep the top of the fringe even. Use your finger to ruffle the stamen fringe so the fringe covers the inner stamen.

5 CUTTING PETALS Take a strip of the prepared crepe paper that is 1¹⁄₂in (3.8cm) tall (I like to use a water-washed one here) in Distant Drums or Tanned Yellow for Peonies. Stretch again. Cut six petals using template A. Notch the petal lips as desired. Cup the top half of the petals by using your thumb pad to shape the cup. Glue two petal bases together, with the bases aligned and the petal lips at slight angles. Reverse-dart the paired petal base and glue to secure. Carefully pull the petal lips apart. Gently pinch the petal lip at the notch.

6 Since the petal bases are reverse-darted with their bases flat on the sides, they will be glued sideways onto the centre fringe. Apply glue to one of the sides of the petal base. Place the petal pairs randomly around the stamen fringe, inserting the petal lips into the fringe, and placing its base just below the fringe. The petals do not have to face the same direction; in fact, the more randomly they appear placed, the better.

7 Cut another eight petals using template A. Notch the petal lips as desired. Reverse-cup the top half of the petals by using your thumb pad to shape the cup. Apply a dot of glue to the petal bases and dart normally. If desired, gently pinch the petal lip at the notches or middle of the petal lip. Pair up the petals by gluing their bases together so the petals pivot from the bases and the petals are angled away from each other; have some pairs with the right petal overlapping the left and others with the left petal overlapping the right.

8 Apply glue to the petal base and distribute them around the centre fringe and between the previous petal pairs. The petals should face the centre; however, I like to slip some of the petals into the fringe when I can. If necessary, reshape the petal lips by gently pinching again and pushing down towards the petal base.

9 Use the 2¹/₄in (5.7cm) tall strip of prepared crepe paper (I like to use a tea-dipped version here). Stretch completely. Cut 12 petals using template B. The petals will be 2in (5cm) tall. Notch the petal lips as desired. Reverse-cup the top half of the petals by using your thumb pad to shape the cup. As you cup, use the top corners of your thumb to stretch out the petal lip. Dart and glue to secure. Again, pair up the petals by gluing their bases together so the petals pivot from the bases and the petals are angled away from each other; have some pairs with the right petal overlapping the left and some with the left petal overlapping the right.

10 The flower petals should shoot upwards as opposed to outwards to the side. Dot glue at the petal pair bases, up ¹/₄–⁵/₈in (about 6–16mm). Distribute the petal pairs ¹/₄in (6mm) below the first layer of petals in no particular order. I have found that, as you place the petals, copying the placement of the petal pairs in the previous layer, then placing them slightly staggered creates a more natural-looking placement. For example, if the previous petal pair was a left-right (i.e. left petal on top of right petal when glued together before attaching to centre or, when attached to centre, the left petal would be closer to the centre than the right petal), then glue a left-right below it, slightly off to one side. If desired, gently pinch all or some of the petal lips while pushing down towards the petal base to shape.

11 To fill in the rest of this layer, take a strip of crepe paper 2¹/₄in (5.7cm) tall, stretch it, and then cut five petals using template C. Reverse-cup the top two-thirds of each petal and then curl the corners of the petal lips. Dart and glue to secure.

12 Dot the petal bases with glue, up ¹/₄in (6mm). Look down at the flower from the top and look for empty spaces between the petal pairs; place the single petals ¹/₄in (6mm) below the previous layer. When possible, slip them between previous petals. Shape each petal as you place it into position; pinch and push the petal lip down, creating an arch in the petal.

13 For the final layer of petals, take a strip of prepared crepe paper 2¹/₄in (5.7cm) tall, stretch it, and then cut 13 to 15 petals using template D. Notch the petal lips as desired. Reverse-cup the petals (not the bases), then curl the corners of the petal lips. Dart and glue to secure. Pair up eight to ten petals as you did in the previous steps, and leave the remaining petals as singles.

14 Dot glue at the petal pair and petal bases, up ¹/₄in (6mm). Distribute the petal pairs ⁵/₈in (16mm) below the previous petals in no particular order, but trying to stagger the previous petal pairs in the technique described in Step 10. When possible, slip them between previous petals. Try to place the single petals on an angle from previously placed petals using the petal base as the pivot point. Shape each petal as you place it into position; pinch and push the petal lip down, creating an arch in the petal.

15 **CALYX** Cut five sepals using template CA from double-sided crepe paper in green, such as Leaf/Moss. Make three short cuts along each side of the sepal to mimic the serrated edges. Lightly apply a brown or burgundy pastel colour to the leaves to create dimension. Cup-stretch the sepal (although not the base) and twist in your hands.

16 Apply tacky glue on the sepal, a quarter of the way up from the base, on the side that will be seen when looking at the rose from above. Glue to the base of the flower, covering the petal bases and the stem wire. Push the sepals into any empty spaces between the petals. Envision the flower base as a clock and distribute the five sepals evenly. Attach the first three sepals at 12 o'clock, 5 o'clock and 7 o'clock; attach the last two sepals at 2 o'clock and 10 o'clock. To finish, wrap floral or crepe tape/glue from the sepal to the end of the stem wire. Pinch the tips of the sepals. Bend the rose stem slightly and tilt the flower head in one direction. If desired, you can attach two or three rose stems together. See Rose Foliage (page 188) for instructions on how to attach a stem of rose leaves to the flower stem below the flowers.

Coral Charm peony

I don't think I could have made this peony with confidence had I not had the real version of it from my garden in front of me as I worked. I noticed that the petals curved and dipped when the flower was in full bloom. To achieve that shape, the petals are glued sideways. My model has only four large pistils with two smaller ones, but some have more, so feel free to vary the numbers of pistils. I use orange pastel here as it is accessible for most people; however, if you find spraying the paper before cutting more efficient than colouring pastels on petals by hand, you could try sprays such as Design Master Colortool or Smithers-Oasis Floral Spray.

YOU'LL NEED

- ✿ Scissors
- ✿ Ruler
- ✿ Tacky glue
- ✿ Hot glue gun and glue
- ✿ Wire cutter
- ✿ Pastel foam applicator or brush
- ✿ Paintbrush or foam applicator for glue

CENTRE – PISTIL
22- or 24-gauge stem wire,
    cut into 2in (5cm) sections
18-gauge wire
180g Italian crepe paper in Pink Suede/Intense
    Fuchsia (#570) or any dark pink
Floral tape in light green

CENTRE – STAMENS
180g Italian crepe paper in Goldenrod/Yellow
    (#576) and Cream/White Cream (#603)
    or any off-white

PETALS
Double-sided crepe paper in Strawberry/Tulip Pink
    (or Rose/Salmon, Salmon/Peach)
Pastels in light orange and orange such as
    PanPastel in Orange Tint and Orange,
    or any peach

CALYX
Double-sided crepe paper in Leaf/Moss or
    Cypress/Green Tea
Pastel in dark brown such as PanPastel in
    Permanent Red Extra Dark
Clear tubing with a diameter of $3/16$ or $1/4$in
    (5 or 6mm)

1 PISTILS To make six pistils, cut one 22- or 24-gauge stem wire to create six 2in (5cm) short stem wires. Cut a strip of 180g Italian crepe paper in Pink Suede/Intense Fuchsia, $^3/_4$in (19mm) tall, across the grain. Try to cut this strip so that the machine grain is on one of the long edges. Then, cut six narrow pieces $^1/_8$in (3mm) wide. Stretch the end with the machine grain to create a fan along that edge. Cut that edge so it looks like the end of a cashew. Apply glue to the piece of crepe paper that has not been stretched and wrap it around a short stem wire.

2 Make the pistils by taking a long strip of light green floral tape and wrapping it around the pink crepe paper until you create a bulbous shape. Make four large and two small pistils: the large ones should be about 1in (2.5cm) long with a $^5/_{16}$in (8mm) diameter; the small pistils should be the length of the pink pistil, with a $^3/_{16}$in (5mm) diameter. To thicken the pistils more efficiently, fold the floral tape lengthwise as you wrap to create a double layer. Use the handle of your scissors to push on the pistils to flatten them so they look like almonds. Flattening the pistils allows them to be grouped and fit together easier.

3 Use floral tape to attach the wires of the two small pistils together. Continue to wrap floral tape around the centre while you attach one large pistil at the stem after every round, until you have four large pistils surrounding two small pistils. The large pistils should sit $^1/_8$in (3mm) higher than the small ones. Squash the pistils together so they are tightly packed. Finally, wrap the tip of an 18-gauge stem wire to the short stem wires; arrange the short stem wires around the 18-gauge stem wire to make the wrapping as smooth as possible.

4 STAMENS The stamen fringe is made of two fringed strips, each covering half of the pistils. Cut four pieces of 180g Italian crepe paper in Cream, $1^1/_2$in (3.8cm) tall along the grain by 6in (15.3cm) long stretched. Cut two pieces of 180g Italian crepe paper in Goldenrod/Yellow, $2^1/_2$in (6.4cm) tall along the grain by 6in (15.3cm) long stretched. The Goldenrod/Yellow piece will be sandwiched by two Cream pieces. To laminate, spread glue with a foam applicator or paintbrush on the entire strip of Cream crepe paper, then place it along the bottom edge of the Goldenrod piece, aligning the long bottom edge and the short side edges. Press and smooth out any ridges. Repeat with the second Cream piece, gluing and placing it on the Goldenrod/Yellow piece and on the other side of the first Cream piece. Trim the edges. Repeat with the second strip.

5 To create the filaments, spread a thin layer of glue on the top of the combined strip, on the Goldenrod section only. Fold the section in half, across the grain. Then apply glue again over that entire section, and fold the section in half again, to create a ridge of Goldenrod. Make a second strip in the same way.

6 For both strips, cut fine fringes along the thin ridge, making cuts two-thirds of the way down the fringe. Trim the short ends even and cut across the base diagonally to reduce bulk. Then, gather the base by folding pleats to make the base narrower; $^3/_4$in (19mm) wide at most. To keep the gather together, apply a thin line of hot glue along the gather and about $^3/_8$in (1cm) above the diagonal edge. Repeat on the other side. Repeat with the second strip.

7 To assemble, first fold the fringe away from you at a 90-degree angle. Apply hot glue to the pleated base facing you, and wrap it around half of the centre pistils with the fold hugging the crease at the base of the pistils. To secure, take a piece of floral tape and wrap it around the stamen base and pistil base. Repeat with the second stamen fringe, wrapping it around the other half of the centre pistil. Again, secure with floral tape.

8 **PETALS** Cut across the fold of double-sided crepe paper in Strawberry/Tulip Pink (or Rose/Salmon or Salmon/Peach), 3^1/$_2$in (9cm) tall grain-wise. Use the strip to cut nine of template A, four of template B, 13 of template C, three of template D and five of template E. (For a larger version, cut the petals ^{1}/$_2$in (13mm) taller and ^{1}/$_4$in (6mm) wider than the templates provided.) It doesn't matter which side of the crepe paper faces you (or what colour it is) when you cut your petals. However, when you are cupping the petals, the Strawberry (or Salmon) side should face the outside of the petal.

9 To tint the petals with a glow, use a foam applicator to apply light orange pastel from the petal base to two-thirds of the way up the petal on both sides; swipe up from the petal base so the colour naturally fades into the top of the petal. Then, swipe a bit of orange pastel one-third of the way up from the base and over the light pastel on both sides. Repeat with all of the petals.

10 Now shape the petals: first, make sure the colour you want on the outside of the petal is facing away from you. Curl the entire petal from its base to its lip with your curling tool. Then, cup the top two-thirds of the petal generously, being careful not to tear at the notches. I find cupping two or three petals at a time helps prevent tearing. If the petal has 'fingers' like those cut with template D, curl the tips of the petal fingers in different directions.

11 Stack the petals into ten sets before placing them into their positions in the flower. Here are the set # and the petal layers (identified by their template letter names), from bottom to top: (#1) A, A, B; (#2) A, A; (#3) A, A, A, B; (#4) A, A, B; (#5) D, C, C, B; (#6), (#7) and (#8) C, C, C; (#9) C, D; (#10) D, C. Once stacked, work on each set separately. Place the petals at different angles within the stack so that the petals fan out from the aligned petal bases. For example, for one set, place the left petal over the right; in another set, place the right petal over the left. For any sets where there are more than two petals, try to designate the outside/bottom petal as the petal staggering the

ones above; place the right petal over the left, then place the third petal behind/underneath those two, to stagger where they overlap. As you stack and stagger, dot a bit of tacky glue on the petal bases to secure. Once the set is secure, reverse-dart the attached petal bases, then apply hot glue to the back of the dart, ^{1}/$_2$in (1.25cm) up from the base, to glue the dart together. I find that darting the petals together creates a built-in stem, strengthens the petal and prevents the cup from drooping. If the petals are hugging each other tightly within a set, peel the petals apart. Repeat with each set.

12 Whether the petal is glued onto the flower stem facing the centre (which is usually the case) or glued sideways (because of the reverse-darted base), the petal base is usually placed and glued parallel to the flower stem. We are not going to do that for this flower; to glue the reverse-darted petal base parallel to the flower stem would make the petals stand upright, which is not what we want. We want the petals to open up, and point almost perpendicular from the flower stem. Hence, we are going to glue the petal bases sideways. Envision the letter 'T' and pretend the long vertical line is the flower stem and the short horizontal line is the petal and petal base. Apply hot glue to one side of the petal base and then place the base on a slight diagonal (or completely horizontal), using the petal base to frame and hug the centre. I suggest you do a trial test on the petal placement before you actually glue it onto the stem, and for all of the petal bases to lie diagonally with the bases pointing the same way. Here I'm gluing the bases all pointing anti-clockwise, but as long as you're consistent it doesn't matter if you glue them clockwise or anti-clockwise. For ease of reference, I will refer to the positions of placement on the flower stem by referring to the stamen fringe as a clock. Choose your 12 o'clock position and indicate it by drawing a line on the stamen base. Use sets #1 to #4 for the first round. Apply hot glue to the base of set #1 and glue it so the petals are at 1 o'clock when looking from the top of the flower but the petal set base is on a diagonal clockwise, pointing towards 2 o'clock.

13 For set #2, apply hot glue and place it so the petals are at 12 o'clock when looking from the top, with the petal set base on a diagonal, pointing towards 1 o'clock. Place set #3 at 9 o'clock, and set #4 at 5 o'clock, with their petal bases on a diagonal clockwise, pointing to the next hour.

14 Now move onto the second layer, comprising sets #5 to #10. Place set #5 at 7 o'clock, set #6 at 3 o'clock, set #7 at 11 o'clock, and set #8 at 6 o'clock. If you find that the petal base you want to glue into a particular position is already occupied by an existing, secured, petal base, simply place the new petal base on an angle or slightly below the existing one with the bases hugging as closely as possible.

15 Place set #9 at 3 o'clock and set #10 at 10 o'clock.

16 You will have a few loose template E petals to fill up any gaps. Reverse-dart each petal and glue to secure. Double-check by looking down at the flower and see if the 'clock' has any odd spaces. A good rule is that if you see too much of the stamen fringe base, it may be in need of a filler petal. Glue these petals so the dart lies perpendicular to the flower stem or on an angle with the petal angling down to the ground so it opens up the petals.

17 **STEM** This flower has a fairly large bloom, so I like to thicken the stem to balance the proportion. First, determine how long you want your stem to be and cut your stem wire to size. Then, cut a length of clear tubing. For an arrangement with a pin frog, cut the length of the tubing 1in (2.5cm) shorter than your stem wire; for an arrangement that does not use a pin frog or a bouquet, cut the tubing and the stem wire the same length. Once the tubing is the desired length, thread the flower stem wire through the tubing. Apply hot glue to the fringed base (the part that protrudes out), press the tubing flush with the fringe base, and hold until the hot glue cools.

18 **CALYX** Cut two of template CA from double-sided crepe paper in green, such as Green Tea/Cypress or Leaf/Moss. Determine which will be the colour showing when viewing the flower from the bottom; that will be the colour away from you as you cup. Here, I wanted the Green Tea side to be the outside. Lightly swipe some dark brown pastel on the edges. Cup the top two-thirds of the sepal on the darker green side. To emphasize the cup, dart and glue the mid-point of the sepal lip. Apply glue to the base of the two cupped sepals, with the cup side facing you, and place them so that the bottom quarter of the sepal hides the space between the petal bases and the clear tubing. Place them directly across from each other.

19 Cut two of template S1, two of template S2, and one of template S3. Lightly swipe some dark brown pastel on the edges of each sepal. For S1 and S2, cup-stretch the sepals with the dark side facing you, and twist to create shape. For S3, crease the leaf as indicated by the dotted lines: pinch the crease with one hand; with the other, gently pull the sides of the leaf to create dimension. Apply hot glue to the bases of the two S1 sepals and place them directly across from each other and perpendicular to the two cup sepals.

20 Apply glue to the bases of these remaining sepals and distribute the sepals around the flower base, hiding any part of the stamen fringe or stem wire that is still showing. Finish by using green floral tape to wrap the base of the sepals down to the end of the clear tubing and stem wire.

ARRANGEMENT TIP

These fluffy bright coral flowers are difficult to hide, so show them off, front and centre. Display only one bloom or arrange in a group. They are perfect year-round, unlike real peonies, which have very short lifespans. As Coral Charm peonies mature, their coral petals start to fade to peach, then cream, so if you experiment with non-coral coloured petals, these peonies can also serve to link cream coloured or pastel peaches to brighter corals within an arrangement.

Chocolate cosmos

I was introduced to chocolate cosmos by floristry. Their long stems allow them to float above an arrangement. They are known to have a chocolate scent; we cannot capture this in paper, although we can recreate their whimsical nature and deep burgundy red colouring. There are more complicated ways to make the centres. However, I usually like to use several chocolate cosmos in an arrangement, so, for the sake of efficiency, these centres are fairly straightforward, coloured with black and burgundy markers to reproduce the depth and colouring of these wonderful flowers.

YOU'LL NEED

✿ Scissors
✿ Ruler
✿ Tacky glue
✿ Curling tool
✿ Wire cutter
✿ Pastel foam applicator or brush

CENTRE
180g Italian crepe paper in Goldenrod/Yellow
    (#576)
Marker in maroon or burgundy,
    such as Copic Marker in Peony, and black
22- or 24-gauge stem wire

PETALS
180g Italian crepe paper in
    Burgundy/Bordeaux Red (#588)
Pastel in red, such as PanPastel in Permanent Red
Marker in maroon or burgundy, such as
    Copic Marker in Peony

CALYX
Double-sided crepe paper in green,
    such as Leaf/Moss
Floral tape or crepe tape in white
Spray paint in green and burgundy or maroon,
    such as Design Master Colortool or Oasis Floral
        Spray in Basil or Olive, and Burgundy or Maroon
Alternatively: floral tape or crepe tape in green

1 CENTRE Prepare the centre pollen by cutting across the grain of 180g Italian crepe paper in Goldenrod/Yellow for a strip 1in (2.5cm) tall grain-wise. Stretch the strip. Cut a piece off 6in (15.3cm) long. Use a maroon or burgundy marker to draw a fine line along the same edge. In addition, paint short lines about $^1/_4$in (6mm) long from the coloured edge along the grain. Turn the strip over and use a black marker to draw a fine line on one of the long edges. Cut fine fringes on the long coloured edge, one-third of the way down from the edge.

2 To reduce bulk, cut the base diagonally across. With the burgundy/maroon details facing up, apply tacky glue to the wider end of the strip to adhere a 22- or 24-gauge stem wire. After the glue dries, dot the rest of the strip base with glue and then roll the stem wire along the strip.

3 To secure the strip, take a piece of floral tape or crepe tape in either white or green and wrap around the base of the fringed centre and just past the stamen base. Do not cover the fringes. Using your fingers, gently spread the fringe into a half-sphere.

4 PETALS Cut across the grain of 180g Italian crepe paper in Burgundy for a strip $^3/_4$in (19mm) tall grain-wise. Stretch the strip. Cut eight petals using template A. For each petal, smooth out the crepe by using your thumbnail to press the paper grain smooth as you slide it along the grain. To create dimension in the petal, use a burgundy or maroon marker to colour the bottom third of the petal, as well as along the top edge. If necessary, use a colourless blender to blend the colour into the petal. Then, using a pastel foam applicator, apply red pastel to the entire petal, two-thirds of the way from the petal base. Repeat with the remaining seven petals. Curl the top edge of the petal with your curling tool. Apply glue to the bottom third of the petal, then pinch and twist to give the petal a concave shape and a narrow petal base. Repeat with the remaining seven petals.

5 Dot the petal bases and attach each of the pinched/twisted bases to the fringed centre, ensuring that the petal bases sit below the fringe. The eight petals should be distributed evenly on one layer. Secure the petal bases with floral or crepe tape dotted with glue in either white or green and wrap the tape just past the stamen base.

6 CALYX Cut a piece of double-sided crepe paper in green such as Leaf/Moss, 1in (2.5cm) tall grain-wise and $^3/_4$in (19mm) wide. Cut eight long triangle sepals using template CA as an example. I usually fold it in half and cut four sepals, which double into eight once I open it up. Alternatively, place template CA on top of the piece of crepe paper and cut. Curl the sepals slightly if you wish. Apply glue to the base and wrap the calyx around the bottom of the petals.

7 STEM As the stem wire is so fine, finish wrapping the stem wire from the calyx to the end by using a narrow strip of crepe tape, in green or white. I tend to make a bunch of chocolate cosmos at one time, pairing up a few of them and leaving others as single. When I attach two chocolate cosmos together, I use crepe tape in the same colour and attach the flowers near the midway point of their stems.

8 If you used white floral or crepe tape, spray the top of the white stem with Design Master Colortool first in Basil or Olive to achieve a smooth transition from the green calyx to the stem, and then in Burgundy with some overlap with the Basil and Olive, to mimic a natural transition. Open up the petals and bend the stems to give the flower character.

Even if I plan to add chocolate cosmos to an arrangement, I tend to add them last as a finishing touch after evaluating the entire arrangement. In fact, I mainly use this flower in two ways: to add visual lightness to an arrangement by having it dance above the other flowers; and to ground the arrangement with a darker colour. They also bring burgundy or red into an arrangement subtly.

ARRANGEMENT TIP

Cupcake cosmos

Cosmos come in all sorts of seed mixes, from cupcake and saucer to double and semi-double. Here, I refer to them as single and double based on how many layers of petals are in the flower. They share the same stamens and calyx. To create a smaller version of either flower, simply fold down more of the base to shorten the length of the petal.

YOU'LL NEED

- ✿ Scissors
- ✿ Ruler
- ✿ Glue stick
- ✿ Tacky glue
- ✿ Floral tape in green
- ✿ Wire cutter

CENTRE

180g Italian crepe paper in Goldenrod/Yellow (#576) and Buttercup/Carminio Yellow (#574) (or a light yellow)
20-gauge stem wire
Black marker

PETALS

180g Italian crepe paper in Bright White/White (#600) and Sweet Pea/Light Pink (#569)

CALYX

Double-sided crepe paper in green, such as Leaf/Moss

1 STAMENS Prepare the centre pollen by laminating one strip of Buttercup/Carminio Yellow (or light yellow) 180g crepe paper and one strip of Goldenrod/Yellow 180g paper together. Cut each piece $1^{1}/_{2}$in (3.8cm) tall along the grain and 3in (7.6cm) wide. Stretch the strips so they are about $7^{1}/_{2}$–8in (19–20.3cm) long. Laminate them together with a glue stick (see page 20). Fold this strip midway along the grain and cut at the fold to get two equal pieces. For the first piece, fringe finely $^{1}/_{4}$in (6mm) down. For the second piece, first draw a broken line along one long edge using a thick black marker and leaving a thin line of yellow on the edge. Turn the piece around and repeat the same on the other side. The dotted lines do not have to be straight or even. Fringe the second piece similarly to the first section. Cut triangle notches into both pieces with the triangle tip just below the fringe.

2 Make a loop at the tip of a 20-gauge stem wire using wire cutters. Dot the Goldenrod/Yellow side of the first fringed piece with glue along the base and triangle sections. Starting on one end, wrap the fringe around the loop. Keep the fringed tips as flush as possible. Press the triangle section down to wrap around the stem wire. Repeat with the second fringed piece, with the fringe tip lying $^{1}/_{16}$in (1.5mm) above the tip of the inner fringe. To secure, wrap a strip of green floral tape about $^{1}/_{4}$in (6mm) down from the fringe tip, pulling tightly. Use your thumb to open out the stamens by spreading the fringes outwards. The tips of the outer fringes should face outward and down so that the fringe is shaped like a dome. If you want a fluffier stamen fringe, wrap the floral tape lower.

3 FULL CUPCAKE For the petals, cut across the grain of 180g Italian crepe paper in Bright White/White or Sweet Pea/Light Pink for a strip 2in (5cm) tall grain-wise. Stretch. Cut two pieces each 5in (12.7cm) long. Pleat each piece accordion-style every $^{1}/_{4}$in (6mm) to create hills and valleys. Keep the pleats flat/closed. Use a pair of heavy-duty scissors to cut through multiple layers as you round off one end to look like a blunted triangle. If you prefer to cut with a template, use template A and mind the dotted lines showing where to fold. Next, hold onto the flat (base) side with your left thumb and forefinger and use your right hand

to open up the pleats, creating a fan. With the fan open in front of you, press the petal base flat. Use your thumb and index finger to pluck the creases on the petals, moving your thumb from the petal base to the petal tip, flattening out the pleats. At the same time, push your thumb to create a slight cup in the petal. Fold the petal at the base to create a 90-degree angle. Repeat with the other petal piece.

4 Apply glue to the petal bases, even between the pleats in the bases. You may need to slightly open up the pleats in the petal bases to stretch them out so that they are wide enough to cover the stamens. For a smaller full cupcake cosmos, simply fold down more of the base to shorten the length of the petal. Place the first petal base around the stamens so it covers half of the stamens' parameter. Place the second petal base around the other half of the stamens' parameter, below the fringe. For both petal bases, place it $^{1}/_{4}$in (6mm) below the fringe bottom so that the fringe just grazes above the petal (instead of the petal squashing the fringe).

5 To create one continuous petal, overlap the two petals on both sides and apply glue to secure them together. Trim the petal tips as necessary.

6 DOUBLE CUPCAKE For the petals, cut across the grain of 180g Italian crepe paper in Bright White/White or Sweet Pea/Light Pink for a strip $1^{7}/_{8}$in (4.8cm) tall grain-wise. Stretch. Cut two pieces that are 4in (10.2cm) long, trimmed to $1^{7}/_{8}$in (4.8cm) tall. Pleat each piece accordion-style every $^{1}/_{4}$in (6mm) to create hills and valleys. Keep the pleats closed. Use your scissors to cut through multiple layers as you round off one end to look like a blunted triangle. If you prefer to cut with a template, use template A and mind the dotted lines showing where to fold. For a smaller double cupcake cosmos, simply fold down more of the base to shorten the length of the petal.

7 Hold onto the flat (base) side with your left thumb and forefinger, then cut two long slits into the fold three-quarters of the way down from the cut edge; cut one slit on one side of the pleated petal at any fold, and turn the pleated petal over and cut another slit at any fold. Repeat with the second petal.

8 Again, hold onto the flat (base) side with your left thumb and index finger, and use your right hand to open up the pleats, creating a fan. With the fan open in front of you, press the petal base flat. Then, use your thumb and index finger to pluck the creases on the petals, moving your thumb from the petal base to the petal tip, flattening out the pleats. At the same time, push your thumb to create a slight cup in the petal. Fold the petal at the base to create a 90-degree angle. Repeat with the other petal strip.

9 Glue the petal strips as per step 4. Curl the petal tips.

10 For the outer petals, use the same crepe paper strip from step 6 and cut 2 pieces 1⁷⁄₈in (4.8cm) tall grain-wise and 6in (15.3cm) long. Pleat and cut the petals like in Step 6. If you prefer to cut with a template, use template B and mind the dotted lines showing where to fold. Then, repeat the petal manipulation in step 7, but make a total of four slits instead of two. For a smaller double cupcake cosmos, simply fold down more of the base to shorten the length of the petal. Repeat the petal manipulation in step 8 and glue the petal strips as per step 4.

11 CALYX Cut across the fold of double-sided crepe in green, such as Green Tea/Cypress, for a strip 1in (2.5cm) tall grain-wise. Place template CA on top to cut a calyx with eight sepals. Curl or pinch the sepal tips slightly. Before attaching the calyx, wrap the entire stem wire in floral or crepe tape in a similar colour to the double-sided crepe paper. Apply glue to the calyx base and wrap it around the bottom of the petals. Stretch the calyx base as you wrap to cover the entire petal base.

12 FOLIAGE Cosmos have thin foliage attached to their fine stems. Cut a thin strip of the same double-sided green crepe paper used for the calyx, 2in (5cm) tall grain-wise and 1⁄8in (3mm) wide. Use scissors to cut a long slit about two-thirds deep from one end. Trim one of the long ends shorter than the other long end, and trim both ends pointed. Curl the long ends or pinch/twist as desired. Try splitting one of the long ends to create another thin piece for interest.

13 Glue one or two pieces of foliage by dotting the foliage base with glue and pressing it into the flower stem wire, 4–6in (10.2–15.3cm) below the calyx.

Collerette dahlia

Many people are not aware that some dahlias come with a collerette, which adds a flourish of texture to what could otherwise seem a rather stiff and flat flower. This collerette dahlia in sorbet yellow is called Clair de Lune. Try not to colour the collerette entirely in yellow; let bits of the white crepe paper show through as highlights that give further dimension to the ruffle. I have not added leaves, since they are always removed for arrangements and bouquets anyway. You can adapt the techniques in this tutorial for other flowers: remove the collerette and you have a single-flower dahlia; make the bubble centre in a different colour for a scabiosa; re-use the shaping technique of the petals and you can make other dahlias.

YOU'LL NEED

- Scissors
- Ruler
- Tacky glue
- Curling tool
- Wire cutter
- Skewer
- Brush for glue and Mod Podge
- Pastel foam applicator or brush
- Narrow paintbrush

CENTRE – FLORET BUDS
180g Italian crepe paper in yellow, such as Lemon/Lemon Yellow (#575), Buttercup/Carminio Yellow (#574) or Goldenrod/Yellow (#576)
Pastel in orange
Mod Podge

COLLERETTE PETALS
Fine crepe paper in Vanilla or Cream, or 60g Italian crepe paper in White Cream (#303)
Pastels in light and dark yellow, such as PanPastel in Hansa Yellow and Hansa Yellow Tint

PETALS
Double-sided crepe paper in Vanilla/Chiffon, Peach/Petal or White/White; or 100g Chinese crepe paper in Yellow, laminated with glue or fusible webbing
Pastels in light or dark yellow, such as PanPastel in Hansa Yellow and Hansa Yellow Tint

STEM
Clear tubing with a diameter of ³/₁₆ or ¹/₄in (5 or 6mm)
180g Italian crepe paper in green, such as Green Leaf/Sage Green (#562)

1 CENTRE Cut a long piece of 180g Italian crepe paper in yellow, such as Lemon/Lemon Yellow, Buttercup/Carminio Yellow or Goldenrod/Yellow, 6in (15.3cm) tall grain-wise and $1/2$in (1.3cm) wide; do not stretch. Dot it with glue and twist it lengthwise to create a twisted piece 6in (15.3cm) long. This will be used like cording for piping (in sewing). Cut across the grain of 180g Italian crepe paper in the same colour for a strip 2in (5cm) tall grain-wise. Stretch the strip. Cut a piece 6in (15.3cm) long. Fold the strip midway lengthwise to crease. Apply glue on one side of the fold, then place the twisted piece along the crease. Fold over the stretched crepe paper at the crease, covering the twisted piece. Using your fingernail, crease just below the twisted piece, pushing it up towards the crease to reduce looseness. Trim the ends.

2 Let dry for a few minutes, then cut fringes from the creased side halfway down. Keep the fringe about $1/8$in (3mm) wide. After a few cuts, shape the tip of each of the fringes you just cut by pushing the twisted piece tightly towards the crease and as high up into the tip as possible. Hold onto the top of the fringe with your thumb and index finger just below the twisted piece; with your other thumb and index finger, mould the tip into a rounder shape. Return to cutting more fringes, and then, after a few cuts, shape the fringes again. Continue to alternate tasks until the entire fringe has been cut and the fringe tips shaped. Trim the bottom of the fringe strip diagonally to minimize bulk at the base of the fringe. The wider side will be the start; the narrower side will be the end.

3 Apply glue on the fringe base at the widest side of the floret buds strip. Place an 18-gauge stem wire with a looped end on the glue and roll it over the fringe once. Press and wait until the glue dries before continuing. While the glue is drying, cut a narrow strip of crepe tape from 180g Italian crepe paper in green, such as Green Leaf. Once dried, dot glue along the bottom of the fringe and wrap the fringe around the stem wire. As you wrap, move the fringe strip down the stem wire about $1/16$in (1.5mm) or less after every round, creating a slight dome shape. If the fringe tip has sunk into the dome, use the end of a skewer to lift it back up. Secure the centre by using crepe tape to wrap around the fringe base; continue to wrap down to the stem wire and a further 2in (5cm) down.

4 If you have a yellow centre, use a brush to apply orange pastel to the fringe tips to make it look more orange, with yellow showing through. Use a brush to paint on Mod Podge to seal the pastel and to create shine. If you do not have Mod Podge, you can skip this or you can spray with a gloss finish.

5 COLLERETTE PETALS Cut across an entire fold of fine crepe paper in vanilla or cream, $1^1/8$in (2.9cm) tall grain-wise. Cut eight pieces, each $1^1/8$in (2.9cm) wide. Place template A on each piece to cut out eight feathery connected petals. If you want, you can split some of the middle petals by splitting them in half along the grain and rounding off the corners. Apply a light swipe of yellow pastel onto one side of the petal, about halfway up from the base, using one hand to hold the petal base to prevent the crepe paper from tearing as you swipe. Flute the petal tip, or curl the petal tip on an angle with a skewer. Then, dot a little glue on the petal base and gather the base by making small folds. Squeeze to secure. Repeat with all the connected petals.

6 PETALS Cut eight petals from double-sided crepe in Vanilla/Chiffon, Peach/Chiffon or White/White (alternatively, you can laminate 100g Chinese crepe paper in Yellow with glue or fusible webbing; see page 21) using template B. Once the petals are cut, determine which side of your petal is the front (e.g., Vanilla) and which is the back (e.g., Chiffon). Use your thumbnail to etch an eye shape onto the back of the petal, from the petal tip to the start of the petal base. Turn the petal so the top is facing up and fold along the etching. Use a pastel foam applicator to swipe light yellow pastel from the petal base to petal tip. Repeat with all the petals.

ARRANGEMENT TIP

Collerette dahlias can look quite flat from the side, yet they are not quite a five-petal flower (they have eight petals). I find they work best in an arrangement by positioning them so they stick out a bit and give them a lot of breathing room, maybe layering a few together. The stems are quite rigid and straight, so bear that in mind. Experiment by turning their faces in different directions and at different angles.

7 Turn the petal so the lip faces towards you and the base faces away. Apply a small dot of glue to one corner of the petal base. Wrap the petal base around the pointed end of a skewer so that the base corners overlap and the tip of the skewer overhangs the base edge by 1/4in (6mm). You can control how wide the petal is by how much the base corners of the petal overlap: the more they overlap, the narrower the petal.

8 Hold the petal with the skewer in one hand and use the other hand to bend the petal so that the tip arches backwards.

9 Finally, use a curling tool to curl the edge of the petal back, gently pulling the curl at the same time. Remove the skewer. Repeat steps 7, 8 and 9 with all the petals.

10 Apply a dot of glue to the base of a collerette petal. Insert the base into the tunnel created by the skewer in one of the petals. Press the base down with your skewer tip to secure. Repeat with each petal and collerette petal.

11 There is only one layer of petals, so all the petals should be on the same plane. Apply glue to the petal bases and then attach all eight petals around the centre so that the petal bases are adjacent to each other and not overlapping. Place the bases 1/4in (6mm) below the centre fringe and in such a way that the fringe tips on the edge of the centre graze the tops of the petals. The petals themselves may overlap each other slightly. To avoid the petals looking as if they are being layered one after the other, reorder how the petals are positioned on top of other petals.

12 STEM Dahlias have a fairly thick stem, especially the first stems that bloom. I use clear tubing to thicken the stem. First, determine how long you want your stem to be and cut your stem wire to size. Then cut a length of clear tubing. For an arrangement with a pin frog, cut the tubing 1in (2.5cm) shorter than your stem wire; for an arrangement that doesn't use a pin frog or for a bouquet, cut the tubing and the stem wire to the same length. Once you have cut the tubing to the desired length, thread the flower stem wire through

the tubing. Apply hot glue to the fringe base (the part that protrudes out), press the tubing flush with the fringe base, and hold until the hot glue cools. Cover the stem with a strip of crepe tape using 180g Italian crepe paper in green, such as Green Leaf, by starting at the base of the petals down to the end of the tubing.

13 BRACTS There are two parts to the bract. To make the first one, cut a piece of 180g Italian crepe paper in green, such as Green Leaf, 1 1/4in (3.2cm) tall grain-wise and 1 3/4in (4.5cm) long. Stretch one long edge, leaving the other long edge unstretched. The piece should look like a fan. Fold short edge to short edge, parallel with the grain, once, twice, and a third time so eight layers overlap. You will cut eight leaves at once, on a continuous strip. Either cut freehand or use template BR1 to cut a narrow leaf shape (like a long triangle) on the stretched edge, with the leaf base ending one-third of the way up from the bottom of the strip. Trim any ragged edges and re-shape the sepals as necessary. Then cup each of sepal.

To make the second bract, cut a piece 1in (2.5cm) tall grain-wise and 3/4in (19mm) long from the same 180g Italian crepe paper. Again, stretch one edge. Fold edge to edge, along the grain, and then fold tri-fold. Use template BR2 to cut a long, narrow leaf shape (like a long triangle) on the stretched edge, with the leaf base ending one-third of the way up from the bottom of the strip. Twist the leaves to create movement.

14 To attach the first bract, have the cupped sepal side facing up and apply glue to the linked bottom edge. Wrap the linked bottom edge around the base of the petals. Stretch the linked bottom edge as you wrap so that four sepals cover one round. The next four sepals become the second round and stagger the first round.

15 For the second bract, apply glue to the linked bottom edge, then wrap it around the first bract, 1/4in (6mm) below the bend. Cover the seam between the first bract and the start of the stem wire. Bend the bracts so their tips face the ground.

Ball dahlia

In late summer, the large stalks of dahlias in my garden suddenly burst alive, prolifically producing bloom after bloom until late into autumn. Each bloom is unique, and from the same bulb and stalk the same dahlia can bloom in slightly different colours. The shape of the florets allow me to shade my dahlias with different colours so that I can easily make them all with one colour of paper with different results. Some dahlias appear to have different colours on each side of their petals, so double-sided crepe paper with bright two-toned colours can be the perfect choice for some dahlia varieties. The secret to making this flower perfectly spherical is the Styrofoam ball base structure and using a tool to apply each petal without squashing them.

YOU'LL NEED

✿ Scissors
✿ Ruler
✿ Glue stick
✿ Tacky glue
✿ Glue gun and hot glue
✿ Pastel foam applicator
✿ Round-head paintbrush
✿ Wire cutter

PETALS
Styrofoam ball ³⁄₄–1in (18–25mm) in diameter
18-gauge stem wire

CREAM OR LIGHT YELLOW DAHLIA:
Double-sided crepe paper in White/White, White/Vanilla or White/Ivory
Pastels in light brown, light yellow and dark yellow, such as PanPastel Bronze Metallic, Hansa Yellow Tint and Hansa Yellow
Coloured pencil in white, slightly blunt

FUCHSIA AND MAROON DAHLIA:
Double-sided crepe paper in Fuchsia/Maroon
Pastels in light and dark purple, or black and dark burgundy, such as PanPastel in Violet Tint and Violet, or Black and Magenta Extra Dark
Coloured pencil in red or a dark colour, slightly blunt

CALYX
Clear tubing with a diameter of ³⁄₁₆ or ¹⁄₄in (5 or 6mm)
Double-sided crepe paper in light green, such as Green Tea/Cypress
Floral tape in light green or Chinese crepe paper in light green, such as Moss Green

1 PREPARE YOUR PAPER Cut across an entire fold of double-sided crepe paper in your desired dahlia colour, 3^1/$_4$in (8.3cm) tall grain-wise; here I used White/White sprayed with Design Master Colortool in Ivory to create a warm off-white base. You will need a section 3in (7.6cm) wide from the prepared strip for the centre and fringes. From this section, cut the following strips across the grain: (A) ^{5}/$_8$in (1.6cm) tall by 3in (7.6cm) wide; (B) 1^1/$_{16}$in (2.7cm) tall by 2^1/$_2$in (6.4cm) wide; and (C) ^{1}/$_4$in (0.6cm) tall by 3in (7.6cm) wide.

2 CENTRE Take the (A) strip. Fold in half midway, long edge to long edge, and apply glue using a glue stick in between. Cut a fringe two-thirds down the strip on the folded side. Dot tacky glue along the bottom of the strip, below the fringe, and roll. Hot glue the bottom of the rolled strip and place it on the top of the Styrofoam ball.

3 INNER FRINGE Take the (B) and (C) strips. Fold each in half midway long edge to long edge, and apply glue using a glue stick in between. For (B), cut narrow triangle fringes two-thirds down the strip on the unfolded side. Keep the fringes as narrow as possible and curl them towards you. For (C), cut narrow triangle-fringes three-quarters down the folded side. Keep the fringes as narrow as possible; curl fringe towards you. Dot glue along the bottom of the (B) fringe, below the fringe, and wrap it around the centre, with the curled fringe facing the centre. Stretch as you wrap so that the fringe goes around the centre twice. The fringe base should sit on the Styrofoam ball. Use your fingers to press the fringe down into the centre of the flower to close the fringe.

4 OUTER FRINGE Dot glue on the base of the (C) fringe, and wrap it around the (B) fringe with the curled fringe facing the centre and the spiky part of the fringe sitting just below the spiky part of the (B) fringe. As you wrap, move the (C) fringe slightly lower than the previous round. The bottom of the fringe won't touch the Styrofoam ball.

5 PETALS Cut two sections 3in (7.6cm) wide from the prepared strip to make any extra petals. Round 1: You will need 11–12 petals, which will go around the outer fringe. Cut a 2in (5cm) wide section from the prepared strip and cut across the grain to get three strips of ^{3}/$_4$in (19mm) by 2in (5cm). Cut four petals from each small strip by accordion-folding along the grain into four layers. Slit the folds and cut a round-arched door shape freehand, with the curve of the arch starting one-third of the way down from the petal.

6 Turn the petal so the lip points towards the ground and the base faces the ceiling. Make sure the colour facing you is the colour you want on the inside of your petals. Trim the left top corner of the petal bottom to reduce bulk. Cup-stretch the petal. Apply white tacky glue on the right corner of the petal. Place the tip of a pencil ^{1}/$_4$in (6mm) below the edge of the top of the petal. Wrap the petal top tightly around the pencil tip by folding the left top trimmed corner of the petal down diagonally to the right, and then the top right corner down diagonally to the left, creating an upside-down V. Press and hold to secure the glue. Leave the pencil in the petal and press the tip flat.

7 Dot hot glue on the flat tip and place it next to the centre so it is sitting straight up; when you look down directly on the centre, you can see inside the petal. Repeat with the remaining 11 petals and try to place them all around the centre.

8 ROUND 2 You will need 12–14 petals for this round. Cut a 2$\frac{1}{4}$in (5.7cm) wide section from the prepared strip and cut across the grain to get three strips of $\frac{7}{8}$in (2.2cm) by 2$\frac{1}{4}$in (5.7cm). Cut four petals from each small strip in the same way as Round 1. Repeat the petal manipulation in step 6 for these petals.

9 Place the petal bases $\frac{1}{16}$in (1.5mm) below Round 1's petal bases, staggering the previous layer's petals, and push them as close to the previous petals as possible, angled slightly less vertically. You may press the flat tip down into the Styrofoam ball.

10 ROUND 3 You will need about 15 petals for this round. Cut a 2$\frac{1}{4}$in (5.7cm) wide section from the prepared strip and cut across the grain to get three strips of 1in (2.5cm) x 2$\frac{1}{4}$in (5.7cm). You will need three extra petals, so use one of the extra strips to cut a fourth strip that is 1in (2.5cm) by 2$\frac{1}{4}$in (5.7cm). Cut four petals from each small strip in the same way as for Rounds 1 and 2. Repeat the petal manipulation in step 6.

11 Place the petal bases $\frac{1}{8}$in (3mm) below Round 2's petal bases and start your first petal staggered. The bases will naturally angle less and less vertically, but should not yet be parallel to the ground. As you place each successive petal close to the previous petal in the round, the petals will no longer be perfectly staggered since you are likely fitting more petals in this round.

12 ROUND 4 You will need 15–16 petals for this round. Cut a 2$\frac{1}{2}$in (6.5cm) wide section from the prepared strip and cut across the grain to get three equal strips 1$\frac{1}{16}$in (2.7cm) tall. You will need three or four extra petals, so use one of the extra strips to cut a fourth strip that is 1$\frac{1}{16}$in (2.7cm) tall and 2$\frac{1}{2}$in (6.4cm) wide. Cut four petals from each small strip as in the previous rounds, except instead of cutting the petal curve at the one-third mark, cut at the halfway mark. Repeat the petal manipulation in step 6, but place the pencil tip flush with the top edge of the petal bottom, hold on to the tip of the pencil with one hand, and wiggle the pencil a bit with the other hand to increase the size of the petal mouth. These petals should look wider than those on the previous round. Place these

petals $\frac{1}{16}$in (1.5mm) below Round 3 and start your first petal staggered. The petals should be close to parallel to the ground.

13 ROUND 5 You will need 15–16 petals for this round. Cut one 3in (7.6cm) wide section from the prepared strip and cut across the grain to get three equal strips 1$\frac{1}{16}$in (2.7cm) tall. You will need three or four extra petals, so use one of the extra strips to cut a fourth strip that is 1$\frac{1}{16}$in (2.7cm) tall by 3in (7.6cm) wide. Cut four petals from each small strip like you did in Round 4. When gluing the petals on the Styrofoam ball, glue in a similar way to Round 4, but turn the flower upside down. Place these petals $\frac{1}{16}$in (1.5mm) directly on top of Round 4. The petals should be parallel to the ground.

14 ROUND 6 Repeat Round 5 so that the petals angle down slightly.

ARRANGEMENT TIP

Real dahlias are challenging to place in an arrangement because their stems are so stiff; paper dahlias made with stem wires are much more forgiving. I designed these to be smaller than most of my flowers, so they make a great addition to any arrangement with other dahlias to introduce variation in scale. Like all dahlias, their petal-dense shape provides visual texture. They come in rich dark burgundy, which I love to bury deep in my arrangements to create an illusion of depth. In cream, they make amazing little textural pieces that can be subtly coloured in different hues. Since they are made from double-sided crepe paper and are petal-dense, they hold their shape quite well when nestled among other flowers.

15 **ROUND 7** Repeat Round 5, although you may need only 13–15 petals to close up the ball shape. The petals may not lie as flush to each other as you want; some may seem to stick out from the flower because they lie slightly higher than the others. In this case, use scissors to trim the petal lips.

16 **STEM** Dahlias have a fairly thick stem, especially the first stems that bloom. I use a clear tubing to thicken the stem. First, determine how long you want your stem to be and cut your stem wire to size. Then, cut a length of clear tubing so that it is 1in (2.5cm) shorter than your stem wire. First, apply hot glue to the looped end of an 18-gauge stem wire and push it into the Styrofoam ball at the bottom of the flower. Then apply hot glue to the Styrofoam ball around the stem wire. Thread the stem wire through the tubing and press the end of the tubing into the hot glue, and wait for it to cool.

17 **CALYX** There are two layers to the calyx: the first layer comprises the ray florets; the second layer is the bracts. Cut eight ray florets using template 1 and double-sided crepe paper in Green Tea/Cypress or in any light green. If you want to cut freehand, take a fold of double-sided crepe paper in Green Tea/Cypress or in any light green and cut a strip 1⁷/₈in (4.8cm) wide along the grain to be used for this step and for the second calyx; cut two pieces of 1¹/₄in (3.2cm) tall along the grain, and 1¹/₂in (3.8cm) wide. Using one piece at a time, accordion-fold (along the grain) into four narrow layers and cut a shape that resembles a spoon with an elongated face and a spoon handle one-quarter of the layer long. With the darker green side facing up, dot glue on the floret handle. Dot glue all over the Styrofoam ball. Cover the Styrofoam ball by placing all eight florets side by side onto the Styrofoam ball with the spoon handles on the clear tubing. Cut and glue more florets as needed. Press to secure.

18 The second layer of the calyx is made up of the bracts that protect the bud. Cut five bracts using template 2 with the same crepe paper as in the previous step. If you want to cut freehand, cut a piece 1¹/₈in (2.9cm) tall along the grain and 1⁷/₈in (4.8cm) wide. Accordion-fold (along the grain) into five layers. Cut a sepal that resembles a spoon with an elongated face, and the spoon handle one-quarter long. Stretch each sepal. With the dark green side facing you, fold in half midway across the grain to divide the piece into the sepal tip and sepal base. Dot glue on the sepal bases and place them around the stem so that the fold sits on the ray florets.

19 Once secure, press down on the folds so the bracts point down. Finish the stem wire by wrapping with green floral tape or gluing a narrow strip of green crepe tape around it.

20 **COLOURING** At this point, I remove any hot glue strings, and I apply colour. Take a paintbrush and charge it with your pastel in the colour you want to layer on to the dahlia. Here, I wanted to create a dahlia with a muddy yellow colour, so I charged my brush first with a light brown to colour the inside of each petal, then I coloured the petals with a light yellow. I highlighted some of the petals with a dark yellow.

Parrot tulip

To mimic the frilliness of parrot tulip petals, each petal consists of two layers of fine crepe paper, with additional very fine 'feathers' glued on the outer petals. When I was experimenting with dip bleaching (see page 30), I found that 60g Italian crepe paper was poor at absorbing liquid and, when bleached, leaves quite a distinctive line; simultaneously, the bleach sometimes draws out unexpected colours from the dye. When this orange crepe paper is bleached, it draws out a muddy sepia colour along the bleached edges that I find irresistible.

YOU'LL NEED

- Scissors
- Ruler
- Tacky glue
- Hot glue
- Glue gun
- Wire cutter

CENTRE
24-gauge stem wire, paper-wrapped in light green, and cut into six sections
18-gauge stem wire
Clear tubing ³/₁₆in (5mm) in diameter; ¹/₄in (6mm) as an alternative
180g Italian or Chinese crepe paper in Black (#602)
180g Italian or Chinese crepe paper in yellow, such as Buttercup/Carminio Yellow (#574) or Lemon/Lemon Yellow (#575)

PETALS
28- or 30-gauge stem wire, paper-wrapped in white, cut into three sections

ORANGE TULIP
60g Italian crepe paper in Intense Orange (#299), bleached on one long edge

DARK PURPLE TULIP
Extra-fine crepe paper in Aubergine, water-dipped on one long edge

STEM
180g Italian/Chinese crepe paper, or 100g Chinese crepe paper in a bright green such as Green Tea
Clear tubing with a diameter of ³/₁₆ or ¹/₄in (5 or 6mm)

1 PREPARE YOUR PAPER To achieve the dual coloration of the parrot tulip, I dip-bleach or water-dip the crepe paper, depending on the flower colour. Cut across an entire fold of 60g or fine crepe paper in the colour of your choice for a strip 3–4in (7.6–10.2cm) tall grain-wise. One long strip should be enough to make one parrot tulip. To make the orange parrot tulip, bleach one long side of 60g orange crepe paper. If necessary, immerse the top half of the paper strip into the bleach to let it soak through more evenly.

2 To make a dark purple parrot tulip, water dip one long side of Aubergine extra-fine crepe paper. Once the paper dries, you can use it as it is or iron it to flatten it. If you choose not to iron it, gently stretch it out to get it smoother for cutting.

3 STAMENS Cut one 24-gauge stem wire, paper-wrapped in green, into six equal sections. Then cut across the grain for a thin strip of 180g Italian or Chinese crepe paper in black, $1/4$in (6mm) tall grain-wise. Stretch and cut this into six $4^{1}/2$in (11.4cm) long strips. Take one strip and dot it with glue, then start wrapping the tip of a short 24-gauge stem wire. Start $1/2$in (13mm) down from the tip, wrap up to the tip, then back down and back up until you get an elongated tip. Repeat for five more stamens.

4 STIGMA Prepare your 18-gauge stem wire by cutting a thin strip of 180g Italian/Chinese crepe paper in yellow, $1/2$in (6mm) tall grain-wise, for crepe tape. Dot with glue and wrap the tip of the stem wire down 2in (5cm). Using that same strip, cut a section 2in (5cm) long, fold midway and laminate with tacky glue. Cut in half across the grain lengthwise to get two narrow strips, each about $1/8$in (3mm) tall grain-wise.

5 We will make a three-prong star for the stigma. Take one strip, dot it with glue, and wrap one end onto the tip of the yellow-covered stem wire. Pinch the strip at $1/8$in (3mm) to create one of the three prongs. The strip should return back to the stem wire. Press to secure, then repeat the pinch at the $1/8$in (3mm) mark.

6 Return the strip back to the stem wire, press to secure, then pinch one last time at the $1/8$in (3mm) mark, for the third and final prong. Have the strip return to the stem wire and then trim off the extra.

7 Take the yellow crepe tape and wrap it around the yellow stem wire, $1/2$in (13mm) down from the three-prong stigma. Start attaching the black stamens around it so that the stamen tips are slightly higher than the stigma. On the first round of crepe tape, tape only one stamen; on the second and third rounds, tape two stamens per round; on the fourth round, secure the last stamen. This should create enough bulk for the clear tubing to slip over. Open up the stamen surrounding the stigma. Trim the stamen stem wires short and staggered before covering with crepe tape.

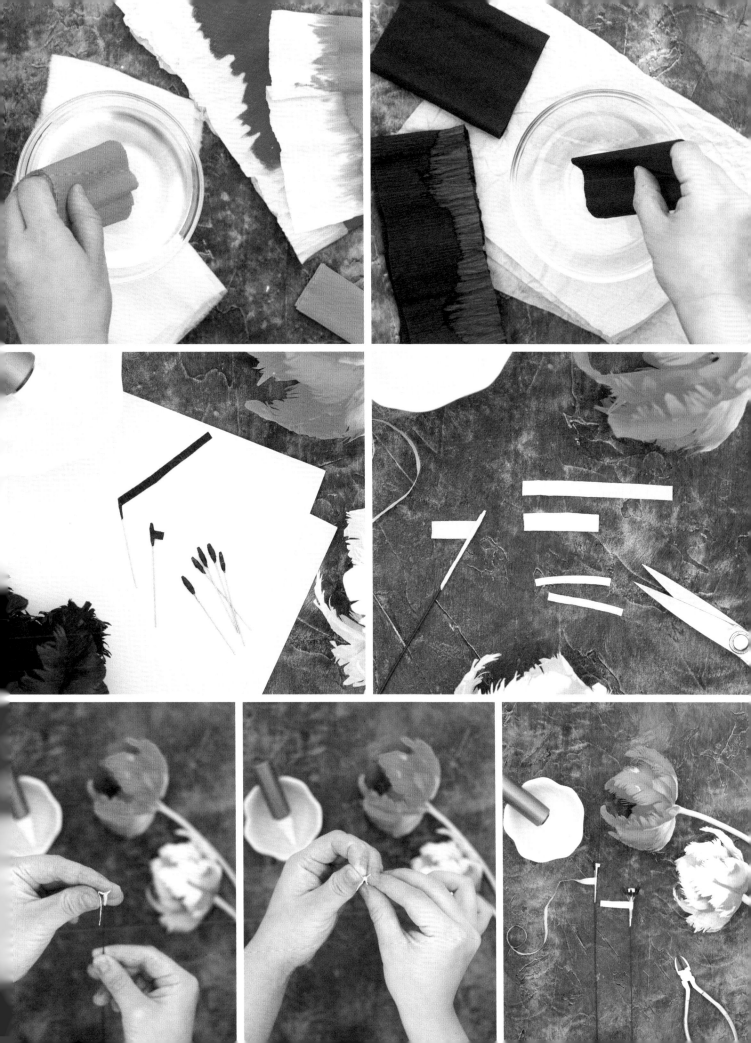

8 **STEM** Tulips, like dahlias, have thicker stems. First, determine how long you want your stem to be and cut your stem wire to size. Then, cut a length of clear tubing. If you intend to use it for an arrangement with a pin frog, then cut the length of the tubing 1in (2.5cm) shorter than your stem wire; if you intend to use it for an arrangement that doesn't use a pin frog or a bouquet, then simply cut the tubing and the stem wire the same length. Apply hot glue to the base of the stamens. Thread through the clear tubing and push the tubing over the stamen base and into the hot glue. Once the glue cools, cut off any chunky bits that may have squeezed out. Then, take your yellow crepe tape and wrap around the seam at the clear tubing to hide the hot glue.

9 **PETALS** As a result of the bleach, the prepared crepe paper should have one long edge of its original colour that lightens to an off-white colour on the other long edge. Because we will be relying on the bias when creating the petal, half of the paper you cut will be lighter and half will be darker. Keep this in mind as you cut and glue the petals. Start by doubling up your strip; fold your long strip midway, along the grain. This ensures that the two layers mirror each other: the same long edge on both layers is dark and the same long edge on both layers is light. Cutting through both layers, cut 12 sections, each 2$\frac{1}{2}$in (6.4cm) wide. You should have 12 double layers.

Cut diagonally across the 12 double layers. You should have two piles of triangles: one pile with a lighter colour on the top edge, one pile with a darker colour on the top edge. Choose one pile to work with for your parrot tulip, and save the other pile for another parrot tulip. (The pile with a lighter top edge will make a parrot tulip with a lighter petal lip; the pile with a darker top edge will make a parrot tulip with a darker petal lip.)

10 I chose to work with the triangles with lighter colouring on the top edge. Take two triangles and glue the diagonal edges together to keep the double layer together. Trim the diagonal edge evenly. Repeat with the other 11 double layers of triangles.

11 Cut two 28- or 30-gauge stem wires (paper-covered in white or bare) into thirds. Turn each triangle double layer so the darker side is closest to you while the lighter bleached side is away from you. Cut $\frac{1}{4}$in (6mm) off the darker tip of the triangle double layer, with the cut line perpendicular to the diagonal edge. Then, match triangle with triangle along the diagonal side, so that both triangles have the dark at the bottom (or the light at the bottom if you are working with the triangles with darker colouring on the top edge). Dot glue on the diagonal edge of one triangle double layer, and place one of the short 28- or 30-gauge stem wires on top of the glue. Dot the stem wire with glue, then place the diagonal edge of the other triangle double layer on top. Press to secure.

Repeat with the other ten triangle double layers.

ARRANGEMENT TIP

I love tulips for their long, elegant stems. When tulips are allowed to display their swan-like necks they often serve to define the perimeters of a composition, emphasize the three-dimensional aspect of an arrangement, and create beautiful and elegant lines for your eyes to follow. Try turning their heads so they face different directions. I particularly love tulips that are bowing their necks with their blooms facing down as if they're gazing at their own reflection on the table. For variety, open up the blooms of some of the flowers so their petals are spread completely apart, leave others closed, or bend and curl the petals backwards from the centre (a technique known as 'reflexing' in floristry).

12 Place template A on top of the petal, aligning the centre line; make sure the grain lines are in the same general direction, then cut. Using the template as inspiration, make short and long cuts into the edges of the petals and round off the cuts. I first cut my longer slits to help me define what the edges will look like. Then, after I round off the slitted edges, I cut fine triangle fringes throughout. One you have cut the fringes, position your scissors perpendicular to the petal side and randomly cut into the fringe to create a more jagged side.

13 Fold the petal in half along the stem wire so that the outside of the petal is folded to the inside. Hold the stem wire with one hand. Use the thumb of your other hand to shape the petal by pulling and cupping the two sides of the petals. You should see a deep valley when you look at the petal from the outside.

14 Take a curling tool and curl the fringed and bottom edges of the petal.

15 You can add 'feathers' to the petals as an option. Cut small and narrow triangles from discarded pieces of crepe paper. Cut them along the grain, and cut their bases slanted. Then dot a bit of glue to the base of the triangle and place it on the outside of the petal.

16 Line up the grain and the colours so that the feather looks as if it is rising naturally from the petal.

17 To assemble the tulip, create crepe tape by cutting across the grain of 180g Italian or Chinese crepe paper or 100g Chinese crepe paper in a bright green (such as Green Tea). The strip should be about $^{1}/_{4}$in (6mm) tall, along the grain, to be used as crepe tape. Stretch and dot with glue. Start wrapping the base of the stamens; add and attach a petal on each round until there are three petals evenly distributed along the same plane. Attach the petals so the white stem wire does not show beneath the petal. Close the petals towards the centre before proceeding to attach the second layer by bending the wired petal into a C-shape; bend the tip of the petal inwards. Use your fingers to pinch the wire as you shape it.

18 The second layer of three petals should stagger the first layer, and be evenly distributed. Once all the petals are secure, trim the white stem wires short, and continue to wrap down to the stem bottom. Again, bend the wired petals into a C-shape, using your fingers to pinch the wire as you shape it; bend the tip of the petal inwards.

19 Tease the petals open and into different positions to give the flower some character. Bend the stem slightly.

Open ranunculus

I'm drawn to flowers with unique colouring, so I am fascinated by the Café Caramel ranunculus, with its muddy gold/yellow colour and dark brown and/or burgundy details. Even with this general colour formula, every flower is slightly different. Experiment using different sides of the double-sided Yellow/Goldenrod paper as the top side; the Yellow side is slightly duller than the Goldenrod so using different sides as the top side will create subtle variation in your flowers. The colour recipe for the centre pistils and stamens of the flower can be used for most other ranunculus types. Use the colour recipes for the purple-burgundy ranunculus and the Eze ranunculus in the Closed Ranunculus tutorial (see page 128) and make them open instead.

YOU'LL NEED

- ❀ Scissors
- ❀ Ruler
- ❀ Tacky glue
- ❀ Hot glue and glue gun
- ❀ Wire cutter
- ❀ Fan paintbrush
- ❀ Flat-head paintbrush

CENTRE
18-gauge stem wire
Floral tape in light green or Chinese crepe paper in light green, such as Moss Green

CAFÉ CARAMEL RANUNCULUS
Extra-fine crepe paper or 180g crepe paper in Bronze Metallic
180g Italian crepe paper in Black (#602)

WHITE RANUNCULUS
Extra-fine crepe paper in Green Tea, 180g Italian crepe paper in Water Green/Lime Pulp (#566), or 180g or 100g Chinese crepe paper in

Moss Green and 180g Italian crepe paper in Goldenrod/Yellow (#576)
Optional: Pastel in bronze or medium brown such as PanPastel in Bronze and Burnt Sienna

PETALS
CAFÉ CARAMEL RANUNCULUS
Double-sided crepe paper in Yellow/Goldenrod
Acrylic paint in burgundy (dark red, dark reddish brown)
Inks in black and deep red, or burgundy

WHITE RANUNCULUS
Double-sided crepe paper in White/White

CALYX
Double-sided crepe paper in light green, such as Green Tea/Cypress
Floral tape in light green or Chinese crepe paper in light green, such as Moss Green

1 **PREPARE YOUR PAPER** For the white ranunculus, take a fold of double-sided crepe paper in White/White and cut a strip across the grain, 1¼in (3.2cm) tall. For the Café Caramel ranunculus, take a fold of double-sided crepe paper in Yellow/Goldenrod and cut a strip across the grain, 1¼in (3.2cm) tall. Cut it into four equal lengths. For each length, apply burgundy acrylic paint roughly using a flat-head paintbrush on one side, letting some of the yellow show through in the strokes. Keep the side that you paint on consistent. Let the acrylic dry. Mix a bit of deep red and black ink or watercolour to create a dark burgundy/brown. Add more black ink if you want the details to look darker; use less if you want them to look more fiery. Use a fan paintbrush and gently graze the bristle along the grain of the crepe paper strip to create a striped effect. Go back and highlight the edges of the petal by applying more colour to one edge of the strip (by going over the edge a few times); this will be your petal tip.

2 **CENTRE** Make the centre pistil by wrapping one end of the 18-gauge stem wire with floral tape to create a small bulb head with a diameter of about ³⁄₁₆in (5mm). Start your floral tape at least 2in (5cm) below the top of the stem wire and go up; then build up the tip. Roll the tip on a hard surface such as your table to shape it further.

3 Cover the bulb head with a square piece of crepe paper dotted with glue; for the Café Caramel ranunculus, use Bronze metallic and for the white ranunculus, use a green colour such as extra-fine crepe paper in Green Tea, 180g Italian crepe paper in Water Green/Lime Pulp (#566), or 180g or 100g Chinese crepe paper in Moss Green. Make the bulb head smooth by slightly stretching the crepe paper as you glue it on top. If you are using a piece of 180g or 100g crepe paper, stretch it first before gluing.

4 Create the stamens around the fringe by cutting a piece of 180g Italian crepe paper across the grain, ¾in (19mm) tall grain-wise by 3in (7.6cm) long. For the Café Caramel ranunculus, use Black; for the white ranunculus, use Goldenrod. Do not stretch. Using scissors, cut a fringe along one long edge, so that it is cut along the grain, about ¼in (6mm) long and ¹⁄₁₆in (1.5mm) wide. To reduce bulk, cut a diagonal line across the bottom of the fringe. Curl the fringe in one direction so that the curl points downwards.

5 Apply glue to the bottom of the fringe on the side where the curl is facing away from you. Wrap the entire fringe around the bulb head so that the bulb head extends about ⅛in (3mm) above the curled fringe; do not move down the stem as you wrap. Once wrapped, re-curl the fringe by pushing the curl down towards the floor; trim the tips of the fringe so they are even. If you are making the white ranunculus, darken the fringe by colouring it with a bronze pastel.

6 This step is structural and will prevent the petals from squashing the fringe. Cut a narrow strip of black crepe paper (or Goldenrod if making a white open ranunculus) ¼in (6mm) tall grain-wise by 3in (7.6cm) long. Do not stretch. Dot it with glue and wrap it over and over around the bottom of the fringe, just below where the tip of the fringe ends to create a doughnut around the stem. Look at it from the side; the doughnut should sit just below the curled fringe and be about flush.

7 **PETALS** Use the entire strip (all four sections) of the prepared crepe paper to cut 30–35 petals. I like to accordion-fold the strip into 1in (2.5cm) widths. After about four to five layers, I cut the petal using template A. Cut the petals so that the edge where you applied more colour and detail is your petal tip (as opposed to the petal base). As you work through the prepared crepe paper, you will end up with small remaining sections that are less than 1in (2.5cm) wide; working freehand, cut out narrower petals with these small strips. I like to place two to three of these narrow petals as my first layer.

8 Randomly cut slits into the petals, going half to three-quarters of the way down from the petal tip, then round off the edges of the petal where it splits. The slits can be in the centre or the side.

9 Flute the petal tips and gently cup-stretch the petals, being careful not to tear at the slits. Curl the edges back in different directions.

10 Dart the bottom of the petals and glue to secure (squeeze and glue the base of the narrow petals). Then glue the petals at the base in pairs. Have the petals with the stripes facing up. As you place the petals into pairs, pivot them from the bases and angle the petals away from each other; have some pairs with the right petal overlapping the left and some with the left overlapping the right. Leave a few unpaired as singles.

11 Apply glue to the bases of the narrow petals. Place them on the doughnut so the petal tops skim the fringe tips. Position them across from each other.

12 Apply glue to the petal bases for a $1/8$in (3mm) base allowance. Take a few of the pairs and randomly glue them between the narrow petals, on the same plane, until the first layer is full. Try to glue so the petal tops are below the fringe tips.

13 For the second layer, glue pairs of petals so their bases lie directly on top of the bases of the first layer. Like the first layer, place the pairs in no particular order, leaving spaces between the pairs and then going back to fill them with a pair. Layer the petals under each layer as tightly as possible and until all of the petal pairs are used or until you are satisfied with the fullness of the flower. As you position the petals, look from the side to gauge the flower's fullness, and look down from the top of the flower to see if the petals continue to create a circle. Your layers will naturally move down the black crepe paper stamens and the petals will naturally be placed closer and closer to the flower stem.

To secure your final petals, you will be pushing the petal bases up from below. If you have gone down to the stem wire, you are leaving too much space between layers. Once dried, open up the bloom by inserting a finger between the petal layers and pushing the petals gently downwards. If necessary, re-curl or flute the petals.

14 **CALYX** Cut a strip of double-sided green crepe paper, $1^1/4$in (3.2cm) tall grain-wise. Accordion-fold into $5/8$in (16mm) wide rectangles, and cut five spade-shape sepals from template CA. Gently cup-stretch the middle and bottom of each sepal. With the cupped side up, apply white tacky glue on the sepal, one-quarter of the way up from the base. Glue the sepal to the base of the flower, covering the petal bases and the stem wire. Envision the flower base as a clock and distribute the five sepals evenly: attach the first 3 sepals at 12 o'clock, 5 o'clock and 7 o'clock; attach the last two sepals at 2 o'clock and 10 o'clock.

15 To finish, wrap floral or crepe tape around the sepal bases to blend it into the stem wire. Bend the stem slightly and tilt the flower head in one direction.

ARRANGEMENT TIP

Ranunculus flowers are very versatile and come in many interesting colours. Their round faces are neither too big nor too small. They have lovely stems that can be straight or winding. As such, they can be used deep in an arrangement, positioned around other flowers or even floating above. I like making them in slightly different colours or shade or tint them to create variation, just like in nature.

Closed ranunculus

Ranunculus flowers that have not yet bloomed are tight balls of petals. The trick to this shape is to imagine the silhouette of your flower, and then imagine the shapes that, together, form that silhouette. The natural tendency is to fixate on the shape of the Styrofoam sphere and try to bring the petals all the way down to the bottom of the Styrofoam ball. However, if we do this, the bud is too big for the flower. Envision the base of the ball being cut flat two-thirds of the way down; then the structure of the flower becomes clear. For this flower, I used fine crepe paper first water-washed or bleached, and then laminated to create double layers. I sometimes find that the fusing is absorbed through the fine crepe paper and creates a plastic layer over the crepe paper, making it difficult to work with tacky glue. I suggest using hot glue if you find it difficult to adhere the petals to the Styrofoam ball. I have also included two sizes of ranunculus for variation.

YOU'LL NEED

- ✿ Scissors
- ✿ Ruler
- ✿ Tacky glue or hot glue and glue gun
- ✿ Wire cutter
- ✿ Fan paintbrush
- ✿ Paint palette or plastic egg container

CENTRE
Styrofoam ball ¾–1in (18–25mm) in diameter
18-gauge stem wire
Fine crepe paper in black or in light green, such as Green Tea

PETALS
PURPLE-BURGUNDY RANUNCULUS
Extra-fine crepe paper in Aubergine or fine crepe paper in Sangria/Merlot, water-dipped along one long side and laminated into double layers with fusible webbing

Fine crepe paper in Burgundy, bleached along one long side and laminated in double layers with fusible webbing
Alternative: Double-sided crepe paper in Aubergine/Sangria water-dipped along one long side

EZE RANUNCULUS
Double-sided crepe paper in White/White
Alcohol ink In sepia or beige such as Copic Refill Inks in Sepia or Beige (or watered-down tea)
Ink in a light muted purple such as Tim Holtz Distress Ink in Milled Lavender
Rubbing alcohol

CALYX
Double-sided crepe paper in light green, such as Green Tea/Cypress
Floral tape in light green or Chinese crepe paper in light green, such as Moss Green

128

1 PREPARE YOUR PAPER Cut across the grain of a fold of fine crepe paper in Aubergine, Sangria/Merlot or Burgundy, and cut it 1½in (3.8cm) tall. Cut across the grain of the fold a second time so you now have two sets. Unroll each fold and cut each into two shorter strips. You will need three strips for this flower. Take each strip and either water-dip it (for the Aubergine or Sangria/Merlot) or bleach it (for Burgundy) along one long edge. Hang and let dry. Once the strips are dry, fold the strips in half along the grain and laminate the strips with fusible webbing (see page 21), making sure that the lighter long edge on one side mirrors the lighter long edge on the other side. You should have eight laminated strips, each no less than 10in (25cm) long.

2 For the Eze ranunculus, cut across the fold of double-sided crepe paper in White/White, and cut it 1½in (3.2cm) tall. Cut across the grain of the fold a second time so you have two sets. Unroll each fold and cut each into four shorter strips. You will need six strips for this flower. Apply a very light brown colour all over the strips using the dabbing technique (see page 36). I use Copic Refill Inks in Sepia or Beige, diluted. Once the alcohol ink is dried, use a fan brush to apply streaks of light muted purple all over the strip. Here I used Tim Holtz Distress Ink in Milled Lavender, and diluted it to get a very light streak. To highlight the edges, I coloured from the edges again, this time using the ink without diluting it.

3 CENTRE PISTIL Glue a Styrofoam ball ¾–1in (19–25mm) in diameter onto the looped end of an 18-gauge stem wire. Cut a small piece of fine crepe paper in light green or black, and cut a small circle with a diameter of ¾in (19mm). Glue it onto the very top of the Styrofoam ball, so it looks like an eyeball. This is to create depth and cover the white Styrofoam ball.

4 PETALS The petals are divided into centre petals and outer petals. There are five rounds of centre petals, each serving to create a round or ball shape in the inside and middle of the flower. You will need 21–24 petals for the first round. Take one laminated strip and cut it in half across the grain to get two narrow strips each ¾in (19mm) tall grain-wise; one of the strips will likely be slightly lighter in colour than the other due to the bleach- or water-dipping. Use the two narrow strips to cut 24 petals, each ¾in (19mm) tall grain-wise and 1in (2.5cm) wide using template A; when cutting, try to have the lighter edge on the petal lip.

5 Look at the colour details on each petal and decide which side you want to be on the outside of the flower so it will be seen. Turn the petal so the side you want to be seen is away from you, then cup the top half of the petal. Dart the petal base, two-thirds of the way up to create a 'super cup' and glue to secure the dart.

6 Apply glue to two-thirds of the inside of the petals. Attach the first petal so that the petal lip covers one-third of the black eye when looking down. The petal base should be at about the 'equator' of the Styrofoam ball. Attach the second petal to the right of the first and overlapping by one third. Look at the flower from the side and with the petal right in front of you as you put it into its place so you can see that the petal lips are parallel to the ground. Then turn the flower so you are looking down and staring at the eye; place the mid-point of the second petal's lip over the first petal's lip by one-third (imagine the first petal being partitioned into thirds).

7 Continue with the third petal, overlapping over the second; again, the mid-point of the third petal's lip should be over the second petal's lip by one third. Continue to overlap the petals until you return to the first petal. When all of the petals are placed in this way, the petal lips create a hexagon (assuming there are only six petals; here I actually used seven). This is round 1.

8 For rounds 2 and 3, repeat the round 1 petal placements, placing the petals ¹/₁₆in (1.5mm) above and ¹/₁₆in (1.5mm) out from the previous layer at each round to create greater depth. Your petals should fall at the equator of the Styrofoam ball.

9 The purpose of the fourth round is to create a larger centre and to define the 'bud' area where the petals are still tight and the bloom closed. You will need eight petals, each 1in (2.5cm) tall grain-wise and 1in (2.5cm) wide, using template B. Again, consider which long edge to cut or place your template higher or lower on the strip with the petal lip along the lighter edge to cut. Cup the top half of each petal. Dart the petal bases two-thirds of the way up to create a 'super cup' and glue to secure the dart.

10 Apply glue to half of the inside of the petals. Glue the first of the eight petals with the lip just below the previous round and hugging the previous round.

11 Glue the remaining seven petals similarly. When looking at the flower from the side, this round of petal lips should lie flush with the previous round. The petal bases should sit at the equator or two-thirds of the way down the Styrofoam ball. Repeat the overlap amount from the previous rounds.

12 We are now at the transition stage when we want the flower to look as if it is starting to open up, so we want some of the petals to be open and some to still be closed and hugging the previous layers. For round 5, cut ten petals, 1in (2.5cm) tall grain-wise and 1in (2.5cm) wide, again using template B. Again, place your template higher or lower on the strip as you choose, with the petal lip along the lighter edge to cut.

13 For five of the petals, cup-stretch, then dart and glue the petal base halfway up ('simple petal'). For the other five petals, take three of them and cut a slit down three-quarters of the petal, making sure to round off the petal corners at the slit; leave the other two un-slit. Then, either cup-stretch the entire petal and slightly flute the top edge, or make a big flute by pulling the entire petal in opposite directions. Curl back the corners as desired, then glue and dart the bottom ('open petals').

14 Glue the petals into pairs with one simple petal and one open petal. Apply glue to all of the open petal bases, then place a simple petal base on top. Position them so the petals are pivoting from the bases and the petals angled away from each other; have some pairs with the right petal overlapping the left and some with the left petal overlapping the right, but always with the simple cup petals at the top of the pair.

15 At this point, you may want to switch to hot glue. Attach the petal pairs by first applying glue to the petal pair base, and then placing them below the previous layer by ¹/₁₆in (1.5mm) and slightly overlapping the bottom of the previous petals. If there are any spots where you can see the Styrofoam ball (such as between the petal bottoms in the previous layer), make sure that is covered by this round of petals. This may require you to apply glue directly to the Styrofoam ball and then press the petal pair onto it. When you press the petal bases, you'll find that the open petals will bend away from the centre, opening up as if they are blooming.

16 We are now at the stage (round 6) where the petals have fully opened. For a larger flower, cut 18–24 petals, each 1¼in (3.2cm) tall grain-wise and 1¼in (3.2cm) wide, from template C; for a smaller flower, cut 24–28 petals, each 1in (2.5cm) tall grain-wise and 1¼in (3.2cm) wide, from template D. For both cases, select a couple of petals to slit. For all the petals, flute the entire petal (this means you will be stretching out the petals as you flute) or reverse-cup. Curl the corners of some of them back a bit. Glue and dart the petal base. Then glue the petals at the base in pairs with the petals pivoting from the bases and the petals angled away from each other; have some pairs with the right petal overlapping the left and some with the left petal overlapping the right.

17 Here are some things to think about before gluing this last round: by round 5, only one-third of the bottom of the Styrofoam ball should be showing. You will be covering the Styrofoam ball with petal bases ¼in (6mm) high. Try imagining a bowling ball sitting on top of a stack of pancakes. The centre of the pancake stack is pressed and gathered together beneath the ball, while the edges of the pancakes are spread open at different angles like a ruffle. This is similar to how you want these petals to be positioned: you want the petal bases to appear to meet under the ball, with the petals in each subsequent layer more and more parallel to the ground. Apply glue to the petal pair base at least ¼in (6mm) up from the base. Stick them, in no particular order, just below the previous layer, making sure to cover any holes. Slip the petals in front of the petals of the previous layer if it feels right. When you are trying to position the petals, imagine using your hand and pushing the petals up from the bottom of the Styrofoam ball. If you want to be exact, glue the petals anti-clockwise, one pair beside the previous pair, slightly overlapping. If there are any areas that look less full, use single petals to fill the gap.

18 Once dried, open up the bloom by inserting a finger between the petal layers and pushing the petals gently downwards. If, when pushing the petals apart, you still see the Styrofoam ball, apply some hot glue to that spot and press the petal onto it to cover.

19 CALYX Depending on the placement of your petals, the Styrofoam ball might be fully covered or a lot of it might be showing. Use the sepals of the calyx to cover it up. Cut a strip of double-sided green crepe paper, 1¼in (3.2cm) tall grain-wise. Accordion-fold into ⅝in (1.5cm) wide rectangles, and cut five spade-shape sepals from template CA. Gently cup-stretch the middle and bottom of each sepal. With the cupped side up, apply white tacky glue on the sepal, a quarter of the way up from the base. Glue the sepal to the base of the flower, covering the petal bases, Styrofoam ball, and the stem wire. If necessary, apply glue directly onto the Styrofoam ball and press the sepals on it to cover and secure. Envision the flower base as a clock and distribute the five sepals evenly: attach the first 3 sepals at 12 o'clock, 5 o'clock and 7 o'clock; attach the last 2 sepals at 2 o'clock and 10 o'clock.

20 Finish the stem by wrapping floral tape from the calyx down to the bottom of the stem. Bend the stem slightly and tilt the flower head in one direction.

Like open ranunculus flowers, closed ranunculus are very versatile in an arrangement because of their round faces and small to medium blooms. They lack the penetrating centre stamens of an open ranunculus, so they are subtler. They are perfect both for layering and drawing lines in a composition. Try making them in a variety of colours for variation and interest; try the colour recipes of the Café Caramel and white ranunculus in the Open Ranunculus tutorial (page 122).

ARRANGEMENT TIP

134

Panicle hydrangea

These blooms are popular where I live (southwestern Ontario, Canada), probably because they are tolerant of both cold and heat. The most common varieties I've seen here are white and pink with tinges of green. These types of hydrangeas have comparatively smaller and more delicate petals than a standard hydrangea. My panicle hydrangea is a stylized dwarf variety; it is not as full as the real panicle hydrangeas, as it has only 40 small flowers. This is the perfect flower to make if you have leftover thin white crepe paper strips. I added leaves to these hydrangeas because they add more visual weight to their base.

YOU'LL NEED

✿ Scissors
✿ Ruler
✿ Wire cutter
✿ Tacky glue
✿ Glue stick (optional)
✿ Pastel foam applicator or brush
✿ Rubbing alcohol
✿ Brushes to apply rubbing alcohol
✿ Paint palette or plastic egg container or cups

CENTRE

24-gauge stem wire, paper-wrapped in light green
  or dark green
Floral tape in white and green
Pink marker or pastel

PETALS

Double-sided crepe paper in White/White
Alcohol ink (or water-based ink) in coral/pink and
  lime/green, such as Adirondack Alcohol Inks in
  Coral, Lettuce and Citrus

STEM AND LEAVES

16-gauge stem wire, cut short
22- or 24-gauge stem wire
180g Italian or Chinese crepe paper in green,
  such as 180g Chinese crepe paper in Moss Green
Pastels in brown and dark green, such as PanPastel
  in Bronze Metallic and Dark Bright Green

1 PREPARE THE CREPE PAPER Take a fold of double-sided crepe paper and cut across the fold for a strip ³/₄in (19mm) tall grain-wise. Cut the length of the strip into thirds to get three strips about 16in (40.5cm) long. Using the dabbing method (see page 36), colour the strip using alcohol inks in pink/coral and lime/green. Colour one strip more green than pink ('green strip'); colour the second strip green and pink in near equal proportions ('green-pink strip'); colour the third strip with more pink than green ('pink strip'). There can be bits of white visible. Overlap the green and pinks to get a muddy antique colour.

2 PETALS Visualize what you want the hydrangea to look like. If you want it to be predominantly pink, cut more petals from the pink strip; if you want it to be predominantly green, cut more petals from the green strip. To achieve a more pink-looking hydrangea, cut 16 pink petals, 16 green-pink petals and eight green petals – this is what I used in this tutorial. To achieve a more green-looking hydrangea, cut eight pink petals, 16 green-pink petals and 16 green petals. In both cases, use template A. Once you feel comfortable with the template, try cutting the petals freehand: cut pieces ³/₄in (19mm) tall along the grain by 1in (2.5cm) wide; fold the piece into four, along the grain; round off one end; then slit the edges of the folds three-quarters of the way down.

3 CENTRES Cut ten 24-gauge stem wires into quarters to get 40 short stem wires. Cut a 16-gauge stem wire in half.

4 Cut half-width strips of white and green floral tape and stretch to activate. Use the half-width strips of floral tape to create small rounded tips on the end of each of the short stems. Shape them with your hands or by pressing the floral-taped centre on a hard surface such as your worktable to smooth it. Use white/pink floral tape for pink tips and green floral tape for green tips. Make the same number of white/pink tips as you need for the pink petals and the same number of green tips as you need for the green-pink and green petals. If you use white rather than pink floral tape, colour the white tips with a pink marker or pastel to achieve a pink tip.

5 ASSEMBLING THE FLOWER STEMS Gather the base of a petal with your hands, then use your thumbnail to flatten the gather. Place a short stem wire on top of the gathered petal base so that the tip of the centre is halfway up the gathered base. Wrap the gathered base around the centre. Take a strip of green floral tape and wrap it around the gathered base so that the top edge of the tape is in line with where the petal starts to open up. Wrap down about ¹/₂in (13mm).

6 Shape the petals by cup-stretching them and trimming the edges to even. Cup the petal by running your thumbnail up the petal from the centre to the lip. Repeat with each of the petals and stems until you have the desired number of flowering stems.

7 ASSEMBLING THE FLOWER Before you start assembling, group your blooms into ones that are predominantly pink, predominantly green, and green/pink. Visualize the cone shape of the flower you are constructing. Begin with the pinkest flower stems at the top, then move to the green-pink flowers that will occupy most of the middle section of the cone shape, and end with the green flowers at the base of the cone. Start by taking a half-width strip of green floral tape and wrap the tip of a short 16-gauge stem wire. Then place a flower stem beside the short stem wire and wrap with the floral tape; the stems should only overlap by about 1in (2.5cm).

8 For the second round, attach the next four flower stems below the first flower stem, lower than the previous round by about ³/₄in (19mm) and angled slightly outwards, and staggering the first round. Start to create a cone shape by slightly bending the head of the flower stem at the 1in (2.5cm) mark; the degree of the bend should become larger and larger as the flower stems are positioned lower and lower on the main flower stem.

138

9 Continue on to a third round, attaching as many flower stems as necessary to stagger and to fill up the round. Again, this round should be $^3/_4$in (19mm) lower than the first, with the flowers angling down more; accordingly, the subsequent flower stems will be shorter and shorter. Usually by the time I get to this round I have used up all of my 16 predominantly pink flowers.

10 The subsequent rounds with the green-pink petals should continue to be positioned about $^3/_4$in (19mm) below the previous round. As you move down the main stem wire, try to continue to stagger the flower stems and fill in any gaps. Keep angling the flowers to be more and more horizontal. You may find that your floral tape is not going down the main flower stem as quickly as the amount you are reducing of the flower stems; this is fine as long as it results in the flower looking like a long cone.

11 The final round with the green petals should fill up the bottom of the flower; it may not be completely parallel to the ground. Once you have finished with the green petals, finish the stem wire with floral tape.

12 **MAKING AND ATTACHING LEAVES** Make three to six leaves per flower, making three leaves at a time. Prepare the stems by taking a 22- or 24-gauge stem wire and cutting it into three equal lengths. Cut across the grain of 180g crepe paper in green for a strip 3in (7.6cm) tall grain-wise. Stretch the strip and cut two pieces each 9in (23cm) long. Laminate the two pieces together with tacky glue or glue stick. Accordion-fold into three layers, slit the folds, and cut the layers diagonally to create six triangles.

13 Take each pair of triangles and flip one vertically. Place the long edges of the pair side by side so that the grain lines of both triangles join together to create a V like a chevron pattern. Cut $^1/_4$in (6mm) off the bottom of the V with the cut line perpendicular to the long edge.

14 Apply glue to one long edge and place a short stem wire on top, $^1/_4$in (6mm) from the top edge. Apply glue on the stem wire and then place the other long edge on top to create a diamond-like shape. Repeat with the remaining leaves.

15 Fold the diamond in half so that the edges are flush. Place template L on top and against the fold and cut. Before the glue dries, unfold the leaf and colour it at the fold and edges with brown and dark green pastels, using a pastel foam applicator to create dimension. Shape the leaf as desired. Let dry before assembly.

16 Attach all three leaves on the same location (called a node) on the main flower stem using floral tape to secure. If you made a second set of three leaves, attach them about $1^1/_2$in (3.8cm) below the first set of leaves. To finish, bend the flower stem and colour the node and the thick stem with brown pastel to suggest a woody stem.

ARRANGEMENT TIP

Real hydrangeas will wither in the heat and in a bride's hand, so these paper ones make a great substitute in bouquets. I love using hydrangeas for their texture and size, and these ones for their colours. With leaves, they look as if the plant is grounded in the arrangement. I would take advantage of the elongated shape of these stylized panicle hydrangeas and show them off, whereas normally with hydrangeas I use them as fillers.

Rosebuds

Showing the same flower at different stages of maturity is something that I'm very keen on. I love to accompany my roses with rosebuds, all on the same stem, as they would be in nature. I also like to use a cluster of rosebuds to bring in colour and texture in a subtle way. Here, I've used a safety swab to quickly create the base structure and foundation for these rosebuds. Although I've used double-sided crepe here, feel free to experiment with 180g florist crepe paper.

YOU'LL NEED

- ✿ Scissors
- ✿ Ruler
- ✿ Tacky glue
- ✿ Hot glue gun and hot glue
- ✿ Wire cutters
- ✿ Safety swabs or toilet paper
- ✿ Curling tool, such as a toothpick
- ✿ Pastel foam applicator or brush

STEMS
18- or 20-gauge stem wire
Floral tape in green

PETALS
Double-sided crepe paper in Rose/Salmon water-washed, or in a colour of choice

CALYX
Double-sided crepe paper in Leaf/Moss or Cypress/Green Tea
Pastels in brown or burgundy, such as PanPastel in Permanent Red Extra Dark

142

1 CENTRE Cut 18- or 20-gauge stem wires in half to create shorter lengths; if you are making a cluster of rosebuds, leave one stem uncut. To create a foundation for the petals to adhere to, cut off the end of a safety swab with $1/4$in (6mm) of the tube attached. Apply hot glue to a stem wire and slide it into the safety swab tube. Repeat for as many buds as you want. Alternatively, use one-third of a sheet of toilet paper, fold over two or three times to create a thin strip, apply glue to it, then wrap it around the tip of the stem wire to create a teardrop shape.

2 PETALS Cut one petal from template A using double-sided crepe paper in your desired rosebud colour. Here I used double-sided crepe paper in Rose/Salmon, water-washed. Have the side you want to be on the outside as you cup the entire petal except the base. The first petal covers the entire safety swab tip. Apply glue to the edges of the petal and wrap it around the safety swab. Pull down the top corners of the petals first and press one corner edge onto the other to secure. Gather the base of the petal, trying to gather it as smoothly as possible. Squeeze to secure. This is the base petal.

3 Cut three petals from template B using the same double-sided crepe paper. Have the side you want to be on the outside as you cup only the middle cross-section of the petal. Number the petals 1, 2 and 3.

4 For the first petal, apply glue only to the left edge of the inside of the petal and its base. Then, place the seam of the base petal directly on top, centred on the first petal and the petal lip about $1/8$in (3mm) higher. Press the left corner side of the first petal onto the base petal. Leave the right side (with no glue) of the petal open like a wing.

5 For the second petal, apply glue to the left edge of the inside of the petal. Then slide that glued side into the open wing of the first petal, pressing the top left corner down onto the base petal. Place the second petal so its lip is slightly below the first petal lip but above the base petal. The right side of the second petal should also swing open.

6 For the third and last petal, repeat the above process, sliding the glued side into the open wing of the second petal so that its lip is slightly below the second petal lip but above the base petal.

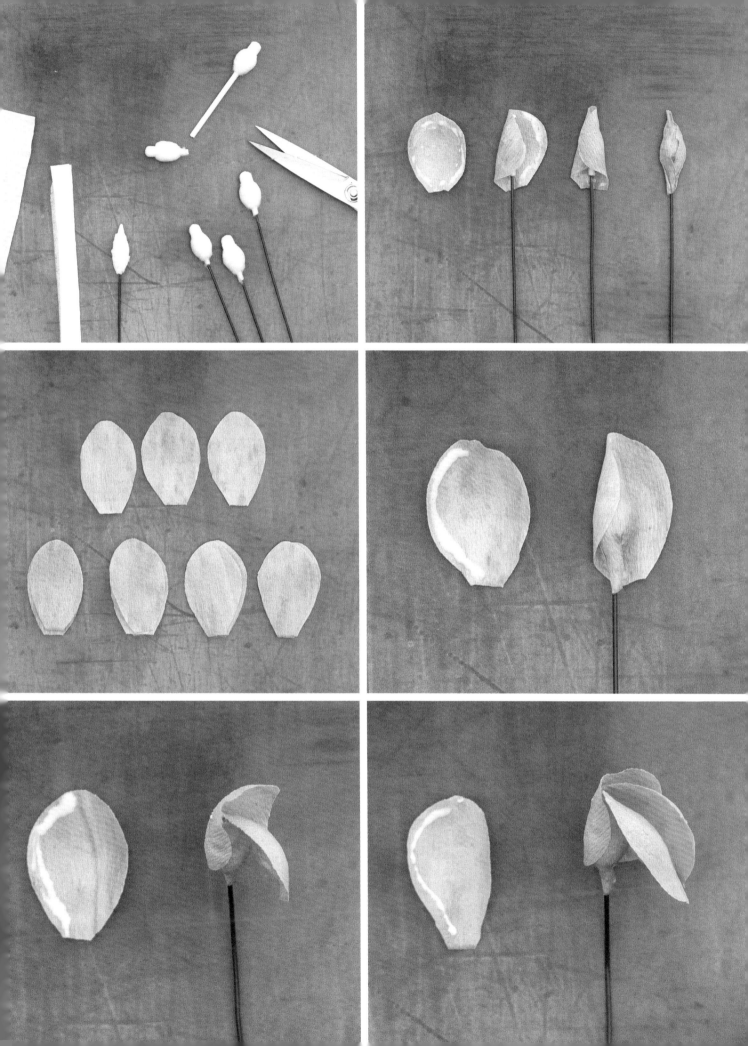

7 To close the petals, first press the left side of the first petal's base against the stem wire; fold/crease the base as necessary to get the base to hug the safety swab and the stem wire. Then apply glue to the right half of the third petal.

8 Pull the top right edge down of the third petal, pressing on the glue to secure. Repeat with the second petal wing in a similar manner.

9 Finally, close the first petal wing in a similar way. As you close, fold or pleat the base of the previous petal under the wing you are closing.

10 Use a curling tool like a toothpick to gently curl back the petal lips.

11 CALYX Cut template CA from double-sided crepe paper or 180g florist crepe paper (stretched) in green. Stretch the middle of each sepal gently. Colour the edges with brown or burgundy pastel. Dot glue on its base and wrap around the flower base. Stagger the sepals if the base overlaps. Twist each sepal to shape.

12 FINISH Finish each stem with green floral tape or green crepe tape. Attach the short-stemmed rosebuds onto the long-stemmed rosebud at random heights or, alternatively, attach the short-stemmed rosebud(s) to a rose stem.

ARRANGEMENT TIP

Rosebuds bring a textural element to a group of roses or flowers. They can break up a mass of fluffy flowers and add contrast in shape and size subtly. If you are looking for a transition flower, try using rosebuds to bring a much-needed mid-tone into your arrangement. The great thing is you can attach as many or as few rosebuds together as you need, depending on their purpose. When rosebuds are attached to a few full-bloom roses, you have something similar to clippings from the garden, with a variety of shape and sizes, all in a handful.

Sweet pea

I tend to use double-sided crepe paper for sweet pea petals. Although they translate better in fine crepe paper, I find them too delicate to hold up in bouquets. I will, however, use fine crepe paper petals for arrangements, where there is less possibility of them being crushed. In this tutorial, I make sweet peas using both double-sided and fine crepe paper, which I double up to give it more strength and to create the illusion of extra ruffles. I have also dyed fine crepe paper with food colouring and alcohol inks with amazing results; it is a testament to the quality of Dennison fine crepe paper to absorb liquids so evenly. If you do not have green paper-wrapped stem wires, you can wrap bare stem wires with green crepe tape.

YOU'LL NEED

- Scissors
- Ruler
- Tacky glue
- Glue stick
- Wire cutter
- Curling tool such as a skewer
- Pastel brush
- Rubbing alcohol
- Paintbrush

CENTRE
24-gauge stem wire, paper-wrapped in
   light green or dark green

PETALS
WHITE SWEET PEA
Double-sided crepe paper in White/White or
   White/Vanilla

Pastel in dark green such as PanPastel in
   Bright Yellow Green Shade

LIGHT PINK-PEACH SWEET PEA
Fine crepe paper in White
Food colouring in peach or pink and orange
Water

DARK PINK SWEET PEA
Fine crepe paper in White
Alcohol ink in bright pink such as Flamingo
   or Coral

CALYX
Double-sided crepe paper in green,
   such as Leaf/Moss or Cypress/Green Tea
Floral tape or crepe tape in a green similar
   to the paper-wrapped stem wires

148

1 **PREPARE THE PAPER** For each of the light pink-peach and pink sweet peas, cut across an entire fold of fine crepe paper in White, 3in (7.6cm) tall grain-wise. Cut the strip into four shorter lengths. Then fold each length in half. For the light pink-peach sweet pea, roll the folded lengths and dip them into orange and pink food colouring that has been diluted in water (see page 31). Unroll and hang to dry.

2 For the pink sweet pea, place the folded strips over craft paper to protect your working surface. Soak the strips with rubbing alcohol using a paintbrush; then, using the direct application technique (see page 37), apply pink alcohol ink by squeezing it on one long edge and using a brush to move the ink up the grain, creating an ombré effect. You can charge your brush with more alcohol to help move the ink more easily. Let dry.

3 Once dry, create a double layer by applying glue stick to the white part of the dyed fine crepe paper where it is just starting to blend with the colour. Hold the top edge of the strip as you swipe the glue stick onto the paper. The glue will keep the layers together as you cut the templates. Sweet peas usually have a lighter colour near the stem and darker edges, which is why we are gluing down the lighter rather than the darker colour.

4 For the white sweet pea, cut across an entire fold of double-sided crepe paper in White/White or White/Vanilla, 2in (5cm) tall grain-wise. Cut a long section of the fold to work with. Trim one long edge to get a narrow strip no more than $1/4$in (6mm) tall grain-wise.

5 **CENTRE** You will need three 24-gauge stem wires paper wrapped in green (or simply wrap bare stem wires in green crepe tape), full length, for three of your blooms. For every additional bloom, cut a 24-gauge stem wire half-length. I have found that three stem wires is sufficient to give the flower stem strength without bulk. Here, to make five blooms, I used three full-length and two half-length 24-gauge stem wires. Bend the tip of each stem wire at the $1/8$in (3mm) mark to create a small circle loop. Then push the loop so it sits evenly on the long stem.

6 Cut off about 2in (5cm) from the narrow crepe strip in double-sided White/White or use the 4in (10cm) long fine crepe in White, whichever applies. Dot this short strip with tacky glue, then wrap it around the circle loop of a stem wire. Keep wrapping it around the loop to create a small bulb-like shape at the tip of the stem wire; go no further down than the loop. Once you achieve about a $1/8$in (3mm) diameter, stop wrapping and cut off the extra strip. The shape might be fatter on one side than the other. Repeat with each stem wire.

7 **PETALS** Using the prepared crepe paper for the white sweet pea, cut five of each template, making sure to place the templates along a fold grain-wise: A (the keel petal), B (the wing petals) and C (the petal). For the wing petal, cut along the dotted lines to split the wing petal so it is attached only at the base.

8 For the light pink-peach and pink sweet pea, cut five of template B (the wing petals) and C (the petal) using the coloured double-layered strip. Place the templates on the strip so that the petal will be coloured at the top and white at the bottom. To make and cut the keel petals and template A, either use the leftover pieces after cutting the ten petals or cut a section off the double-layer strip; in both cases, apply glue to the parts that are not glued together. Once dry, use this double-layer section to cut the keel petals using template A.

150

9 Once the keel petals are cut, take one and cup. Apply a bit of glue to the inside and place the bulb-like tip on top in the middle. Have the flatter side of the bulb on the petal, so the wider side faces you. Fold the petal in half to enclose the tip and press to secure. Trim the shape if necessary. If you are making a white sweet pea, apply a bit of green or brown pastel to the tip of the keel petal with a brush. Repeat with each keel petal.

10 Take a pair of wing petals and curl the top edge of the wing petals diagonally and towards you. Then flute the top and bottom edges gently. Repeat with each wing petal. Apply a dab of glue at the base between each wing and place the keel petal on top so that a bit of the base shows at the bottom. Squeeze the base from behind so that the base wraps around and meets itself. Repeat with each keel and wing petal.

11 Take a petal and apply a bit of glue to the inside edge of the top where it dips. Pinch it from the back. If you are using a double layer, first apply a dab of glue between the double layer at the dip, then dab a dot of glue to the inside edge at the dip. Continue to hold that section with your one hand, then use the other hand to flute the petal lip. Turn the petal around to flute the bottom edge. Once the glue dries, open up the petal and see if you need to trim the top edge to make it even. Repeat with the other four petals.

12 Apply a line of glue at the base/stem of the petal. Place the stem wire on top with the bottom edge of the wing petal flush with the bottom edge of the petals. Squeeze the petal base/stem from behind to create a flat base/stem. Let dry and trim off an extra base/stem so it hugs the stem wire and is nice and smooth. Repeat with the remaining stems.

13 **CALYX** Cut five pieces of double-sided crepe paper in Leaf/Moss or Green Tea/Cypress, $^{1}/_{2}$in (1cm) tall grain-wise and $^{3}/_{8}$in (9.5mm) wide. Cut five narrow triangle sepals starting on one side and cutting down along the grain, ending halfway down the piece. I usually fold the piece in half and cut two and a half of a sepal, through both layers. Trim the sides of the base to reduce bulk. Apply glue to the base, and wrap it around the base of the flower, covering the petal stem. The colour facing outwards should be similar to the colour of your stem wire or the colour of your crepe tape.

14 Take one of the longer flower stems and use it as the main flower stem. Attach your first stem about 3in (7.6cm) down from the flower of the main stem by wrapping it around the main stem with the crepe tape. From there, go down a bit, and attach another stem and so on. Stagger the heights of the blooms. Use up all of your short stems before moving on to attach your remaining two long stems. Concentrate the flowers near the top third of the main flower stem. Once all five flowers are on the stem, trim to even out the end of the stem wires. Once assembled, bend the stems to create soft curves.

ARRANGEMENT TIP

I think of sweet peas whenever I want ruffles or waves of colour in my compositions. Sweet peas are perfect for creating texture that is soft, wavy and frilly. I vary the number of blooms per stem to give me flexibility. To cover a lot of space, I will group stems together in twos or threes; to fill up a gap between blooms, I slip in a stem with fewer blooms. Sweet peas are a great way to add intentional dabs of colour, and they are particularly effective as a transition colour. In nature they also come in a vast array of colours, even grey.

Phlox

Phlox appear deceptively simple, with only five petals, yet these flowers come in a wide range of sophisticated colours, including the wonderfully muddy tone seen in the cherry caramel version shown here. When grouped together, phlox add subtle texture and a nice contrast in size. Cherry caramels come in a toffee colour, marked with red-pink and purple; however, I encourage you to make them in other colours such as purple, blue and yellow. I have suggested using alcohol inks for colouring; you could also use pastels or food colouring added to alcohol inks.

YOU'LL NEED

- ✿ Scissors
- ✿ Ruler
- ✿ Tacky glue
- ✿ 16-gauge stem wire
- ✿ Skewer
- ✿ Floral tape in a colour similar to the stem wire, cut to half-width
- ✿ Wire cutter

CENTRE
180g Italian or Chinese crepe paper in light yellow, such as Lemon/Lemon Yellow (#575), or fine crepe paper in yellow
22- or 24-gauge stem wire, paper-covered with green

PETALS
CHERRY CARAMEL PHLOX
Double-sided crepe paper in White/White
Alcohol ink in light brown, such as Copic Marker Sepia or Tim Holtz Alcohol Inks in Sepia, Ginger or Caramel, or, alternatively, watered-down tea

Rubbing alcohol
Paintbrush for alcohol ink and paint
Alcohol ink marker in burgundy and light purple, such as Copic Marker in Peony and Mallow
Alcohol ink blender
Acrylic paint in white

BLUE PHLOX
Double-sided crepe paper in White/White
Alcohol ink in light blue, such as Copic Phthalo Blue
Rubbing alcohol
Paintbrush for alcohol ink

PURPLE PHLOX
Double-sided crepe paper in Lavender/Lilac, water-washed

LIGHT YELLOW PHLOX
Double-sided crepe paper in Vanilla/Chiffon or Blush/Chiffon

1 PETALS Cut across the fold of double-sided crepe paper, 1in (2.5cm) tall grain-wise. For a cherry caramel or blue phlox, use White/White; for a yellow phlox, use Vanilla/Chiffon. Place template A on top and cut any number of petals divisible by five. I made 10 blooms, so I needed 50 petals. If you wish to cut freehand, cut pieces 1/2in (13mm) wide and in a shape similar to template A.

To assemble, start with one petal as the base petal, with the petal colour facing up (for a yellow phlox, have the Vanilla side facing up; if you are using Blush/Chiffon, have the Chiffon facing up). Envisage this base petal being divided into thirds, lengthwise, then apply glue to the outer thirds. Place one petal on top of the right third and a second petal on top of the left third, with the middle third still showing slightly. The petal bases of the first and second petals should be angled towards each other, creating a V-effect, and nearly touching. Apply glue on the left half of the first petal and on the right half of the second petal. Then place a third petal on top of the first petal so it covers half of the first petal, and place a fourth petal on top of the second petal so it covers half of the second petal. Again, angle the petals so they point towards each other, creating a V-effect. This will naturally narrow the flower base. Repeat with the remaining petal sets and let dry.

2 CENTRE Prepare the stamens by cutting each 22- or 24-gauge stem wire (paper-covered in green) into four. You will use one short stem for each flower; to make ten blooms, I needed ten short stem wires. Cut across the grain of 180g crepe paper or fine crepe paper in a light yellow for a strip 3/4in (19mm) tall grain-wise. Cut narrow pieces 1/8in (3mm) wide; you will need as many as you have flowers, so I needed ten. Make three short cuts on one end, in the direction of the grain, then use your thumbnail to press down the grain below the fringe. Apply glue below the grain and wrap it around the tip of a short stem wire so that the stem sits halfway up the fringe base. To narrow the stamens, twist the part of the fringe base that is below the fringe and above the stem tip.

3 FLOWER Apply a thin line of glue to one long edge of the petal set. Then wrap the petal set around the pointed tip of a skewer so that the tip of the skewer is flush with the petal base or just hanging over by 1/4in (6mm) (this will depend on how narrowly you glued the petals together). Press the other long edge of the petal set on the line of glue. Press down. Roll the skewer so it does not stick to the petals, and remove. Once dry, bend the petals back to open up the flower.

4 If you are making a light yellow or purple phlox, skip to step 5. To colour the petals for a cherry caramel phlox, first create the base colour of muted caramel/toffee. You can dye it with watered-down tea; however, you will have to wait for it to dry, and I would recommend that you dye the paper before cutting petals out, otherwise it may affect the glued parts. For post-assembly, I recommend you use an alcohol ink in brown such as Tim Holtz Alcohol Inks in Sepia, Ginger or Caramel, or Copic Marker in Sepia, and using the bottles or refill tubes to pour the ink into rubbing alcohol to lighten. Otherwise, if you are working with an alcohol ink pen, simply rub the ink into a paint palette so it drips into the palette and then add the alcohol to mix. Once you have your light brown mixture, apply it with a brush directly onto the flower. You will find that the double-sided crepe paper absorbs it very quickly.

Once the petals are dry, apply the cherry-pink or light purple marks. Use an alcohol ink pen in those colours, such as Copic markers in Peony and Mallow. Starting at the centre, make light strokes of different length outwards as if the centre is the sun and you are drawing rays from it. If desired, use an alcohol ink blender pen to blend the strokes into the petal. For a blue phlox, I dyed crepe paper in the same way as the cherry caramel phlox, except with an alcohol ink in blue instead of brown.

5 The last detail is to use a fine brush to paint a ring of white acrylic around the edge of the centre to highlight the stamens. You can paint into the funnel of the flower to cover any alcohol ink strokes if necessary. You can leave this step out, but I find the white ring accentuates the centre of the flower.

6 Once the white paint is dry, gently flute-stretch each petal to create movement. Pinch the tip of the petal lips.

7 **CALYX** Cut across the fold of double-sided crepe paper in green for a strip $1/2$in (13mm) tall along the grain and $1^1/4$in (3.2cm) long. Make two cuts along the grain to obtain three equal pieces. For each piece, cut five narrow triangle sepals freehand, with the sepal bases ending halfway down the piece. I find it is easier to visualize the five sepals when I fold the piece in half, along the grain, and cut two full sepals and one half sepal on the fold. Trim the two sides of the base inwards to reduce bulk.

8 The calyx base will attach the stem wire and the flower together. Slip the stem wire base through the top of the flower. The fringe should lie flush or slightly below the white ring, and the stamen base should not show more than $1/4$in (6mm); if the stamen base shows too much, trim the fringe shorter. Determine which side of the calyx will be seen from the outside; here, I used the dark side as the outside. Dot glue on the calyx base and place the stem wire with the flower on top so that the calyx base covers both equally and can hide the seam. Wrap around the flower base. Stretch the base as needed to cover the entire flower base. If the base is a bit longer than needed, simply continue to wrap it around until the end.

9 **ASSEMBLY** Using green floral tape, tape the top 3in (7.6cm) of a 16-gauge stem wire, and wrap up towards the tip. Place one flower stem base beside it, overlapping by $1^1/2$in (3.8cm), and wrap both stems at least once to secure.

10 Continue wrapping the other flower stem bases, two at a time, staggering the heights.

11 Once you have attached your desired number of flowers, take a wire cutter and cut off the stem bases so they are staggered, creating a smooth transition from base to stem wire.

12 Wrap the floral tape down to the end of the stem wire. Open up the group of flower by gently moving the flower stems into place. I tend to open and spread my flowers so they form an asymmetrical shape as opposed to a sphere. This is because I like to slip them between flowers to fill in spaces whereas a sphere would create more space between flowers.

ARRANGEMENT TIP

I tend to use phlox to add texture and visual interest, so I don't usually make a full head of bloom and I don't make any leaves. I generally like to make a few stems so I can scatter them about in an arrangement, and on each of those stems I have only seven to ten little flowers. I vary the number of flowers per stem to create interest. If you want to make a full head, you will need about 30 flowers; for half a head, you need about 18–20 flowers.

Campanula

I am drawn to flowers that dangle from long stems, such as this campanula. I particularly like *Campanula takesimana*, which originates from Korea. It comes in a beautifully muted purple and purple-pink, with slim, drooping bells that add interest to any arrangement. The colouring technique for this tutorial can be used on other flowers with muted colours. You can also easily adapt this tutorial to make *Campanula ponctata*, which are spotted, by splattering burgundy paint or ink onto the crepe paper before assembling.

YOU'LL NEED

- ✿ Scissors
- ✿ Ruler
- ✿ 24- or 26-gauge stem wire, in green or white, plain, paper- or cloth-wrapped
- ✿ Tacky glue
- ✿ Wire cutter
- ✿ Hot glue and glue gun
- ✿ Paintbrush

CENTRE
30-gauge stem wire, in green or white, plain, paper- or cloth-wrapped
Styrofoam balls, ³/₄in (19mm) in diameter
Design Master TintIt in Purple for muted purple and purple-pink *Campanula takesimana*

PETALS
30- or 33-gauge stem wire in white, paper-wrapped for the petals
Green floral tape, cut into half-widths, or narrow green crepe tape/glue in the same colour as the calyx leaves

MUTED PURPLE *CAMPANULA TAKESIMANA*
Fine crepe paper in Orchid or English Rose
Design Master TintIt in Plum (Oasis Just for Flowers in Purple Pansy), or any spray paint in purple
Design Master TintIt in Sepia (optional)

PURPLE-PINK *CAMPANULA TAKESIMANA*
Fine crepe paper in French Violet
Pastels in pink, such as PanPastel in Magenta

WHITE SPOTTED *CAMPANULA TAKESIMANA*
Fine crepe paper or 60g crepe paper in White (#330), spotted with alcohol ink, watercolour ink or acrylic paint in burgundy or light brown, such as Tim Holtz Alcohol Ink in Cranberry or Sepia

CALYX
180g Italian or Chinese crepe paper in dark green or light green, such as Moss Green
Green floral tape, cut into half-widths, or narrow green crepe tape/glue in the same colour as the calyx leaves

1 PREPARE THE PAPER If you are making the muted purple or purple-pink *Campanula takesimana*, just use the paper as it comes from the manufacturer. If you are making the white spotted *Campanula takesimana*, cut a large piece of fine crepe or 60g crepe paper in white, at least 5in (12.7cm) wide and $6^{1}/_{2}$in (16.5cm) long grain-wise if you want to make six bellflowers. Using the flick method (see page 37), flick paint or ink dots all over the white fine crepe paper strip with a paintbrush. To get light brown or burgundy spots, use burgundy alcohol ink, watercolour ink or acrylic paint. Here, I diluted alcohol ink in Cranberry to achieve light sepia-coloured dots. Let dry completely before using.

2 CENTRE STEM Cut the 30-gauge stem wire, cloth- or paper-wrapped in green, into lengths of around 3in (7.6cm). Cut as many stems as your desired number of bellflowers. I like to use between three and six bellflowers on one long stem. Apply hot glue to the tip of stem wire. While the glue is still hot, insert it into a Styrofoam ball, going in about $^{1}/_{4}$in (6mm). If you are making the muted purple or purple-pink *Campanula takesimana*, apply colour to the top of the Styrofoam ball with purple spray paint and let dry. Repeat with each cut stem wire to create these centre stems.

3 PETALS Cut the desired number of bellflowers from the prepared fine crepe paper strip using template A. Then, cut five short stem wires, paper-wrapped in white, per bellflower. Each stem wire should be about $2^{1}/_{2}$in (6.4cm) long. For example, for six bellflowers, you will have to cut 30 short stem wires. Working with one petal piece and five short stem wires at a time, apply a thin line of glue onto one side of the short stem wire.

Place each short stem wire, glued side down, into its position from the pointed petal lip to the petal base and along the grain line as per the dotted line on template A. The end of the stem wire should not extend past the petal lip. Let dry. The side with the stem wire visible will be the outside of the flower. If you are making the purple-pink *Campanula takesimana*, use a foam applicator to apply pink pastel on the petal halfway up the base that fades into the petal.

4 Crease the petal at each stem wire ('hill'). As you crease, gather the hills together so you are also creasing the 'valleys' of the petal and creating accordion-style folding. Repeat with each petal.

5 Dot a bit of glue along one long edge of the petal and overlap it onto the other long edge to create a tunnel. Press the overlap to secure. Repeat with each petal.

6 To create a bellflower bud, insert a short stem wire into the tunnel. Gather the short stem wires together, folding the valleys as if closing an umbrella. Then, take a piece of half-width green floral tape, wrap it around the gathered petal base and the short stem wire to secure, and continue to wrap the rest of the 30-gauge stem wire.

7 To create an open bellflower, insert the centre stem into the petal base end of the tunnel, with the Styrofoam going in about $^{3}/_{4}$in (19mm).

8 Using both hands, gather the short stem wires at the petal base by pushing the valleys in with your index fingers and creating a five-pointed star shape with the hills.

9 Pull the centre stem towards the gathered petal base and smooth down the folds of the gather using the Styrofoam ball as counter-pressure. To achieve the shape of the bellflower, the roundest part of the flower should not be at the top, where the gathered petal base is, but just below it; gently push the centre stem away from the gather so it is about 1in (2.5cm) from the petal lip. Take a piece of half-width green floral tape, and wrap it around the gathered petal base and the centre stem to secure; continue to wrap the rest of the 30-gauge stem wire.

10 Further shape the flower by pinching each petal lip at the white stem wire. As you pinch, bend the stem wire into the centre of the flower, and lift the stem wire up slightly at its tip to create a gentle curve. The bellflower should look a little like the bottom of a ladies' fluted skirt. Alternatively, you can push the tips of the stem wires close together to mimic a flower that hasn't yet opened.

11 For the muted purple *Campanula takesimana*, you can colour the petals at this point by spraying it with a dark purple spray paint. Spray from the petal bottom to almost the tip of the petals, leaving the tips uncoloured. If the white short stem wires show, they will look like highlights.

12 Cut across the grain of 180g Italian or Chinese crepe paper in dark green or light green for a strip ³/₄in (19mm) tall grain-wise. Stretch the strip and then laminate it with tacky glue (see page 20). For every flower, cut two calyxes using template CA and two leaves using template L. Apply glue to the base of the first calyx and wrap around the base of the petal, hiding the seam. Apply glue to the base of the second calyx and wrap it around the first calyx, placing it slightly higher. Try to stagger the sepals.

13 Apply glue to the leaf bases and glue them across from each other, on top of the second calyx.

14 If desired, spray the entire flower, bloom and calyx, with a sepia colour spray paint.

15 To finish, use green floral tape or crepe tape/glue (in the colour of the calyx and leaves) to group two or three flowers together at the stem, staggering their heights. Let each stem hang 1–1¹/₂in (2.5–3.8cm). I like to then attach two to three of these groupings on a main flower stem using a 24- or 26-gauge stem wire. Stagger the placement of these groupings as you use the floral tape to wrap each group onto the main flower stem. Bend the bellflowers to look as if they are hanging with their heads towards the ground and bend the main stem to give it character.

ARRANGEMENT TIP

I like to drape these bellflowers onto other flowers, so I use very thin stem wires in their construction. If using a pin frog, you will need to reinforce the end of the flower stem so it is strong and thick enough to be inserted deep into the arrangement. Even if you are not using a pin frog in your arrangement, you may find that the flower stem needs some weight to prevent it from being jostled by other, larger flowers.

Clematis

Clematis grows prolifically throughout the summer with vines that are strong and long. There can be many blooms on one vine, each at different stages of maturity. My favourite clematises are small-flowering, but I also like the double-petal types. In this tutorial, I use laminated 180g crepe paper for the petals; however, sometimes, I use double-sided crepe paper, without laminating, and it works wonderfully wired with a 30-gauge stem wire. Experiment with the length of your vine and the number of clematis, buds and leaves. I used a floral tape in the same green colour as the paper-covered stem wire so the tape blends seamlessly into the stem wire.

YOU'LL NEED

✿ Scissors
✿ Ruler
✿ Tacky glue
✿ Paintbrush for glue
✿ Glue stick (optional)
✿ Pastel foam applicator or brush
✿ Wire cutter
✿ Safety swabs or toilet paper

CENTRE STAMENS
180g Italian crepe paper in light green, such as Water Green/Lime Pulp (#566), or light yellow, such as Buttercup/Carminio Yellow (#574)
Marker in dark yellow-orange, such as Copic alcohol ink marker in Honey
24-gauge stem wire, paper-wrapped in green

DRIED STAMEN BLOOM
180g Italian crepe paper in off-white, such as Cream/White Cream (#603)
Pastel in light brown, such as PanPastel in Bronze

PETALS
WHITE CLEMATIS
180g Italian crepe paper in white, such as Bright/White (#600)

BURGUNDY CLEMATIS
180g Italian crepe paper in burgundy, such as Burgundy/Bordeaux Red (#588)
Pastel in dark burgundy, such as PanPastel in Permanent Red Extra Dark

LILAC PINK CLEMATIS
180g Italian crepe paper in light purple, such as Lilac/Light Lilla (#592)
Pastel in dark pink, such as PanPastel in Magenta

166

1 **INNER STAMENS** You will make two large clematises, one small clematis, two buds, one dried stamen bloom, and five leaves. To make the inner stamens, cut a strip of 180g crepe paper in light green or light yellow, 1in (2.5cm) tall along the grain. Stretch and then cut four pieces each 4in (10.2cm) long and trimmed down to 3/4in (19mm) tall. Finely fringe along one long edge, halfway down. Curl the fringe, then cut the fringe base diagonally to reduce bulk.

2 Create a small loop on the end of a 24-gauge stem wire with your wire cutter. With the curled fringe facing up, dot the fringe base with glue, then place the loop of the stem wire onto the widest part of the fringe base. Keep the fringe as flush as possible as you wrap the entire fringe strip around the loop. Pinch the fringe base to secure. Gently press the top of the fringe to create more roundness.

3 **OUTER STAMENS** Using the same pre-stretched crepe strip from the previous steps, cut four pieces 4in (10.2cm) long. Fold each piece midway along the grain, and laminate using tacky glue or glue stick (see page 20). Run the side of a marker tip in dark yellow-orange over the edge of one long side to paint a thin line. Crease the strip midway across the grain. Finely fringe along the coloured edge, with the fringe ending at the crease. With the crease folding away from you, curl the fringe towards you. Cut the outer fringe base diagonally to reduce bulk.

4 Re-fold the crease of the outer stamen fringe so that when it wraps around the inner stamens the fringe will be open as you wrap. Dot the fringe base with glue and wrap the base around the inner stamens, aligning the fringe bases. Keep the fringe flush. Use your fingers to open up the outer fringe. To mimic a fading clematis bloom without petals and with dry stamens, wrap a half-width floral tape in green (in a green similar to the green paper-covered stem wire) around the base of the stamens and down about 2in (5cm), blending in with the stem wire; if you wish, colour the stamens with brown pastel to make them look dried. You will need one dried stamen bloom.

5 **PETALS** There are two templates sizes: template A is for a larger clematis; template B is for the smaller one. You will need two large and one small clematis. Before you can cut the petal templates, first prepare the paper for cutting and laminating. Cut a strip of 180g crepe paper in white, burgundy or lilac, 2in (5cm) tall along the grain. Stretch. To make one large clematis, cut a section 16in (40.5cm) long. To make two large clematis, you will need two of these strips. To make one small clematis, cut a section 10in (25cm) long. For each strip, fold it in half, along the grain, and laminate the two pieces with tacky glue or glue stick. Once laminated, accordion-fold each strip along the grain into four layers; cut the folds to get four separate rectangles per strip. You should have two sets of four larger rectangles and one set of four smaller rectangles.

6 For each set, cut the rectangles diagonally to create eight triangles per set. Take the pair of triangles, flip one vertically, then place the long edges of the pair side by side so that the grain lines of both triangles join together to create a V in a chevron pattern. Apply glue to one long edge and place the other long edge on top to create a diamond shape. Repeat with each set of triangles.

7 Fold a diamond in half along the seam. Place the template on top of the diamond, aligning the fold with the side of the template and matching the grain lines on the diamond. Cut. Unfold the petal. Press your fingernail into the petal, running it from the petal lip to the base, creating a slight curve away from the centre fold line. Do the same on the other side of the centre fold line to create an eye-like shaped crease in the middle of the petal. Repeat with each diamond.

8 If you are making the burgundy and lilac pink clematises, colour the petals to create more depth and highlight the eye-like shaped crease. For the burgundy clematis, colour two-thirds of the way up from the burgundy petal base with a dark brown or burgundy pastel. For the lilac pink clematis, lightly swipe a magenta pastel along the entire lilac petal from the base up, highlighting the eye-like shape crease; then apply a vibrant magenta swipe up the middle of the petal. Leave the white petals uncoloured.

9 Flute the edges of the petals. Curl the petal lips back and pinch them. Shape them to your desired shape. Let the petals dry in that shape.

10 Bend the petal bases slightly, but do not crease. Apply glue to the bases. Place the four petals on the fringe base, evenly spaced, just below the fringe. Wrap the petal bases and the stamen base with a half-width green floral tape, going 2in (5cm) down the stem.

11 **BUDS** Make two buds to create interest. Begin with the foundation from Rosebuds (see page 142). Cut off the end of a safety swab, leaving no tube. Apply hot glue to the end of a 24-gauge stem wire, cut to 4–6in (10.2–15.3cm), and slide the stem wire into the safety swab tube. Alternatively, use one-third of a sheet of toilet paper: fold it on the long edge two to three times to create a thin strip; apply glue to the strip; then wrap it around the tip of a stem wire to make a teardrop.

12 Cut two of template C for each bud for a total of four pieces from fine crepe in the same colour as the flowers or in green. Cup each template deeply in the centre. Starting with the first bud piece, apply glue along its bottom edge and about $1/2$in (13mm) up the right edge. Place the safety swab in the middle of the cup and $1/8$in (3mm) down from the bud top. Pull the left edge over the swab and then the right edge over the swab and on top of the left edge so that you create a tip at the top of the bud. Squeeze the bud base to secure. Take the second bud piece and do the same, but place it directly on the other side of the first bud piece. Once the second bud piece is secured, wrap the base with green floral tape, going down about 1in (2.5cm).

13 **LEAVES** Make three small and two large leaves using the same technique as for the petals. Prepare the stems by cutting one 26-gauge stem wire into thirds and cutting one 26-gauge stem wire in half for a total of five short stem wires. Cut two strips of 180g crepe paper in green, one 2in (5cm) tall and one 3in (7.6cm) tall, along the grain. Stretch both. Cut a piece 8in (20.3cm) long from each strip. Fold each strip in half, along the grain, and laminate with tacky glue or glue stick. Take the 3in (7.6cm) strip and fold it midway along the grain. Slit the fold. Cut both layers diagonally

to create four triangles. Likewise, take the 2in (5cm) strip, fold and cut into three equal parts. Cut the three rectangles diagonally to create six triangles. Take each pair of triangles, flip one vertically, and then place the long edges side by side so that the grain lines join together to create a V in a chevron. Apply glue to one of the long edges and place a stem wire on top, $1/4$in (6mm) from the top; dot the stem wire with glue again; then place the long edge of the other triangle on top to create a diamond. Use the shorter 26-gauge stem wires for small leaves and use the half-length 26-gauge stem wires for the large ones. Repeat for all the leaves.

14 Fold each diamond in half along the seam. Turn so the stem wire points away from you. Use scissors to cut an elongated D-shape starting at the triangle tip to the stem. If desired, brush a light brown and dark green pastel onto the centre of the leaves. Flute the leaf edges and twist. Let dry in those shapes.

15 **ASSEMBLY** Before assembly, open the petals of each bloom, and spread the outer stamens open. Assemble the leaves by using half-width green floral tape to wrap into two sets. In the first, group together one small and one large leaf; in the second, group two small and one large leaf. Using the longer stem wire as the main leaf stem, attach the smaller leaf/leaves 1in (2.5cm) below the main leaf, leaving about 1in (2.5cm) of the smaller leaf/leaves stem hanging.

16 Group the flowers, dried stamen bloom, bud and leaf stem into two sets. In the first, group one flower, one dried stamen bloom, one bud and one leaf set; in the second, group two flowers, one bud and one leaf set. For both, use one of the flower stems as the main stem, securing the other stems onto it at about the 4in (10.2cm) mark using half-width green floral tape; leave about 2in (5cm) of the leaf set hanging. Attach the two main stem wires together with half-width green floral tape so that one set is higher up on the main stem than the other. The flowers should not overlap significantly and this should create one long continuous stem. Bend the stem wires to create a slight J-shape, then adjust each stem so that they stagger at different heights and planes when you view it straight on. Finish the main stem with half-width green floral tape.

Berry branch

I love this technique for branches because it doesn't require you to cut multiple stems, make small twigs and then make a big branch. Instead, if you plan ahead a bit, you can create twigs as you go. I prefer to use 36in (1m) fabric-covered stem wires because I often don't need to extend the stem wire. I'm not normally a fan of fabric-covered stem wires, but I like how the fabric naturally thickens the stem and creates bulk. You can use this branch technique for more than just berries; in Fruit Blossom Branch (see page 178), I teach you how to make a flowering branch.

YOU'LL NEED

- ✿ Scissors
- ✿ Tacky glue
- ✿ Wire cutter
- ✿ Toilet paper or paper towel
- ✿ Pastel foam applicator or brush
- ✿ Paintbrush
- ✿ Styrofoam block

BRANCH
20- or 18-gauge stem wire, fabric-wrapped, preferably 36in (1m) long
Floral tape in any colour
180g Chinese crepe paper in brown or 180g Italian crepe paper in Fawn Grey (#16A/5)
Pastels in brown and dark green, such as PanPastel in Dark Permanent Red and Dark Bright Green

BERRIES
22-, 24-, or 26-gauge stem wires, paper-covered in brown or green
Crayola Magic Clay, polymer clay or air-dry clay in blue or in the desired berry colour
Acrylic paint in phthalo blue or in the desired berry colour
UV protector spray

LEAVES
26-gauge stem wires, paper-covered in brown or green
Pastels in brown and dark green, such as PanPastels in Dark Red Permanent and Dark Bright Green)

1 **BRANCH** A small 10in (25cm) branch can be made from one 36in (1m) stem wire without cutting or attaching a separate stem wire to it. For a larger or longer branch, you can use two 36in (1m) stem wires, or attach a 16-gauge stem wire to the branch bottom to lengthen and strengthen it. Start by folding the wire so that one side of the stem wire is about double the length of the other side. As you work on the branch, have the fold facing you and the two ends facing outwards. Visualize where you want the lateral shoots to come out of the two wires. Create a split at about 4in (10.2cm) for a short branch base.

2 To give you some guidance, I double the wire for the thicker parts of the branch, and use a single wire for the thinner parts. When you have one long section that consists of both a double and a single wire, it creates a natural thinning of the branch. To create a lateral shoot that extends out from the branch, take a length of the stem wire and fold it to create a double stem. Repeat on a small scale if you want a twig to extend out of that lateral shoot. Use a wire cutter to help push the wires together and flatten the folds.

3 Once you have your structure, wrap it with floral tape as you would finish a stem. The floral tape keeps the structure in place, smooths out any kinks, and grips the paper towel in the next step. If you need more length to the branch base, attach a 16-gauge stem wire, cut to length, with floral tape.

4 To thicken the branch, I use strips of paper towel, some 2in (5cm) wide and some 1in (2.5cm) wide. Apply glue on the long edge of each strip and fold it over three to four times, each time applying glue between the folds. Apply glue to one side of the strip, and wrap the strip on an angle around the areas of a branch that may be bulkier, such as the base of the branch (where it would have been attached to the tree trunk), or the lateral shoots that are closer to the branch base. Use the wider 2in (5cm) strips first. Then, as you move to narrower parts of the branch, switch to the 1in (2.5cm) strips. Wrap as smoothly as possible; start above the end of the 16-gauge stem wire base, leaving 3in (7.6cm) of the end of the stem wire bare. For more delicate work, you can create bulk with the floral tape instead.

5 To cover the stem, cut very thin strips of a brown crepe paper across the grain, about ¹/₄in (6mm) tall grain-wise. I like to use the 180g Chinese crepe paper in brown (alternatively, you can use 180g Italian crepe paper in any brown-grey, such as Fawn Grey). Dot the brown crepe paper strip with glue and wrap around the thickened branch, on an angle, like crepe tape. Wrap the entire branch, leaving 3in (7.6cm) bare above the end of the 16-gauge stem wire base. Leaving the base free of crepe paper (and only wrapped with floral tape) lets you easily cut and adjust the length of the stem wire when you are arranging them. Try to wrap in the same direction on an angle so that the grain is the similar throughout. Use as many crepe tape strips as you need to fully cover the branch smoothly. Do not worry too much if the branch looks a bit bumpy; real branches are not smooth! If a bump or kink bothers you, you can always hide it with berries or leaves.

6 To create dimension, use a small brush to apply pastel in brown and dark green onto the sides of the branch and around the base of the off-shoots.

ARRANGEMENT TIP

For a lush branch, make more leaves and berries than suggested. If you want to emphasize weight, cluster several berries as opposed to two or three. Adding more berries to a branch will make it look fuller and feel deliciously overgrown, while leaving some of the branches bare creates an entirely different feel. If your branch base is too short and it makes the branch sit too low in an arrangement, extend the branch base by attaching an 18- or 16-gauge stem wire, cut to length, with floral tape.

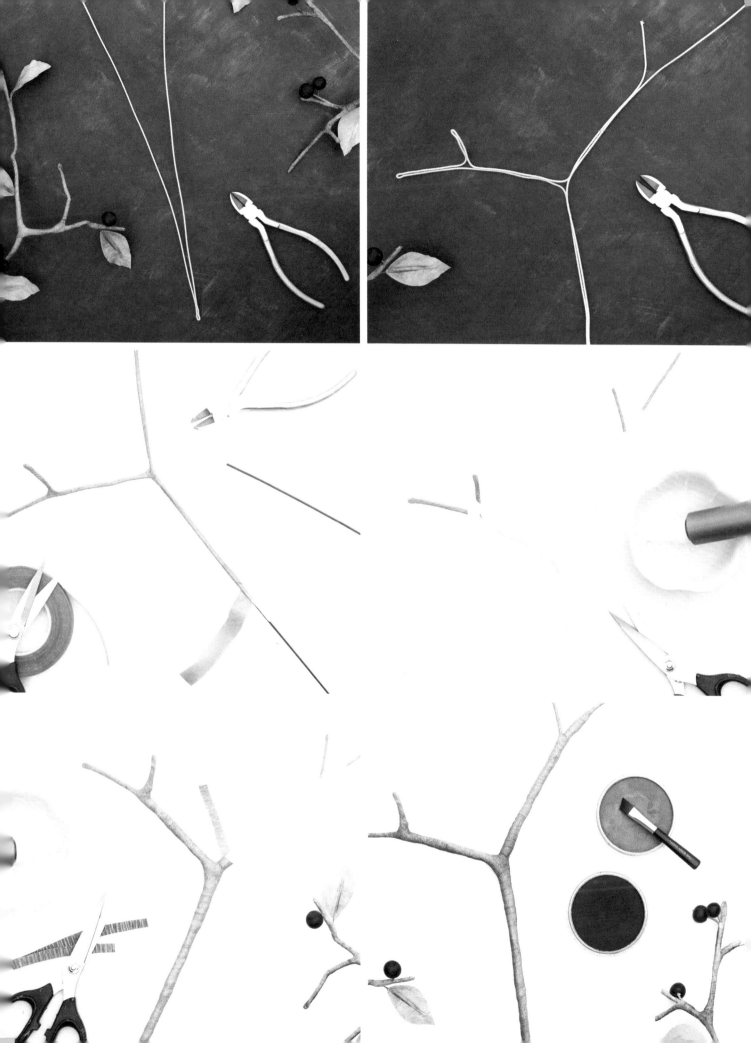

7 **BERRIES** Prepare your stem wires by cutting short pieces around 2in (5cm) long. For efficiency, take a stem wire and cut it into eight equal pieces. Pinch off a small piece of clay and roll it between your hands until you have a ball the size of a blueberry with a diameter of 1/2in (13mm). I like to make mine slightly elongated so that when I insert a short stem wire through the elongated end, the clay ball condenses into a proper sphere. Insert the stem wire three-quarters of the way into the ball, not all the way through. Insert the other end of the stem into a Styrofoam block to air dry the clay ball. It should take 12–24 hours to dry completely.

8 Once dry, you can colour the berries with acrylic paint or spray paint in the colour of your choosing. For the blue-coloured berries, I painted a phthalo blue over the white clay and let the white glow from beneath the blue. The acrylic paint has a shine to it that mimics the subtle gloss of berry skin. To make the green berries, I sprayed them in a chartreuse-coloured paint; in this case, I used Design Master Colortool in Olive Green. To create a glossy berry, spray it with a UV Protector spray in gloss, or paint it with Mod Podge. Although I use a white clay here, you can try using clay in the colour you want. I have pre-dyed white clay with food colouring paste with great results. You could also paint clay in different colours for different types of berries.

9 **LEAVES** Make three to five leaves per branch. Similar to the leaves for the clematis, prepare the stems by cutting two 26-gauge stem wires into quarters to make eight short stem wires. Cut across the grain of 180g crepe paper in green for a strip 2in (5cm) tall grain-wise. Stretch the strip and cut two pieces each 6 1/2in (16.5cm) long. Laminate the two pieces together with tacky glue or glue stick (see page 20). Accordion-fold into five layers, slit the folds, and cut the layers diagonally to create ten triangles.

10 Take each pair of triangles and flip one vertically. Place the long edges of the pair side by side so that the grain lines of both triangles join together to create a V like a chevron pattern. Apply glue to one long edge and place a short stem wire on top, 1/4in (6mm) from the top edge. Then place the other long edge on top to create a diamond-like shape.

11 Fold the diamond in half so that the edges are flush. Turn the leaf so that the tip is facing towards you and the stem wire is facing away from you. Take your scissors and cut the folded double-layered triangle into an elongated D-shape. Unfold the leaf. Flute the edges of the leaf by holding the edge with your thumb and index finger and making a tearing motion. Twist the leaf and shape it any other way you like. Repeat with each leaf.

12 While wet, colour the leaf at the fold and edges with brown and dark green pastel with a brush to create dimension. Let dry before assembly.

13 **ASSEMBLY** Group the berries in different numbers and attach them together using a thin strip of brown crepe paper dotted with glue. Attach one or two single berries to the branch at random spots by wrapping the crepe tape around the stem wire and branch. Trim the stem wire short as necessary for ease. Turn the berries.

14 Attach the leaves in the same way. Place the leaves on the branch as desired. I like to place them close to the berries. If necessary, re-shade the brown crepe tape parts with brown and dark green pastel to blend in the new tape with the existing tape.

Fruit blossom branch

I adore blossoms that are fluffy and pink, and so full and heavy that they look as if they are going to fall off the branches. To create depth, position the fruit blossoms at different heights and planes, and face them in different directions on the branch. Emphasize the weight of the flowers by placing more of the details, like the fruit blossoms, buds and leaves, at the tips of the branches rather than the branch base. I made these fruit blossoms using the same fine crepe paper in two colours: the original dark pink and an ombré dark pink achieved by bleaching; I like to vary the shade of my flowers to add more colour dimension. I use brown-covered stem wires, but you could also use bare stem wire and wrap it with a brown floral or crepe tape before using or as you finish the stems.

YOU'LL NEED

- Scissors
- Ruler
- Wire cutter
- Brown floral tape, cut into half-widths
- Tacky glue
- Cotton wool balls

CENTRE

180g Italian crepe paper in light green,
   such as Water Green (#566), or Cream (#603)
Pastel and oatmeal mix in dark yellow-orange
   or goldenrod
24- or 26-gauge stem wire, paper-covered in
   brown, cut into fifths

PETALS

Fine crepe paper in hot pink, and hot pink bleached
   on one long edge

BUDS

Fine crepe paper in hot pink
Double-sided crepe paper in Green Tea/Cypress
   (or any light green)
24- or 26-gauge stem wire, paper-covered in
   brown, cut into fifths
Pastels in dark green and dark brown, such as
   PanPastel in Bright Yellow Green Extra Dark and
   Permanent Red Extra Dark

LEAVES

Double-sided crepe paper in light green,
   such as Green Tea/Cypress
26-gauge stem wire, paper-wrapped in light green

178

1 **PREPARE THE PAPER** Cut across the fold of fine crepe paper in hot pink for a strip 2^1/$_4$in (5.7cm) tall grain-wise. You can make your fruit blossoms entirely with the hot pink crepe paper; however, I like to bleach my fine crepe paper to give it an ombré effect. To bleach, cut a fold of fine crepe paper across the grain for a strip 1^1/$_2$–2in (3.8–6.4 cm) tall grain-wise; then cut the strip into four equal sections and dip one long side into bleach using the dip-bleaching technique (see page 30).

2 **STAMENS** Cut five 26-gauge stem wire (paper-covered in brown) into five small stem wires, about 2^1/$_2$–3in (6.4–7.6cm) long, for a total of 25 stems. For 16 of the stem wires, create a ^{1}/$_2$in (1.3cm) loop at one end using a wire cutter.

3 Cut across the grain of 180g Italian crepe paper in a light green for a strip 1in (2.5cm) tall grain-wise. Cut 12 pieces, each 2in (5cm) wide. Finely fringe each section halfway down from the long edge. Roll the fringe, with the fringed tips flush, and dip the tips into tacky glue. Immediately dip the tips into a pastel-oatmeal mixture in dark yellow-orange for pollen. Cut the fringe base diagonally to reduce bulk. Dot the fringe base with glue and wrap it around the loop of the stem wire; keep the fringe tips flush as you wrap.

4 **PETALS** There are two layers of double-layered petals. For the first petal layer, use your prepared crepe paper and cut it into 12 sections 1^1/$_2$in (3.8cm) wide. Fold the piece in half, across the grain, long edge to long edge. The folded base will keep the double layer together as you work with it. Place template A on top of the piece, with the folded base at the bottom, and cut through both layers of crepe paper. Repeat with all 12 sections. For the second petal layer, use your prepared crepe paper and cut it into 12 sections 3in (7.6cm) wide. Again, fold the piece in half, across the grain, long edge to long edge. Place template B on top of the piece, with the folded base down, and cut through both layers of crepe paper. Repeat with all 12 sections. Note that if you are using a bleached strip, one edge will be lighter than the other. The lighter side should be the petal lip and the darker side the petal base. Instead of folding the paper in half horizontally, double the width of the crepe paper and fold it in half

vertically on the grain; then place the templates on top, placing it along the fold. If you want the petals to be lighter, simply move the template closer to the lighter edge; if you want the petals to be darker, move the template closer to the darker edge.

5 Gather the base of a first petal layer section by making small folds at the folded base. Once gathered, hold the top section of the petal strip with your non-dominant hand, and use the thumb of your dominant hand to flatten the gather with your thumbnail. Place the stamen stem wire on top of the gathered base, ^{1}/$_4$in (6mm) down from the petal lips. Align the crepe paper so that the slit between petals ends where the fringe base begins, then wrap the gather around the stamens. Secure it with a half-width strip of brown floral tape. Repeat with the remaining 11 petals.

6 Gather the base of a second petal layer section by making small folds at the folded base. Flatten the gather with your thumbnail. Place this gathered base around the first layer's base so that the petal lips on both layers are flush and even. Secure the gather with a half-width strip of brown floral tape. You may find it easier to cover the flower base with the floral tape if you turn the bloom upside down as you wrap. Repeat with the remaining 11 petals.

7 Fluff the petals by first cup-stretching the double petals together, then gently pulling the double petals apart. Finally, ruffle the stamens with your finger to loosen up.

8 **BUD** Cut four pieces of fine crepe paper in hot pink, 2in (5cm) tall along the grain and 1^1/$_2$in (3.8cm) wide, one for each bud. Stretch each gently. Take one-third of a large cotton wool ball, roll it in your hands to form a ball, and place it in the centre of a crepe square. Pull the edges of the crepe paper around the cotton wool ball, and place the looped end of a short stem wire into the cotton wool ball. Gather the edges of the crepe square around the stem wire and pull it to smooth out the gathers around the cotton wool ball. Cut some of the crepe paper to remove bulk. Wrap a strip of half-width floral tape in brown around the gather to secure the ball shape on the stem wire. Repeat with the remaining three crepe squares.

9 CALYXES To make the calyxes for the buds, cut along the grain of double-sided crepe paper in green, such as Green Tea/Cypress for a strip ³/₄in (1.9cm) wide, from the end of a fold. Accordion-fold into four layers, folding across the grain into squares ³/₄in (1.9cm) tall grain-wise. Place template CA on top of the squares and cut four calyxes. Cup the three calyxes with the lighter side facing away from you. Dot glue on the calyx base and wrap it around the base of the bud, covering part of the pink bud. Repeat with the other three calyxes and buds.

10 LEAVES Make seven to eight leaves per branch. Prepare the stems by cutting two 26-gauge stem wires into quarters to make eight short stem wires. Then cut across an entire fold of double-sided crepe paper in green for a strip 2in (5cm) tall grain-wise. Accordion-fold the crepe paper strips into eight layers, each layer 1¹/₂in (3.8cm) wide, and slit the folded edges. Cut four layers at a time and cut across diagonally to create two sets of triangles.

11 Take each pair of triangles and flip one vertically, then place the long edges of the pair side by side so that the grain lines of both triangles join together to create a V like a chevron pattern. Apply glue to one long edge and place a short stem wire on top, ¹/₂in (1.3cm) from the top edge. Dot glue on the stem wire, then place the other long edge on top to create a diamond shape.

12 Fold the diamond in half so that the edges are flush. Place template L on top, aligning the base of the template with the base of the diamond. Cut. Unfold the leaf. Colour the leaves at the fold and edges with brown and dark green pastel with a brush to create dimension. Repeat with each leaf.

13 ASSEMBLY To create a branch for your fruit blossoms, refer to steps 1–6 of Berry Branch (see page 172). You can group the stems before attaching them to the branch, or you can attach them individually. In both cases, use a very thin floral tape, no wider than ¹/₄in (6mm) wide, in the same brown as the branch to attach stems together; here, I used crepe tape from the 180g Chinese crepe paper in brown. Trim the stem wires for the flowers, buds and leaves short.

14 When attaching the flowers, buds and leaves, I suggest you vary the number and type clustered together. For example, cluster four blossoms and a leaf on one tip; three blossoms, one bud and two leaves on another tip; and two blossoms, a bud and a leaf on a third tip. Add a blossom and bud pair closer to the base of the lateral shoots. Vary your formula so that not every branch looks the same; also, don't feel compelled to attach all of the flowers, buds and/or leaves you have made. When you attach the blooms to the branch, attach the flower stem wire at 1in (2.5cm) below the flower base, so that the flower hangs off the branch as opposed to being flush against the branch. In contrast, when you attach the buds and leaves, attach them just below the green calyx or leaf so that the bud and the leaf base look connected to the branch. If necessary, re-shade the brown crepe tape parts with brown and dark green pastel to blend in the newly taped with existing tape.

ARRANGEMENT TIP

These branches have bold, bright and big blooms, so they will make a statement in any arrangement. You can use them to define the height and diameter of the arrangement, or simply as one of the focal points. These pink blooms look magnificent when the branches are layered from front to back, similar to what you would see if looking at them on a tree.

Basic leaf foliage

This is a basic five-leaf stem blueprint that I use to make different types of foliage, by changing the type of crepe paper or colour, replacing the leaf shape, adding details, or creating branches. Each leaf is wired and it is a fairly flat structure. Here I used 180g Chinese crepe paper in Moss Green, but this can easily be replaced depending on what type or colour of leaf and/or branch you want. To create a variegated leaf, I simply paint the edges white. To create a large branch, I attach three to four of these stems together on a 16-gauge wire or a metal stake to define the main stem. I sometimes add berries in clusters to give the branch some visual weight and a feeling of abundance. Experiment with different leaf sizes by varying the height and width of the crepe paper.

YOU'LL NEED

✿ Scissors
✿ Ruler
✿ Tacky glue
✿ Wire cutter
✿ Pastel foam applicator, paintbrushes, palette

STEM

24- or 26-gauge stem wire, paper-wrapped in green or brown, for the leaves
18- or 20-gauge stem wire for the leaf stem
16- or 18-gauge stem wire for a branch (or metal orchid stake for a large branch)
Floral tape or crepe tape in green or brown

LEAVES

Any crepe paper including 180g Italian crepe, Chinese crepe paper or double-sided crepe paper in green, dark green, yellow, burgundy or brown
Colour with pastels, alcohol inks, watercolours or acrylic paint

ARRANGEMENT TIP

The possibilities are endless with this foliage shape, which has all of its leaves lying flat. By placing it vertically, horizontally or sideways, it can create dramatic lines, hide the edge of your vase or stems, and/or add a vital colour to any composition. My favourite way of using this form of foliage is to define the boundaries of the composition and layer branches together to create fullness.

1 PREPARE THE PAPER Cut a large section off the end of a roll of 180g crepe paper, then cut across the grain to get a strip 3in (7.6cm) tall grain-wise. Stretch the strip. Accordion-fold it into five layers with each layer 2^1/$_2$in (6.4cm) wide across the grain as per template A. Cut the accordion folds from the end of the strip and slit the folded edges. Now cut all five layers at once across diagonally so you have two piles of five triangles.

2 Use one 18- or 20-gauge stem wire about 12in (30.5cm) long (for a long branch, use an 18-gauge stem wire). Cut two thinner-gauge stem wires such as a 24- or 26-gauge wire, preferably paper-wrapped in green or brown, into three equal pieces to make a total of six short stem wires. Take each pair of triangles and flip one vertically. Place the long edges of the pair side by side so that the grain lines join together to create a V like a chevron. Apply glue to one long edge and place a stem wire on top, ^{1}/$_4$in (6mm) from the top edge; dot glue on the stem wire and place the other long edge on top to create a diamond shape.

3 Before the glue dries, fold each diamond in half so the edges are flush. Either cut an elongated D-shape freehand starting from the tip of the diamond, or place template B on the fold, aligning the bases of the template and the diamond, and cut. Unfold the leaf.

4 Use the leaf on the long stem wire as the spine of the leaf stem. Take a length of floral tape or glue-dotted crepe tape and wrap just below the bottom of the leaf on that stem and down about 2in (5cm). Take one of the shorter stem leaves and place it to the right of the long stem. Then wrap the floral or crepe tape around both stems to secure. You can either wrap the tape to cover the entire short stem, just below the leaf, or you can let some of the short stem show. If you are using this on the outside of the bouquet like a skirt hiding the outer stems, start the first leaf higher on the long stem, about 1in (2.5cm) instead.

5 Wrap the floral tape 1–2in (2.5–5cm) down the main stem wire, then place a second leaf stem on the left of the main wire. Wrap around both the stem wires to secure, and then down another 1–2in (2.5–5cm). Repeat with the third and fourth short-stemmed leaves,

alternating sides of the main stem. Finish the stem by wrapping all the way to the end of the main stem wire. For a bouquet, consider attaching only two stems if you are using this between flowers as fillers or as a skirt.

6 COLOURING OPTIONS Create other coloured leaves by using other crepe paper colours. So the leaves don't look flat, colour them with pastels or alcohol inks. Here, I coloured the 180g Chinese crepe paper in Moss Green with alcohol inks in Meadow, Lettuce, Sunshine Yellow and Rust; for the yellow leaves, I used 180g Italian crepe paper in Buttercup/Carminio Yellow (#574) coloured with alcohol inks in Citrus, Lettuce and Rust; for the burgundy leaves, I used 180g Italian crepe paper in Burgundy/Bordeaux Red (#588), coloured with PanPastel in Black Fine Pearl Medium sprayed with Krylon UV Resistant spray in Gloss; for the variegated leaves, I used 180g Italian crepe paper in Ivy Green/Leaf Green (#591), with the edges coloured with white acrylic paint applied twice along the grain.

7 LARGE LEAF BRANCH There are two ways to create a larger leaf branch. For both, I recommend using an 18-gauge stem wire as the main leaf stem to avoid drooping. The first method is to attach more leaves to the branch and create a 7-, 9- or 11-leaf branch using the alternating method. The second method is to attach three to five of the five-leaf stems to add a branch with multiple shoots. Continue to wrap floral tape down 5–6in (12.7–15.3cm) on one five-leaf stem. Attach the end of it to a 16-gauge (or thicker) stem wire with floral or crepe tape. At the same location, attach a second five-leaf stem either in front or behind the main branch and wrap down all three stems to secure. Wrap down another 5–6in (12.7–15.3cm) or so, then attach another five-leaf stem in front of or behind the main branch and wrap with tape. Repeat, alternating until you have the desired number of five-leaf stems on the branch. Finish the stem wire with floral tape. To finish, push the stems away from the main branch and turn the leaves towards the ceiling. For really large branches, use an orchid support stake, available at garden centres.

8 ADDING BERRIES For extra interest, make berries in your desired colour (see Berry Branch, page 172), then attach them between or beside the leaves.

Rose foliage

When I make roses, I often add a stem of leaves to it so it looks as if it has just been plucked from the garden. I find that rose foliage helps to cover the stems of the rose and other flowers, especially in bouquets. I make my rose leaf stems the same way as the Basic Leaf Foliage with wired leaves (see page 184). The only differences are that the leaf has notches on the edges, and the leaves are not placed alternating along the main leaf stem but sit opposite/adjacent from each other. I prefer to use double-sided crepe paper in Leaf/Moss for my rose foliage. When using double-sided crepe paper that has different colours on each side, you will need to cut an even number of rectangles in order to properly pair up the triangles of the same colour.

YOU'LL NEED

✿ Scissors
✿ Ruler
✿ Tacky glue
✿ Wire cutter
✿ Pastel foam applicator or brush

STEM
24- or 26-gauge stem wire for the leaves
20- or 22-gauge stem wire for the leaf stem
Floral tape or crepe tape in green or brown

LEAVES
Double-sided crepe paper in Leaf/Moss
Pastels in brown (Pan Pastel in Dark Red
    Permanent)

1 Use the same method as the Basic Leaf Foliage (see page 184), with slight variations. Cut an entire fold of double-sided crepe paper in Leaf/Moss, 2¹/₂in (6.4cm) tall grain-wise. Accordion-fold into six (instead of five) rectangles, each 2in (5cm) wide as per template A. Cut the accordion folds from the end of the strip and slit the folded edges. Cut all six layers at once across diagonally. You will have two piles of triangles consisting of three pairs of triangles.

2 Turn the triangle pile so the grain line is running from the southwest corner to the northeast corner of the triangle, and the diagonal cut line is vertical. Cut ¹/₄in (6mm) off the tip of the triangle at the southwest corner, with the cut line perpendicular to the diagonal cut line.

3 Cut one piece of 20- or 22-gauge stem wire about 6–8in (15.2–20.3cm) long. Cut a 24- or 26-gauge wire into four equal short stems. Take the top two triangles from one pile and place them side by side along the long edges. The colour facing up should be the same for both triangles, and the grain lines of both triangles should join together to create a V like a chevron pattern. Apply glue to one long edge and place a stem wire on top, ¹/₄in (6mm) from the top edge. Dot glue on the stem wire, then place the other long edge on top to create a flat-bottomed diamond shape. Repeat with the other four pairs. You should have one pair of triangles left over for another rose stem.

Rose foliage is a perfect way to hide stems in a bouquet, to fill in the spaces between flowers, and, if using dark-coloured foliage, to create shadows and an illusion of depth within the composition. If the rose is near the edge of an arrangement, I turn the leaf stem so it covers the edge. If the rose is placed in the centre of the arrangement, look for any emptiness between the rose and other flowers where the foliage could assist in filling it up.

ARRANGEMENT TIP

4 Before the glue dries, fold each diamond in half so that the edges are flush. Place template B (or template C for smaller leaves) on the fold, aligning the base of the leaf template with the base of the flat-bottomed diamond. Cut. Unfold the leaf. Colour the leaves with a little brown pastel along the edges and in the centre to give it dimension by scraping the pastel foam applicator on the edge of the leaves.

5 To assemble the leaf stem, use the leaf on long stem wire as the spine of the leaf stem. Take a length of floral or crepe tape and wrap just below the bottom of the leaf on that stem and down about 1–1¹/₂in (2.5–3.8cm). Take two of the shorter stem leaves and place them on top of each other, then on top of the long stem wire where the floral or crepe tape is at the long stem. Wrap the floral or crepe tape around all three stems, completely covering the short stems.

6 Continue to wrap the floral or crepe tape down the long stem wire, another 1–1¹/₂in (2.5–3.8cm). Take the last two remaining shorter stem leaves and attach them in the same way. Spread the leaves outwards.

7 Attach the rose foliage leaf onto the flower stem of the rose. In most rose species, the first stem of leaves normally sits quite low on the flower stem. I like to place the foliage stems higher, about 2–3in (5–7.6cm) below the calyx, so that when you look down on the flower you can see the rose foliage peaking from underneath. I also do not want to put it too low because it might interfere with or hide a flower that sits next to this rose in an arrangement. After securing the remaining two leaves, continue to wrap the floral or crepe tape down the long stem wire for about 1¹/₂–2in (3.8–5cm). Place the flower stem next to the long stem wire and continue to wrap both stems with the floral or crepe tape. Wrap until the rose foliage stem wire is completely covered.

8 An alternative is to make the leaves a bit smaller using template C and/or to have three instead of five leaves on the stem. I usually prefer to use the smaller and/or three leaves on the stem when I am working with smaller flowers such as the wild rose. Try cutting the leaves freehand to create variations.

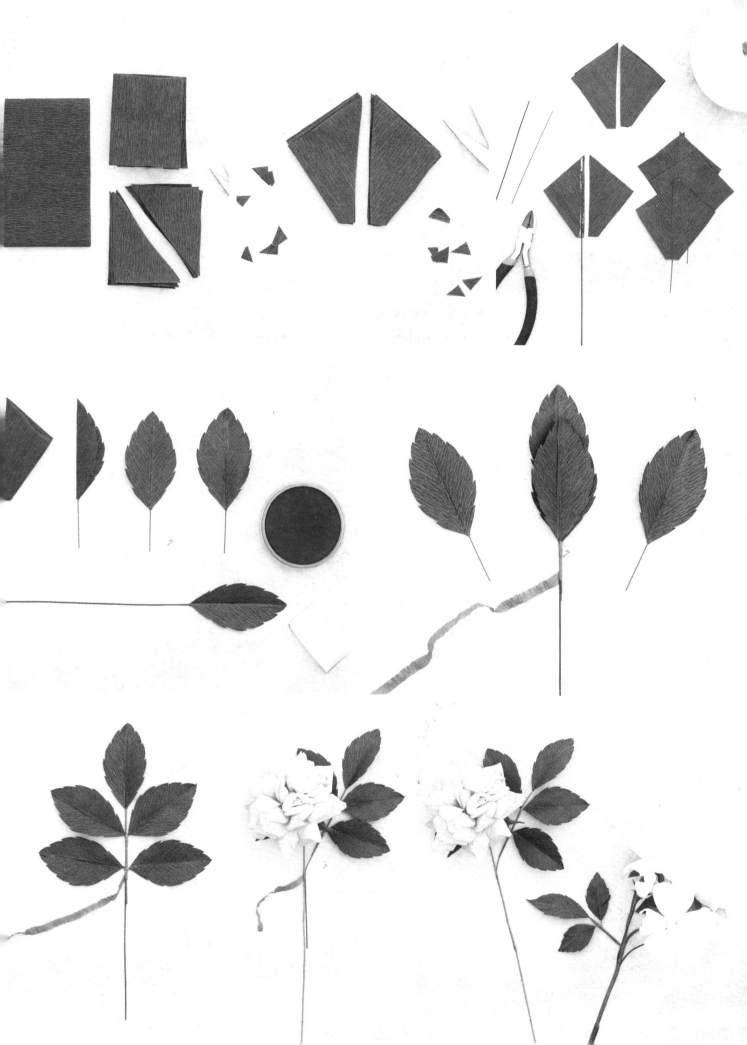

Eucalyptus leaves

I love using foliage to add colour and interest to a floral composition, so I started to experiment with cool-toned foliage. Most of the greens that are available in crepe paper tend to be in a warm tone with a yellow base. To create a blue-based petal or leaf, you have to colour it yourself. To mimic the powdery effect of eucalyptus leaves, I apply a pastel in a light blue tint on top of an existing green colour that also has a blue base to create a powdery blue-green. This is a perfect example of how to layer colours to create new ones.

YOU'LL NEED

- ✿ Scissors
- ✿ Ruler
- ✿ Tacky glue
- ✿ Paintbrush for glue
- ✿ Wire cutter
- ✿ Pastel foam applicator

STEM
20-gauge stem wire
180g Italian crepe paper in Twig/Nut Brown (#567)

LEAVES
180g Italian crepe paper in Ivy Green/Leaf Green
   (#591)
Pastel in light blue such as PanPastel in
   Ultramarine Blue Tint

1 Cut across the grain of an end of a roll of 180g Italian crepe paper in Ivy Green/Leaf Green for a strip 3$\frac{1}{2}$in (9cm) tall. Stretch the strip and cut off a section about 5in (12.7cm) long/wide. Fold the strip in half midway, short edge to short edge. Apply tacky glue with a paintbrush to laminate the strip (see page 20).

2 Before the glue dries, paint a light blue on both sides of the strip using pastels so there is a blue powdery layer over the green leaves. I like to use PanPastel in Ultramarine Blue Tint with a pastel foam applicator.

3 Accordion-fold the laminated strip along the grain into four or five layers or rectangles, each $\frac{3}{4}$in (1.9cm) wide. Cut off the strip. Then, cutting freehand or using template A, cut through the four or five layers into the shape of a long, pointed leaf. Repeat folding the laminated strip to cut more leaves. You should be able to cut between eight and nine leaves from the laminated strip. Pinch the base of each leaf to crease/fold the base in half. Run your thumb under the bottom of the leaf to give it a curve.

4 Cut a narrow strip of 180g Italian crepe paper in Twig/Nut Brown for crepe tape; make sure to stretch it before use. Dot some glue on one end and wrap it around the tip of a 20-gauge stem once or twice. Place the folded base of a leaf on its tip and wrap the tape around both the base and the wire. Apply more glue as needed on the crepe tape. Wrap down $\frac{1}{2}$in (1.3cm), attach a leaf on one side of the stem wire and wrap with crepe tape to secure. Wrap down another $\frac{1}{2}$in (1.3cm) and attach a leaf on the other side of the stem wire. Continue alternating the placement of the leaves, right and left of the stem wire, as you go down the stem wire. Finish the stem with the crepe tape. Bend the stem to create dimension.

ARRANGEMENT TIP

This is one of the few types of foliage that has a blue base or cool bias, so take advantage of it. I like to use it in compositions that have a lot of sour or chartreuse tones. It cuts through the sourness and brings some warmth back into the arrangement. It is also such a pretty turquoise that it complements pinks and peaches very well. I like using this foliage because its shape is distinct from most other foliage – it has skinny leaves that hang down and is almost grass-like – so it offers a good contrast.

Olive leaves

I use this foliage to create movement in arrangements, as the line it creates draws the eye in different directions. I prefer to use the finer double-sided crepe paper for the leaves, but you could also use 180g crepe paper. When I had to name this foliage for my workshops, I looked around for foliage similar to this and thought the leaves (if not the movement) resembled olive leaves, although I have never attempted to attach olives to it.

YOU'LL NEED

* Scissors
* Ruler
* Tacky glue
* Wire cutter

STEM

18- or 20-gauge stem wire
Floral tape or crepe tape in green, brown or
   a metallic colour such as extra-fine crepe
   paper in Bronze Metallic

LEAVES

Double-sided crepe paper in Leaf/Moss or Green
   Tea/Cypress, or 180g in Green Leaf, Dark Green
   or any other green

1 LEAVES Cut across an entire fold of double-sided crepe paper in Leaf/Moss, for a strip 3$^{1}/_{4}$in (8.3cm) tall grain-wise. Fold the strip accordion-style into $^{3}/_{4}$in (1.9cm) wide strips and cut six to eight leaves per leaf stem freehand or by using template A. Decide which side of the double-sided crepe paper will be the front and which will be the back, so that you are consistent when attaching the leaves to the stem. Pinch the leaf base in half, then run your thumb under the bottom of the leaf to shape.

2 ASSEMBLE THE STEM Cut a strip of floral tape and stretch it to activate the glue. Alternatively, use crepe tape (here I used crepe tape made from extra-fine crepe paper in Bronze Metallic). Wrap it around the tip of an 18- or 20-gauge stem wire to secure. Attach the first leaf by pinching the bottom of the leaf and placing it beside the tip of the stem wire, then wrapping the floral tape or crepe tape tightly around it. Wrap the tape down the stem wire about 2in (5cm). The closer together you attach the leaves, the denser they will appear.

3 Place a leaf on the right side of the stem wire so that the leaf top faces you, and wrap the tape around the bottom of the leaf. Wrap the tape down the stem wire another 2in (5cm) down. Place a leaf on the left side of the stem wire, and tightly wrap the tape around the bottom of the leaf. Continue to alternate the placement of the leaves, right and left of the stem wire. I attach around three to four pairs of leaves 2in (5cm) apart for a long branch; for a shorter branch, I attach at $^{1}/_{2}$–1in (1.3–2.5cm) apart. Finish the stem with the tape to cover the bare wire.

4 Bend the stem wire gently in one direction to create shape and movement.

ARRANGEMENT TIP These branches can appear wispy, so I prefer to use them in pairs or triplets and layer them at different lengths. Bend them in different directions to create movement. When used in opposite directions, they can create a dramatic effect, widening an arrangement and even mimicking a cascading bouquet. Support the branches with Italian ruscus (see page 200) so that they don't move around.

Italian ruscus

Italian ruscus is a popular filler foliage. Its leaves are positioned so they are parallel to the ground on the main stem, thereby maximizing the coverage. I make it with unstretched 180g Italian crepe paper because this is crunchy and stiff – everything that I dislike for flowers, yet perfect for structural reinforcement. As it is mainly a structural piece, I use floral tape to attach the leaves around the stem; if the lower leaves obstruct the flowers in an arrangement, I simply pull the leaves out to shorten the height of the foliage. If you are not using this foliage for structural reasons, you can use this template and technique using double-sided crepe paper, which is softer.

YOU'LL NEED

* Scissors
* Ruler
* Tacky glue
* Wire cutter

STEM

18- or 20-gauge stem wire
Floral tape in green or brown

LEAVES

180g Italian crepe paper in Green Leaf/Sage Green
(#562), Olive Green by Tiffanie Turner (#17A/8),
Amazon Green/Forest Green (#561, 16A/8) or any
other green (alternatively, use double-sided
crepe paper in Leaf/Moss or Cypress/Green Tea)
Optional: Spray paint in green or burgundy such as
Design Master Colortool in Basil or Burgundy

1 Cut across the grain of a roll of 180g Italian crepe paper in green, 3^1/$_2$in (9cm) tall grain-wise. Do not stretch the strip. Cut 10–12 leaves using template A. Cup the middle of the leaf but leave the tip and base uncupped. Trim the edges even.

2 Cut a strip of floral tape in green or brown and stretch it to activate the glue. Wrap it around the tip of an 18- or 20-gauge stem wire to secure. Attach the first leaf by pressing the top of the leaf base against the stem wire, at the tip. Wrap the floral tape around it once tightly, then place a second leaf opposite the first, again, by pressing the top of the leaf base against the stem wire, then wrapping tightly with floral tape.

3 Wrap the tape down the stem wire about 1–1^1/$_2$in (2.5–3.8cm), then attach another pair of leaves in the same manner, except when you look down the leaf stem from the top this second pair should appear to cross-hatch the first. Continue in this manner until all of the leaves are attached. Attach more leaves for a long stem, and fewer leaves for a shorter one. Note that the closer together you attach the leaves, the denser they will appear. Finish the stem wire with the floral tape.

4 If desired, spray the foliage with a burgundy/maroon spray paint to create an ombré effect or, if you are using a lighter green crepe paper, spray the bottom of the foliage with a darker green to create an ombré effect that will mimic shadows when used within an arrangement.

ARRANGEMENT TIP

You may find this foliage too stiff to use in an arrangement. However, I rely on it heavily when I need to prop up tall branches or long stems and keep the branch and/or stem from moving around. I like to place them deep in the arrangement so they don't show too much from the top, and sometimes I even wrap them around the bottom half of the branch or stem. This foliage is particularly effective for bouquets that are wide or cascading. It can be used like stakes to keep flowers or foliage in line so they don't swing about when a bride walks with it in her hands, either by placing multiple stems of Italian ruscus stems behind the swinging flower or foliage or wrapping it around the swinging flower or foliage (or vice versa).

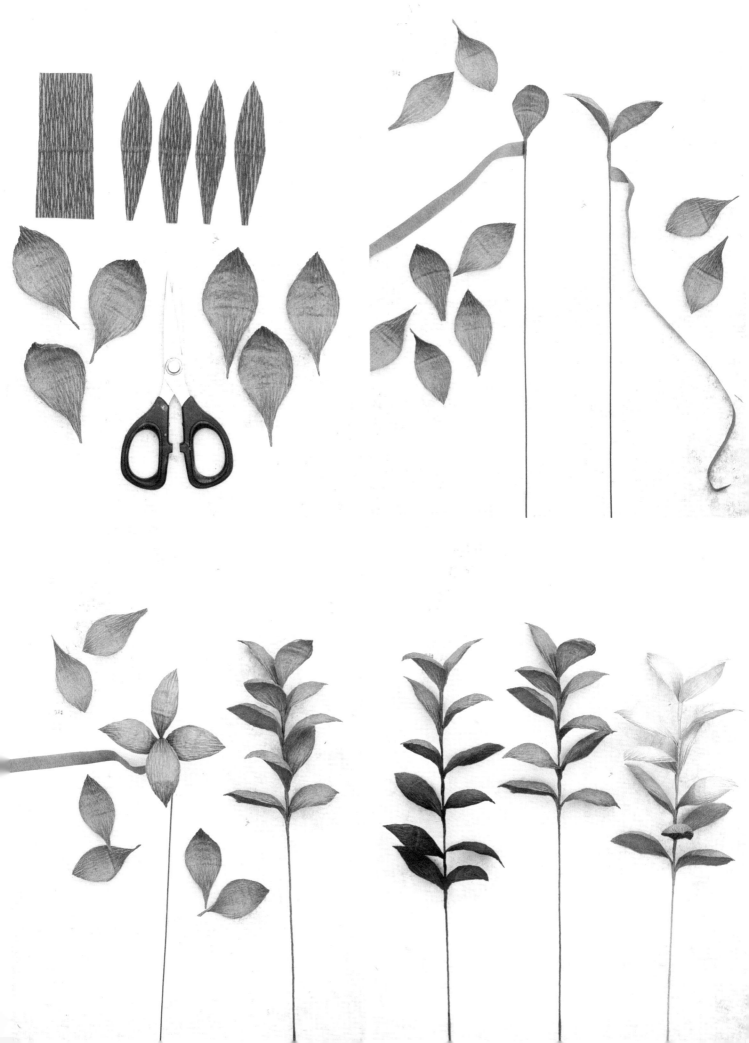

Variegated boxwood

There are two things I like about this structure. One: the leaves are perpendicular to the ground so, when you look down on it, the layers of leaves form a cover over the foundation of the arrangement, similar to Italian ruscus (see page 200). Two: since there are three stems that meet at a notch on a thicker stem, I can position these in different directions, giving an arrangement a look of ease. I use 26-gauge stem wires for the leaves and stem to permit agility and a 16-gauge main stem to insert into a pin frog. The technique used to make the leaves is the same as the Basic Leaf Foliage (see page 184). In larger arrangements, I use the same structural principles to make similar fillers on a larger scale. For lighter variegation, use a lighter green or cream crepe paper and colour it with a dark green centre.

YOU'LL NEED

- Scissors
- Ruler
- Tacky glue
- Glue stick
- Wire cutter

STEMS
26-gauge stem wires, paper-wrapped in green
16-gauge stem wire

LEAVES
180g crepe paper in bright green, such as 180g Chinese crepe paper in Moss Green
Floral tape in green or crepe tape in 180g Chinese crepe paper in Moss Green
Alcohol ink, watercolour ink, or acrylic in dark green (or a green darker than the crepe paper), such as Adirondack Tim Holtz Alcohol Ink in Meadow
Paintbrush

1 PREPARE THE PAPER There are three sizes of leaves. Cut across the grain of a piece of 180g crepe paper (here I used 180g Chinese crepe paper in Moss Green) into three strips with the following heights along the grain: (small) 1in (2.5cm); (medium) 1$^{1}/_{2}$in (3.8cm); and (large) 2in (5cm). Stretch each strip of prepared paper.

2 LEAVES Cut the following lengths from the stretched strips: for six small leaves, cut two strips 6in (15.3cm) long from the small strip, for eight medium leaves, cut four strips 7in (17.8cm) long from the medium strip; for six large leaves, cut two strips 12in (30.5cm) long from the larger strip. Laminate the two small, two medium (do this twice), and two large strips individually with a glue stick.

3 For the small and large leaves, fold the laminated strip midway, short side to short side. Then, fold into three to get a total of six layers of rectangles about 1in (2.5cm) and 2in (5cm) wide, respectively. Slit the folds. For the medium leaves, fold one of the laminated strips midway, short side to short side, then again midway, to get four layers of rectangles about 1$^{3}/_{4}$in (4.5cm) wide. Slit the folds. Repeat with the second laminated strip of the medium leaves. Slit the folds. Cut each layer diagonally to get two piles of triangles for each size.

4 STEMS Use five 26-gauge stem wires paper-covered in green. Cut each wire into four equal pieces for a total of 20 short stem wires. Cut the 16-gauge stem wire in half (you will only need one). Take a half-width length of green floral tape or narrow crepe tape and wrap the entire length of the short 16-gauge stem wire.

5 Make the leaves using the same techniques set out in steps 2 and 3 of Basic Leaf Foliage (see page 184), cutting the leaves freehand into a elongated D-shape with a rounded tip. Alternatively, use templates A, B and C for small, medium and large leaves, respectively.

6 COLOURING To create the variegated detail, dab a dark green ink or paint onto the centre of the leaf with a brush. I use alcohol ink in Meadow.

7 ASSEMBLY Assemble one stem at a time, attaching the leaves to a long 26-gauge stem wire using narrow crepe tape in the same colour as the leaves to wrap around the leaf stem and the main stem. Attach each leaf so that the top faces the main stem and the leaf is perpendicular to the floor when you bend it open.

For the first stem: attach two small leaves to the tip of the main stem on opposite sides; wrap down about $^{3}/_{4}$in (1.9cm), then attach two medium leaves on the opposite sides of the main stem and cross-hatching the first set of leaves; wrap down about 2in (5cm) and attach two medium leaves on the opposite sides of the main stem and cross-hatching the previous set of leaves; wrap down 1$^{1}/_{2}$in (3.8cm) and attach two large leaves on the opposite sides of the main stem and cross-hatching the previous set of leaves; and finally, wrap down another 1$^{1}/_{2}$in (3.8cm) and attach two small leaves on the opposite sides of the main stem and cross-hatching the previous set of leaves.

For the second stem: attach two medium leaves to the tip of the main stem on opposite sides; wrap down about 1in (2.5cm), then attach two large leaves on the opposite sides of the main stem, cross-hatching the first set.

For the third stem: attach two medium leaves to the tip of the main stem and on opposite sides; wrap down about 2in (5cm) and attach two large leaves on the opposite sides of the main stem and cross-hatching the previous set of leaves; finally, wrap down another 2in (5cm) and attach two small leaves on the opposite sides of the main stem and cross-hatching the previous set.

8 To finish, attach all three stems to the 16-gauge stem wire. Take a length of narrow crepe tape and secure the first stem by attaching it 1in (2.5cm) below the tip of the 16-gauge stem wire; the last pair of leaves on the first stem should be no higher than 2in (5cm) above the notch. Wrap the crepe tape around both a few times to secure. Attach the second stem around the same notch with its last pair of leaves no more than 2$^{1}/_{2}$in (6.4cm) above the notch, and wrap a few times to secure. Lastly, attach the third stem around the same notch with its last pair of leaves no higher than 1in (2.5cm) above the notch. Try to distribute the three stems around the 16-gauge stem wire. Finish covering the stems with the crepe tape and trim off any wire that extends past the end of the 16-gauge stem wire.

Fern

This fern is modelled on the Boston fern. It is simple to create and you can make a lot in a short time because there are only two parts to assemble. Also, ferns take up a lot of space and come with natural movement and shape. I love this chartreuse colour because it is so vivid and sour, and it cuts through the other colours in an arrangement. It is also easy to dye and colour because it is a lighter green; I can layer other colours on top and let some of this bright green show through.

This colour comes only in extra-fine crepe paper; however, there is an equally bright green in the 180g Chinese crepe paper called Green Tea, and a lighter version in 180g Italian crepe paper called Water Green/Lime Pulp (#566). Otherwise, use any green crepe paper that you like.

I laminated the paper with fusible webbing. If you use any other type of crepe paper, you can simply stretch it and then use a glue stick or tacky glue to laminate. I have given dimensions for two sizes of ferns; however, I urge you to consider what sizes might be right for your arrangement. Read the instructions first and pay attention to the measurements before cutting the paper. In order to get the leaves to stay rigid, the grain lines on the crepe paper must run perpendicular to the stem wire.

YOU'LL NEED

✿ Scissors
✿ Ruler
✿ Wire cutter

STEM
20-gauge stem wire
Crepe tape in light brown or dark green, such as 60g Italian crepe paper in Musk Green (#264)

LEAVES
Extra-fine crepe paper in Green Tea (or 180g Chinese crepe paper in Green Tea, or 180g Italian crepe paper in Water Green/Lime Pulp (#566))
Fusible webbing, tacky glue or glue stick
Rubbing alcohol
Alcohol inks in greens and browns, such as Adirondack Tim Holtz Alcohol Inks in Lettuce, Willow and Rust
Paint palette or plastic egg container
Paintbrush

1 PREPARE THE CREPE PAPER To make one fern, cut two pieces of extra-fine crepe paper in Green Tea, 4$\frac{1}{2}$in (11.5cm) tall grain-wise and 10–12in (25–30.5cm) long. Cut a piece of fusible webbing in the same dimensions and place it between the two pieces of crepe paper. Fuse to laminate (see page 21). If you're using 180g crepe paper, stretch it before cutting out the pieces and laminating. For smaller ferns, cut the crepe paper and fusible webbing 3–3$\frac{1}{2}$in (7.6–9cm) tall grain-wise and 6–7in (15.2–17.8cm) long. Experiment with other dimensions.

2 CUTTING THE FERN I like to cut my leaves by folding the leaf in the middle and cutting two layers (the right and left side) at once. For the fern, fold the laminated crepe paper in half across the grain. First define the shape of the fern. Since I cut with my right hand (do the opposite if you are left-handed), I hold the paper with my left hand, with the folded side facing the inside of my left hand and the open side facing my right hand. Make a diagonal cut from the bottom left corner (and no more than $\frac{1}{4}$in/6mm away from the folded edge) to the opposite side at the top right corner.

3 After defining the shape of the fern, define the individual leaves. Make a diagonal cut coming from the bottom left corner at the fold up towards northeast, creating a small V. Make the second from the open side of the crepe paper on the right, directly parallel to the ground to where the scissors ended on the first cut (at the end of the V).

4 Flip the fern over so the folded edge is at the top. Subsequent cuts run parallel to the second cut, moving further and further away from the tip. Cut from right to left, stopping about $\frac{1}{8}$in (3mm) from the folded edge. These look like fringes, except the further away from you the thicker the fringe. The third cut makes a fringe about $\frac{1}{8}$in (3mm) wide; the fourth cut makes a fringe about $\frac{3}{16}$in (5mm) wide. I suggest you err on the side of cutting thicker fringes rather than thinner ones, as you will be trimming the fringes in the next step. At the end of the strip, the fringe should be about $\frac{1}{2}$in (1.3cm) and no wider.

5 TRIMMING THE LEAVES To shape the leaves/fringe, I prefer to work backwards, from where I end at the thickest fringe. With the folded side facing the inside of your left hand with the fringes facing your right scissor hand, trim one side of the fringe for all of the fringes before trimming the other side of all of the fringes. I like to trim so that my scissors are always cutting towards the left. This means that I cut the top edge of the fringe first, with the fringe horizontally, rounding off the top right corner, and smoothly along the top edge of the fringe, at a slight angle. Repeat with all of the fringes.

6 Flip the crepe paper so that you're working from the V tip upwards, with the fold facing the inside of your left hand. Repeat the cutting method used for the other edge of the fringe so that your right hand is always cutting left and cutting the top edge of the fringe. You should end up with fringes with rounded tips. Trim the V tip if necessary to obtain a clean tip.

7 ASSEMBLING THE FERN Cover a 20-gauge stem wire by wrapping narrow crepe tape in a darker green. Open up the fern and flatten the centre crease. Apply glue along the crease and place the stem wire on it, leaving a $\frac{1}{8}$in (3mm) allowance below the V tip. Press to secure.

8 COLOURING AND FINISHING To create a fern with a muddier or browner complexion, dab rubbing alcohol all over the fern. Then use a combination of alcohol inks in the colours of your choice. I used Lettuce, Willow and Rust. I dilute the colours slightly so that they aren't too dominating, then dab those colours onto the leaf. To finish and to give the fern dimension, I like to squeeze and crease each leaf in its centre, along the grain, with the stem wire facing up. I then bend the stem wire to create movement.

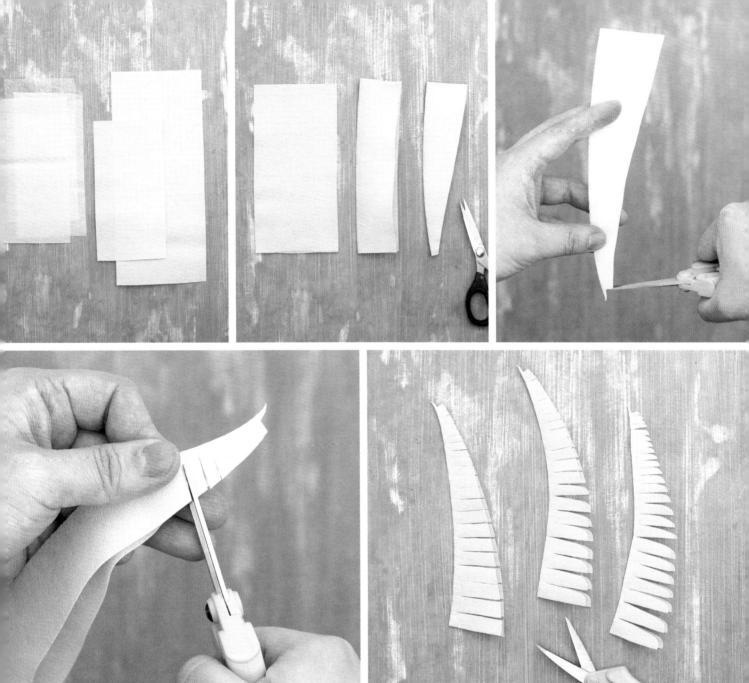

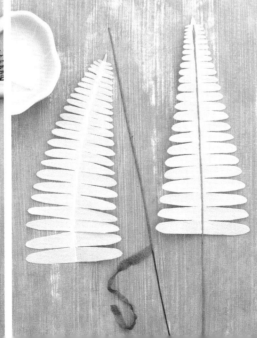
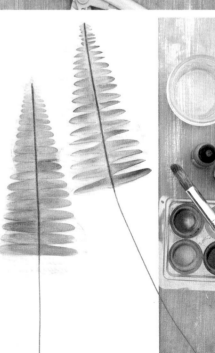

Arrangements

Fine art principles

When I plan out my floral compositions, I always use fine art principles to guide me. These principles are the foundation for a balanced composition. You may have learned about these in fine art classes or read or heard about them. Regardless of your familiarity with these principles, it takes time and practice to create a balanced design. Try looking at other people's compositions and analysing them to work out what is pleasing to your eye.

COLOUR

Colour is the basis of all of my compositions. I like working tone on tone; this means I work with one or two colours that are close to each other on the colour wheel and then add other tints or shades in similar colours. This naturally creates a cohesive colouring.

When working with two colours that do not fall beside each other on the colour wheel – such as blue and yellow, orange and green, or white and black – I prefer to use 80 per cent of one colour and 20 per cent of the other colour. I also prefer not to use two main colours of the same saturation, such as bright yellow and bright blue; the colours fight each other too much for attention. I either go lighter on the yellow or lighter on the blue. To help blend or transition the colours of one flower to another, I usually try to use a flower with lots of texture and a colour that falls between the two colours and/or a flower that incorporates both colours.

MOVEMENT

Movement can be created in many ways. An arrangement that transitions from a dark colour on one side to a light colour on the other will lead your eyes to move from one side to the other. An arrangement with all of the flower stems or blooms pointing in one direction will create the feeling of an arrangement moving in that direction, or it can suggest that the viewer look in the direction that the flower is facing. Placing flowers with long stems just above an arrangement can create a feeling of airiness or dancing flower heads. Vines draping over the ledge of a vase or bouquet can create a sense of expansion or growth from below. Spires that sit tall and are layered from shortest to tallest move your eye to the back of the arrangement.

TEXTURE

Texture can be created by using fine crepe paper instead of heavy crepe with deep ribbing; using flowers with fluffy petals such as peonies instead of flowers with stiff petals such as collerette dahlias; or using flowers with large, smooth petals such as anemones instead of flowers with lots of small petals like ball dahlias. Sweet peas, with their ruffled petals and painterly colours, are a perfect example of a textural flower. Varying flower sizes in an arrangement can also create texture. Texture can also be conveyed through colour such as using a spotted or patterned petal like a spotted campanula.

LEFT
Anemones placed in a line at different depths create subtle movement of flowers shooting outwards.

DEPTH

To create physical depth, try to place your flowers at different planes or levels so they are not all side by side. Paper flowers can look very flat even when positioned at different depths and planes, so I try to create perceived depth through colour: for example, by spraying the bottom of the foliage darker, placing dark foliage or dark-coloured flowers inside the arrangement to create shadows, and positioning lighter-coloured flowers above darker ones to create highlights.

SHAPE

Your composition can take on many shapes. It can be symmetrical or asymmetrical and still be a balanced composition. It can be round, flat or diagonal in shape. It can dip in the middle or fan out from the centre. The shape can be determined by the types of flowers you include – for example, using a large focal flower that dominates the composition. There are no rules in terms of what shape the final composition should form, only that it should appear balanced and in proportion. The bouquets and arrangements that I make normally have a front side and a back side. Such a bouquet allows a bride, for example, to hold the bouquet close to her body; such an arrangement would also work well when placed against a wall.

LINE

Lines draw your eyes from one point in a composition to another. Lines can be straight or curvy; they can go in any direction, left, right or diagonally; they can point up or down; they can be high or low. The most obvious way to create a line is using foliage such as olive branches that extend out of the sides of an arrangement, thereby extending the width as well. Another way is using the same flower and lining them up across an arrangement on the same or different planes. This immediately draws your eyes left to right or right to left.

Another way is by using the same colour: several flowers adjacent to each other in the same colour and intensity would create a strong line; a softer line would be one where the flowers of the same colour are spaced apart like dots or nodes, but you can visually draw a line between those dots. Long stems of floating flowers draw your eyes upwards, softening the edges of the arrangement. Long vines that hang from a vessel and/or draw along a tablescape make you want to follow that line to see what is at the end. Even the vessel or base that you use for your floral composition has lines. A tall vase draws your eyes upwards, whereas a low compote vessel forces your eyes to look sideways.

SPACE

Positive space is when an object occupies a space; negative space is when there is no object in the space. Too much positive space can feel tight and busy; too much negative space can feel empty and minimal. There needs to be a balance between positive and negative space, although this does not mean that there should be an equal amount of positive and negative space in a composition.

SCALE AND PROPORTION

When we speak of proportion in compositions, this relates to the proportion of flowers to vase/base; of flowers to foliage; and to the shape of a composition. I like my flowers to be no more than two to two and a half times the height and twice the width of the base. Any larger and the arrangement would look too small for the base. Using very large flowers for a small bouquet with a small base or with small-leaved foliage can exaggerate the flower's size and look out of proportion. Likewise, using too many small textural elements with a large vase would look too busy.

RIGHT

These ball dahlias that are lined up on different visual planes with the lighter and brighter one on the edge emphasizing and creating depth.

BELOW
Use the five arrangement recipes as inspiration
for your own paper flower arrangements.

MY GENERAL FORMULA

The difference between a good composition and a great one is planning and careful consideration of the fine art principles; it's not enough to make a bunch of flowers you like and hope that they work out together.

I have a simple formula when deciding what types of flowers to include in a bouquet. I start by considering the colour(s) of the composition. I like working tone on tone, and this automatically narrows down the type of flowers that I might use because flowers come in certain colours and not in others. I think of what colour would work for the flowers I decide to include. I generally will repeat the colours or shapes of the flower so there is overlap in both throughout; this makes the arrangement visually cohesive. For example, instead of making a rose in one colour, I'll make it in two with slight colour variations.

Then I consider what the focal flower will be. Generally, I use a larger flower with a particular colour (such as the Coral Charm peony or Koko Loko roses), or a flower with a strong centre (such as an anemone). Sometimes, I use a cluster of smaller flowers, which, when placed together has more dominance (such as small garden roses or wild roses). The focal flower does not have to be the main colour, but it should occupy a prominent position in your arrangement. Also, sometimes an arrangement will not have a focal flower or focal point. This is acceptable as long as there are other elements in the composition that are interesting and that permit your eyes to move around.

Along with focal flowers, I consider what accent flowers would work with the focal flower. You could use an accent flower (such as a closed ranunculus) with a similar shape as the focal flower (such as a Juliet rose), like a round face. If I bring in another accent flower, it will either have a round face as well or have a different-shaped face with a similar colour to the focal or accent flower. Too many round faces can mean there is no place for your eyes to rest. To mix things up, I either bring in a round flower with a strong centre (like an open ranunculus) or a five-petal flower that

has a visible centre. If the flowers are not round, the only way they will fit with other round flowers is if they are the same colour or a similar tone of those colours. I always make these flowers in slightly different sizes and, if possible, different stages of maturity; this usually means slight variations in colour as well.

I love to use accent flowers for lines; for example, any flower with long stems. Sometimes they can make strong statements (such as parrot tulips and foxgloves); sometimes, they float above the arrangement and soften up the edges (like chocolate or cupcake cosmos).

Next comes texture, which I think has been the key to elevating my floral compositions. Texture is a challenge for paper flower artists because texture flowers usually have smaller petals, numerous petals or parts, and are more intricate to make. Yet it is this intricacy that expresses an elevated art form. At the very least, it presents a variation in size and shape that creates interest: it breaks up colour blocks; brings in bits of colour; acts as a transition piece; and can change the lines of a composition. Texture flowers can also include flowering stems.

Sometimes foliage can be an afterthought, but I urge you to think carefully about its form and function. By function I mean how it supports the composition or structure. The main structural challenge in paper flower compositions is stems that swing around and shift; my solution is to place Italian ruscus beside or behind these stems to prop them up and limit their movement.

As for form, foliage is a great source of colour and dimension. If I want to add a darker colour to the arrangement, I can do so through foliage instead of flowers; it is subtle and sophisticated. If I want a loose, flowy feel to my bouquet, I add wispy bits and long narrow foliage such as olive leaves. Variegated foliage is effective at breaking up large swaths of foliage in the same colour.

The last thing I consider is what type of vessel or base to use for an arrangement, or a ribbon for a bouquet to complement what I'm visualizing in my mind.

Preparation and tools for bouquets

I prefer to build my bouquets like an arrangement – in a vessel rather than in my hands. I find that when a bouquet is in my hands, I am too close to it to see whether or not the placement of the flowers works with the overall composition. Also, paper flower stems can be so thin that it can be quite difficult to hold them and maintain the position that you placed them in.

The following method is what I used to make the purple and mauve bouquet on page 240.

I take a large long-necked milk jar (or bottle) and fill it with rice, which will effectively hold the stems inserted into it. You could also use dried beans or small beads. I cut short lengths of floral tape and place them across the round mouth to narrow it and create a square shape over the lip. I pull the floral tape as I work so that it is taut and will hold the stems within the square, until the bouquet stem is thick enough to push open the floral tape. Once I have set up the milk jar, I insert stems into the jar and start arranging.

At the beginning, I find that the stems (especially the long ones) will shift around, and I need to reposition them until enough stems have been placed that they fill up the narrow mouth. One way to minimize the movement is by inserting Italian ruscus foliage as a placeholder to hold the stems in place. I add as many stems as I need while I arrange, especially as the stems are pushed back when new additions are added to the front. The Italian ruscus can be cut short and placed deep so the tops are not seen from the front. If necessary, I wrap it around the flower or foliage to keep it from swinging around.

Once I am satisfied with how the bouquet looks in the jar, I use a floral wire with a cutter to wrap it. I cut a long length and fold it in half to make a double strand with one end loose and one end with a loop. I wrap the double strand around the bouquet at the point where the bride will hold it (generally just below the leaves or the flower blooms), thread the loose end through the loop, and pull to tighten. Once it feels as if the stems are fairly tight together, I pull the bouquet out of the jar. I then split the double strand into two strands of floral wire, each wrapping around the stems in opposite directions, creating a band no more than 2in (5cm) tall. I tie a knot when I'm satisfied that the flower stems are tightly bound. I cut off any excess, then wrap the band with floral tape to smooth out any bumps.

I make final adjustments at this point. The binding of the stems will usually shift the positions of the flower. I hold the bouquet in front of a mirror to give a different perspective; it helps me visualize where I might be missing flowers or where the shape might look odd. To finish, I trim the ends of the stem wires even. Then, I wrap a long ribbon around the floral tape band to cover it up, tie a knot, then a long bow, then trim the ends.

I generally make hand-tied bouquets that have a front and a back. If it has a back, it can lie fairly close to a bride's body. It can also be placed on the hook of the arm sideways, with its foliage pointing towards the ground like a cascading bouquet. In fact, my cascading bouquets are just bouquets built sideways and then turned so the foliage points to the ground.

220

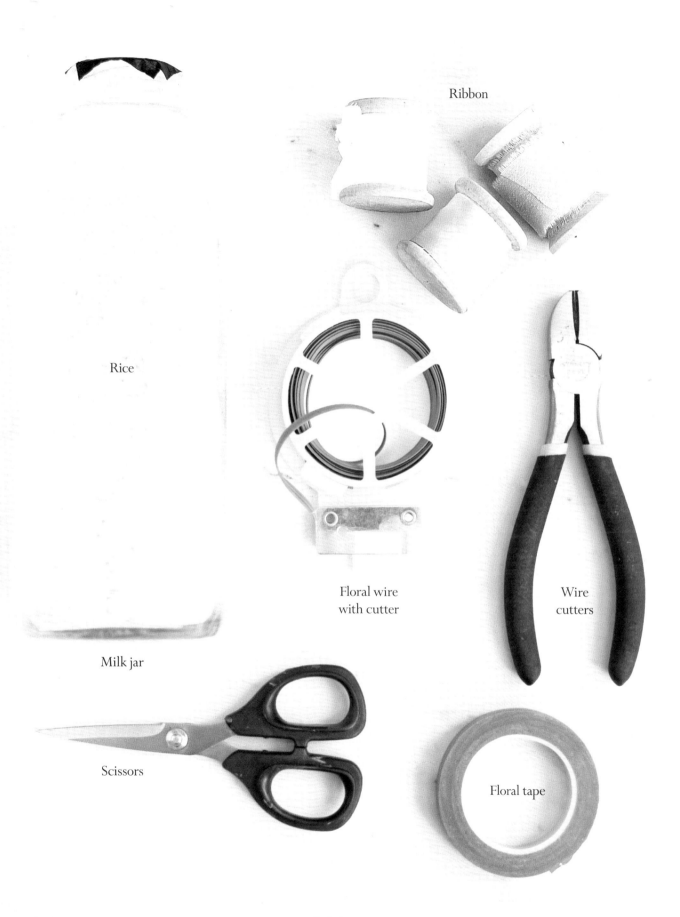

Ribbon

Rice

Floral wire
with cutter

Wire
cutters

Milk jar

Scissors

Floral tape

221

Selection of vessels

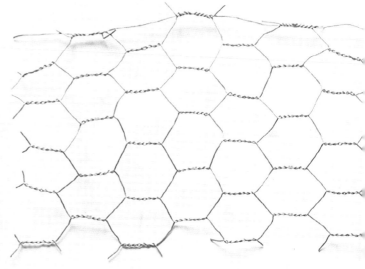
Chicken wire

Floral tape – clear and coloured

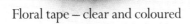

Pin frogs

Floral putty

Preparation and tools for arrangements

When I arrange my paper flowers, I like to create a structure that keeps the stems in place without them pressing into each other. I build them in a similar way to bouquets, except I use mechanics that I have learned from floristry.

There are many different vessel shapes to choose from: tall, short, round, square, low or raised. Some have very narrow mouths, like bud vases, which are perfect to display one or two flowers. Some have wide mouths that allow for stems to be placed almost horizontally. Vessels can be made from various materials, ranging from glass to ceramics to terracotta.

When I use shallow vessels that have wide mouths, such as compotes or bowls, I use a combination of pin frog and chicken wire, such as in the yellow and blue arrangement (page 224). For a vessel that has a mouth smaller than its body, such as the Delft blue vase I use for the coral and magenta arrangement (page 232), I create a grid at the mouth and I might use a pin frog.

A pin frog helps keep the stems in position when they are inserted in between the pins. The taller the pins, the more likely they can restrain the stem wires from falling over. I use pin frogs that have taller pins $^3/_4$ and 1in (19 and 25mm) as opposed to the normal shorter pin frogs. Some of these pin frogs only come in very small diameters, so I use multiple ones to cover the vessel base as needed. To use, simply stick the bottom of the pin frog to the base of the vessel using floral putty. I push the pin frog down using the cap of a glue stick so it lies even.

To use chicken wire, I cut a piece one and a quarter times the diameter of the mouth of the compote or bowl. I fold the edges in under to create a ball shape

(you may want to wear heavy-duty gloves to protect your hands if you do this, as the cut wire can be quite sharp). I press it into the compote or bowl to conform to the shape of the vessel and then secure using two pieces of floral tape across the mouth in an X, holding the chicken wire in place. You can purchase chicken wire (also known as poultry netting) in the fencing department at a hardware store. I buy the 1in (2.5cm) hexagon-shaped type. You can also buy floral chicken wire, which is softer to work with.

Some vessels are not suitable for chicken wire, such as vessels with mouths smaller than their bodies. In these cases, I create a grid at the mouth of the vessel crisscrossing four pieces of floral tape. You can use green floral tape, but I prefer clear floral tape because it is easier to hide. Stems are inserted between the grid lines and the floral tape holds the stems in place. If you use a mason jar, you can buy mason jar frogs that can be screwed on like a lid.

My personal preference is to use wide-mouth compotes. The pedestal base creates a dramatic effect, lifting the arrangement closer to eye level and allowing space for trailing branches and vines to hang freely. However, as it has a wide mouth, it can be quite challenging covering the mechanics, unlike a bouquet in which the bottom of the stems are bound together so all there is to hide is the transition on the edge of the bouquet.

Yellow and blue arrangement

This is a great example of the use of lines to draw the eye from one side to the other of an arrangement. Here, the lines are created by the berry branches, which point in different directions. Your eyes naturally move from the top left to the bottom right of the composition.

The ball dahlias also create a line across the bottom; they are staggered with one deep in and one protruding out of the arrangement. The eye is drawn to the mature wild rose diagonal from the deep-set ball dahlia because the other flowers around it are facing away, thereby forming a V with the wild rose at the base of that V.

The chartreuse-coloured foliage balances out the arrangement by filling in the negative space between the berry branches. The colour is slightly darker and greener than the yellow flowers so acts as a background colour. All of the main flowers are in a yellow tone but in various shades and tints. The mature wild rose and white/cream ball dahlias act as highlights and together create a triangular shape.

The darker blue phlox in the centre of the arrangement creates shadows under the flowers, while the lighter blue-coloured phlox link together the blue berry branches.

RECIPE

6 berry branches (see page 172)
3 golden chartreuse basic leaf foliage branches
  (see page 184)
3 yellow ball dahlias (see page 106)
2 white/cream ball dahlias (see page 106)
4 collerette dahlias (see page 100)

4 blue phlox (see page 154)
1 yellow phlox (see page 154)
4 wild rose stems (1 stem with 1 mature rose;
  1 stem with 3 mature roses; 1 stem with
  3 yellow roses and a rosebud; 1 stem with
  2 yellow roses with a rosebud) (see page 54)

1 Using a pedestal compote, with a 4½in (11.5cm) diameter mouth, place the pin frogs in the centre of the base. Cut a piece of chicken wire and fold it into a small, squat ball. Press it into the compote and secure with floral tape. Define the shape and scale of your arrangement by first inserting the berry branches of various sizes and shapes so one set points in one direction (top left) and one set points in another direction (bottom right). To define the top boundary, position a tall berry branch at the back left. To define the width of the arrangement, place three other branches on the left side extending over the edge of the compote. Place a long branch on the opposite side extending over the right edge of the compote. Take a shorter branch and insert it in front of that long branch to create a smooth transition from the compote edge to the long branch.

2 There should be a large space between the branches. Place three golden chartreuse basic leaf foliage branches in that space. Layer the branches so they are placed successively more forward than the previous branch.

3 Now for the flowers. Place three yellow ball dahlias near the centre, creating a triangular shape with their placement. Have one positioned on the edge of the compote at the front; another staggered above it and facing front right to start a line of ball dahlias; and another placed at the back, mid-height between the berry branch and the compote. Place the two white/cream ball dahlias on opposite sides of the arrangement. Have one positioned on the right side and shooting outwards past the two yellow dahlias to end the line of ball dahlias, and have one on the left side, shooting downwards.

4 Position a pair of collerette dahlias at the top of the arrangement, facing right and staggered in height. For the other two dahlias, have one facing the front slightly off-centre and facing the bottom left; place the other on the left side facing left, mid-height.

5 Use the phlox to add blue into the arrangement and to cover the mechanics. Fill in the centre of the arrangement with the darker blue phlox; place the lighter blue phlox just below the yellow ball dahlia in the ball dahlia line covering the edge of the compote. Position another blue phlox on the left of the centre yellow dahlia and on top of the collerette dahlia just covering the ledge. Finally, place a yellow phlox on the left side covering the mechanics and edge.

6 Finish the arrangement with the wild roses. Insert the stem with three mature wild roses deep in the mid-left and just above the centre yellow ball dahlias and dark blue phlox. Place the three yellow roses in the left, so they are layered above the mature roses. Place a stem with two yellow wild roses on the right between the collerette dahlias. Lastly, place a single mature wild rose just below the collerette dahlia that is hanging over the edge on the front left.

Peach and pink arrangement

The colours here are peach and pink, with a lot of green and a pop of both pink and orange. The orange parrot tulips might be an unexpected addition, but they work because orange and peach are the same tone in different tints. Also the parrot tulip is not completely orange; it has a bit of cream in it, which goes perfectly with the cream/peach small garden roses. A large peach-coloured Juliet rose links both the orange parrot tulip and other more pink-coloured Juliet roses together, complementing the pink sweet peas. The pops of pink coral, the dusty Koko Loko roses, the dark rose foliage on the Juliet roses, and the muted chartreuse ferns ground the composition and give it depth, preventing it from becoming too sweet. The ombré colouring of the panicle hydrangeas links the pinks with the chartreuse ferns.

There are a lot of lines shooting out of the arrangement, from the ferns to the parrot tulips, to the rosebuds and the pink double cupcake cosmos. The flower heads face in every direction, duplicating the fan shape of the lines of the ferns. The coral-coloured rosebuds provide texture, as do the horizontal lines on the ferns, and the folds of the rosettes in the Juliet roses. Placing the large peach Juliet rose near the front of the composition and at the rim of the compote makes it look closer than it actually is.

The overall composition appears quite large because the ferns and parrot tulips take up so much space, but it is still proportionate to the size of the compote.

RECIPE

7 ferns in chartreuse (6 large, 1 smaller) (see page 208)

4 orange parrot tulips (see page 114)

3 panicle hydrangeas (see page 136)

2 Koko Loko roses (see page 76)

3 peach and/or pink Juliet roses (1 large, 2 small) (see page 60)

1 blush pink small garden rose (see page 68)

3 peach small garden roses (1 stem with 3 roses, 1 stem with 2 roses, 1 stem with 2 roses and bud(s)) (see page 68)

6 pink sweet peas (see page 148)

1 pink single cupcake cosmos (see page 94)

1 pink double cupcake cosmos (see page 94)

5 small ferns in muted chartreuse (see page 208)

Italian ruscus (see page 200) and Variegated boxwood (see page 204) as required

1 Using a pedestal compote with a 4in (10.2cm) diameter mouth, place the pin frogs in the centre of the base. Cut a piece of chicken wire and fold it into a small squat ball. Press it into the compote and secure with floral tape. Define the shape and scale of your arrangement by first inserting the chartreuse ferns so they fan out. Place three ferns over the left edge of the compote with their tips pointing left. Then, position two ferns at the back so they are not standing straight up but bending gently back. Place two at the right side hanging over the edge, with one pointing to the front; the top fern should be slightly smaller than the bottom fern. If necessary, attach two together with floral tape before inserting to thicken the stems for the pin frogs. Next, place all four orange parrot tulips in different directions with the back ones with more straight stems and the front ones with stems that are bending more; have the front right parrot tulip dipping downward.

2 Before positioning the focal flowers, define the structure further by inserting the panicle hydrangeas; these can be bulky in size and shape. Position one on the left side and between the parrot tulips and two on the right side with one pointing higher and one pointing lower, and both between the two parrot tulips. Place the panicle hydrangea so there is space for a Juliet rose to fit between them. Use the leaves to cover the edge of the compote.

3 Place the two focal flowers – the Koko Loko roses – together so they are staggered in height (with the more muted one behind the more pink one if possible). Place them off-centre and have their blooms facing slightly to the right.

4 The other large flowers are the peach and/or pink Juliet roses. To create a triangular shape, place the largest Juliet rose closest to front; place one at the back with a long stem and its face facing left; then insert the third Juliet rose on the right side, deep between the panicle hydrangeas. Turn the rose foliage down to cover the edge of the compote. If the parrot tulips are shifting around or backwards, use a few Italian ruscus to prop them into their place. I've put two Italian ruscus behind the parrot tulips and the ferns at the back of the arrangement to keep them in place.

5 Fill in the empty spaces with small garden roses. Place a stem of three peach-coloured small garden roses in the big hole on the left side and just above the large Juliet rose, mid-height. Then, place a stem of two peach small garden roses in the centre-right position, leaving the rose blooms protruding out a bit. Place the blush pink small garden rose below the set of two peach small garden rose; using it as a transition flower, set it in deep between the Juliet rose at the back and the Koko Loko roses at the front. If you look down on the arrangement, you should see a line of flowers coming from the centre to front. Finally, place a stem of two peach small garden roses with three rosebuds on the right side, behind the panicle hydrangea closest to the front.

6 Add some pink sweet peas to cover some of the mechanics. I paired up a few by taping their stems with floral tape to thicken their stems. Place one near the back left side between the orange parrot tulip and the ferns at the back. Position another two stems at the front and another two stems left of centre to hide the mechanics and add more pink.

7 To include more pink in the arrangement, place one pink cupcake cosmos behind the peach small garden roses at the top. Place another pink cupcake cosmos on the right above the panicle hydrangea and pointing its face to the right. Bring in a pop of coral pink by adding clusters of rosebuds in three locations: one in the very back right side, placed high enough to be able to be seen when viewing the arrangement from the front; one in the middle just below the Juliet rose at the top of the triangular shape; and one on the left behind the large Juliet rose and in front of the parrot tulip on the left. This positioning creates a link from the top right/back of the arrangement to the bottom left.

8 Lastly, ground the colour of the arrangement using small muted chartreuse ferns. Place three at the front just below the Koko Loko roses, covering the edge of the compote; another between the large Juliet rose and the peach small garden rose above it; and another one at the back by the Juliet rose facing the back. Fill in any empty spots using variegated boxwood.

Coral and magenta arrangement

This composition is in a tall vase with a mouth that is smaller than the body of the vase. The height of the vase allows for taller and more substantial branches to be layered in front of one another. The fruit blossom branches look balanced in this heavier-set vase and are layered asymmetrically on only one side of the composition. The branches almost seem to divide the arrangement in two diagonally from the bottom left to the top right.

The flowers fill in the negative space under the fruit blossom branches. The eye is automatically drawn to the focal flowers: the three Coral Charms that create a triangular shape. Their stamens and centres are highlights to an otherwise pink composition. Surrounding these peonies are hot pinks and magenta flowers with round faces.

To bridge the coral and pink colours are dark pink coral sweet peas with a neutral colour base that have a light ombré to them, mirroring the ombré of the blue-based dark pink fruit blossoms. The sweet peas provide a ruffled texture and create shadows deep inside the arrangement. The ball dahlias too, with their multiple florets, add shadows and depth to the arrangement.

After your eyes move away from the coral charm peonies, they are drawn to the river of light pink lavender on the bottom right. Alone, the lilac pink clematis would look out of place; however, the purple-pinkish phlox bridges the lilac pink with the hot pink of the small garden roses. The clematis flowers draw your eyes downwards on the opposite side of the fruit blossom branches to balance out the arrangement.

RECIPE

5 fruit blossom branches (see page 178)
3 Coral Charm peonies (see page 82)
3 fuchsia and maroon ball dahlias (see page 106)
2 magenta Juliet roses (see page 60)
4 magenta small garden roses (1 sets with two flowers and a bud; 1 set with one flower and one bud; 1 set with three flowers) (see page 68)

2 purple phlox (see page 154)
1 lilac-pink clematis vine with 3 flowers, mature stamen(s) and bud(s) (see page 166)
7 dark pink sweet peas (see page 148)
5 variegated boxwood sprayed dark green at base (see page 204)
Italian ruscus (see page 200) as required

1 Prepare your tall vase by making a grid on the mouth with floral tape. This vase has a 4in (10.2cm) diameter mouth. If you like, also place frog pins at the bottom of the vase. Define the shape and boundary of the composition by placing the largest element first: the fruit blossom branches. I made five branches, each of which has smaller stems on the left side of the branch. Place the tallest one at the back in the centre, then place the remaining four in front of it on the left side, layering in front of the previous one, with the ones in the back taller than the ones in the front. Position one of them near the front, extending its reach towards the left side.

2 Place the three Coral Charm peonies in a triangle shape with one in the front, slightly off to the left side; one at the top with its bloom facing right; and one at the right side, positioned lower than the other two and hanging off the edge of the vase.

3 Distribute the three fuchsia and maroon ball dahlias around the Coral Charm peonies, staggering their heights.

4 Position one magenta Juliet rose in the centre slightly off to the right side, diagonal from the Coral Charm peony, and another magenta Juliet rose on the right and further back than the Coral Charm peony. Turn its bloom so it is looking more towards the front than the side. If you find that the branches are moving around, place two or more Italian ruscus behind and/or around the branches to support them.

5 Insert a set of three magenta small garden roses at the very top of the Coral Charm peony triangle. Then, at the front, place a set of two roses with a bud(s) that hangs slightly over the magenta Juliet rose. Place another two roses with a bud(s) at the left side between the fruit branches to emphasize the depth between the branches. Finally, place one stem of rose with a bud between the Coral Charm peony on the left centre and the fruit blossom branch at the left.

6 Position the two purple phlox so they sit between the Coral Charm peony at the top and the Coral Charm peony at the right side. Place them together, staggered in height, creating a stream of lavender pink down to the edge of the vase. Then insert one lilac-pink clematis vine at the end of the stream.

7 To bring all the coral and magenta colours together, add some dark pink sweet peas below the Coral Charm peony on the left and then fill in some of the spaces around the other two Coral Charm peonies; insert them deep into the arrangement to cover the mechanics.

8 Finally, insert about five variegated boxwoods to fill the empty spaces and cover the mechanics.

White and green arrangement

The anemones are the focal flowers here, with their dark black centres creating a curving line across the arrangement. The greener anemones create this line, while the white ones are used elsewhere. The anemone line deviates on the right side and points to a white clematis vine, which continues the line down to the table. It mirrors the berry foliage branch on the top left of the composition. To balance out the clematis vine at the base of the arrangement, another vine is added on the left side, pointing down in the other direction, although it is slightly shorter to create asymmetry.

The berry foliage branches echo the line of the anemone shooting outward towards the top left and bottom right of the composition. A touch of blue from the variegated foliage keeps it from being too sour. The spots on the white campanula also bring a bit of muddy brown that suits the terracotta compote perfectly. Variegated boxwood sprayed dark at the base creates shadows inside the arrangement. Although the anemones form a line, they are staggered at different heights and distances from the front. They are dynamic because they face different directions, and the right one looks as if it wants to shoot right out.

This arrangement, being wider than tall, is proportionate given that the compote sits lower and its mouth suggests a wider proportion. Although this arrangement consists mainly of white flowers, it is interesting because of the variety of petal shapes. In fact, most of the flowers are not pure white but have a touch of green, chartreuse or yellow.

Finally, the white sweet peas, with their ruffled petals, echo the ruffles of the ranunculus and the inner rosette petals of the Juliet roses. Together, they provide a romantic fluted texture to the arrangement.

RECIPE

2 basic leaf foliage branches with berries (see page 184)
5 basic leaf foliage (see page 184)
1 long basic leaf foliage with berries (see page 184)
2 variegated basic leaf foliage (see page 184)
3 white Juliet roses (see page 60)
10 white and green anemones (see page 48)
4 white closed ranunculus (see page 128)
2 white open ranunculus (see page 122)

2 white clematis vines, one with 5 flower buds and mature stamen(s), and one with 3 flowers with mature stamen(s) and bud(s) (see page 166)
2 white spotted campanula (see page 160)
2 variegated boxwood sprayed dark green at base (see page 204)
4 white sweet peas (see page 148)
2 white double cupcake cosmos (see page 94)

1 Using a low and wide compote with a 5in (12.7cm) diameter mouth, place the pin frogs in the centre of the base. Cut a piece of chicken wire and fold it into a small squat ball. Press it into the compote and secure with floral tape. Define the shape and scale of your arrangement by positioning two large branches with berries at the left back, layered so one is further back than the other. Place some basic leaf foliage in front and behind the two branches with at least one piece hanging over the edge of the compote at the back and one on the left also hanging off the edge. Position the basic leaf long stem with berries on the right side with the branch facing the front. Place two pieces of basic leaf foliage just behind and under the long berry branch so they hang off the edge of the compote. To bring in some cool and blue tones, place the variegated basic leaf foliage on the centre left, covering the edge.

2 Create a triangular shape using three white Juliet roses. Place the larger one at the front, facing slightly right and hanging off the edge. Place a second one on the left, above the variegated foliage, facing up and left. For the last rose, position it on the right side near the back, facing backwards and sitting low.

3 Here I've used ten anemones in white, white and green, and green, but you can use as many anemones as you want. Position a line of anemones off-centre on the right side above the Juliet rose hanging off the edge on the centre-right side. Insert one anemone deep in the right side and one anemone layered higher up as if shooting out of the centre. Insert another anemone near the back facing sideways or towards the back. On the left side of the arrangement, create another line of anemones going down; stagger the heights so they are not on the same planes as the anemones on the right side of the arrangement. Place a final one in the back, midway between the branches.

4 Insert the ranunculus so they are distributed between the anemones and Juliet roses. Place a pair of staggered closed ranunculus on the left between the branches and anemones to emphasize the depth. Place another at the front above and between the Juliet roses so it protrudes outwards, although not as much as the anemone sitting just above. Position another closed ranunculus on the right side layered on top of the anemone above the long berry branch. Take the two open ranunculus flowers and place them staggered at the back, sitting low just above the Juliet rose and creating a line moving upward.

5 Place the longer clematis on the right side, at the bottom of the stream of anemones and just beside the long berry branch. Place the shorter clematis on the left side beside the Juliet rose to balance out the composition.

6 The campanulas should sit above or appear to jump out between flowers so they can be seen. Place one near the front between the anemones and the Juliet rose that faces the left. The second one should go on the right side and above the clematis. Adjust them as you insert the subsequent flowers/fillers.

7 At this point, you may want to add some variegated boxwood as fillers throughout the arrangement. I used two and placed one on the left side and one on the right side, moving the stems around flowers as necessary. You can also add the white sweet peas so they hide stems and the mechanics. I added four sets of sweet peas and placed them fairly deep in the arrangement so they create shadows. If you place them too high between the flowers, and they're too visible, you will lose shadows.

8 Finally, add the two white double cupcake cosmos as the final touch. Position them on the right side, layered above the anemones so they float above the arrangement.

238

Purple and mauve bouquet

Unlike a round traditional bouquet, this one is defined by the dynamic lines created by the olive leaf foliage and the parrot tulips. These guide your eyes outwards from the centre, and also form a looser shape. They also create negative space around the outer edges, softening the transition.

Although this is mainly a purple bouquet, there is a variety of shades of purple, from the purple pink campanula to the blue purple of the parrot tulips and the burgundy red of the chocolate cosmos and clematis vine. The dominant flowers are the Koko Loko roses at the front, which represent the lighter tint of the spectrum. To tie them in, purple pink Eze ranunculus are added to the top and back; they serve as highlights above the darker flowers, and they link the top of the bouquet with the bottom Koko Loko roses, one of which lies near the back right. Likewise, the pink purple campanulas were added near the Koko Loko roses to add some lightness. Muted purple campanulas serve as transition pieces between the Koko Loko roses and the darker purple ranunculus and parrot tulips.

The bright purple anemones are separated from the yellow burgundy Café Caramel ranunculus. However, each flower has one single flower near the middle linking the pair of flowers on each side. Cherry caramel phlox sit under the Koko Loko roses; their coffee colours with purple and burgundy details perfectly bridge the muted purple pinks. Placed significantly deeper than the roses, they create distance and depth. The clematis vine hanging at the bottom right balances the campanulas hanging at the bottom left. Italian ruscus is sprayed burgundy at the base to tie in the burgundy touches throughout the bouquet. Proportionately, all the flowers are about the same size, thus, it is not too difficult to maintain balance in the composition.

RECIPE

4 purple parrot tulips (see page 114)
3 Koko Loko roses (see page 76)
3 purple-burgundy closed ranunculus (see page 128)
3 purple-burgundy open ranunculus (see page 122)
1 Café Caramel closed ranunculus (see page 128)
2 Café Caramel open ranunculus (see page 122)
2 Eze closed ranunculus (see page 128)
3 purple anemones (see page 48)
3 cherry caramel phlox (see page 154)

3 muted purple campanula (see page 160)
1 purple-pink campanula (see page 160)
1 lilac-pink clematis (see page 166)
3 chocolate cosmos (see page 90)
6 olive leaves (see page 196)
4 Italian ruscus, sprayed burgundy at base (see page 200)
4 eucalyptus leaves (see page 192)
2 burgundy basic leaf foliage (see page 184)

1 Prepare your milk jar by adding rice to it, three-quarters of the way up. Apply floral tape on top of the mouth to narrow the opening. Determine which side will be the front of the bouquet. Place the parrot tulips at four opposite points, staggering their heights. Position them so they reach outwards.

2 Place one set of Koko Loko roses on the left side, near the front but not facing you directly. Place the other Koko Loko rose on the right back side, just under the parrot tulip at the back. This will create a line from the front bottom left to the mid-right side. Turn the foliage down and over the edge of the bouquet to cover the stems.

3 Place one pair of purple-burgundy ranunculus with one higher than the other at the front right side. Place the other ranunculus in a similar manner around the bouquet, distributing them higher or lower than the first two pairs. Have at least one ranunculus at the back of the bouquet, facing the back. Place one pair of Café Caramel ranunculus on the right side, between the parrot tulips. This will be the yellow side. Place another Café Caramel ranunculus on the left top side so it links the yellow from the right side to the left.

4 Place the purple anemones on the left and opposite side of the yellow Café Caramels. Position two of them on the very left side, with one of their heads turned towards the front; position the other one, barely open, by the Café Caramel at the front. This will be the purple flower linking the left with the right. Take the two Eze ranunculus flowers and place them at the top of the arrangement, as if floating. They will act as highlights on top of the darker flowers, and will draw the eyes from the Koko Loko roses upwards.

5 Insert some blue-green eucalyptus leaves by the olive leaves and anywhere else that complements it. If you want, you can do this last.

6 Place the cherry caramel phlox between the Koko Loko roses and the purple-burgundy ranunculus and anemone; they are the transition flowers bridging the muddy mauve of the Koko Loko roses and the purple and purple-burgundy of the anemones and ranunculus. Place another one above the pair of Café Caramel ranunculus on the right side. Then, place one muted purple campanula and one purple-pink campanula on the left bottom side, below the cherry caramel and between the Koko Loko rose and anemone; arrange them with their heads hanging down. Place another muted purple campanula on the top right side, on top of the cherry caramel phlox; have the heads pointing upwards. Place one more at the back by the purple-burgundy ranunculus.

7 Insert the two burgundy-coloured elements at the same time. First, insert the clematis on the bottom right side, letting it hang and trail down the bouquet. Then, place one piece of burgundy basic leaf foliage directly on the opposite side, on the edge with the leaves hanging down and covering the stems. Place another piece of burgundy basic leaf foliage at the very back by the purple-burgundy ranunculus, also at the edge with the leaves hanging down.

8 The last step is to place three chocolate cosmos near the back, floating above the other flowers.

Templates

All templates are shown here at actual size. Continuous lines show where to cut, dotted lines show where to fold and arrows show the direction of the grain.

ANEMONE page 48

WILD ROSE page 54

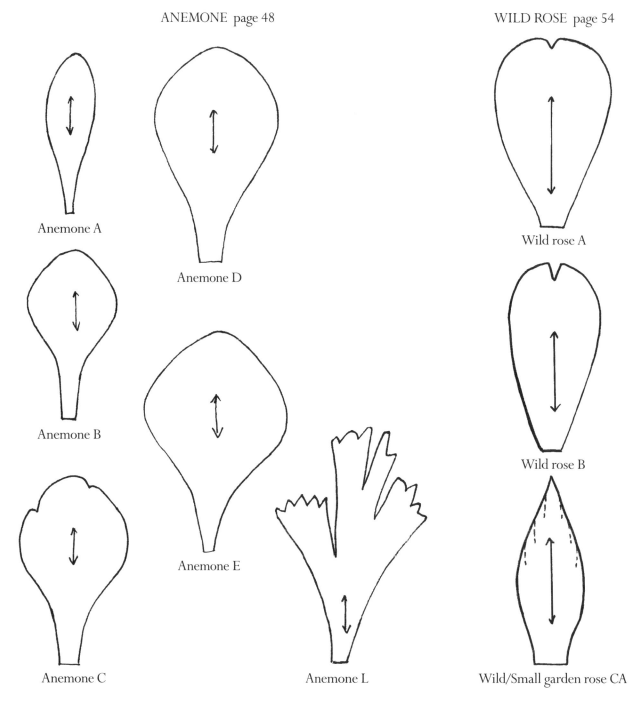

Anemone A

Anemone D

Anemone B

Anemone E

Anemone C

Anemone L

Wild rose A

Wild rose B

Wild/Small garden rose CA

244

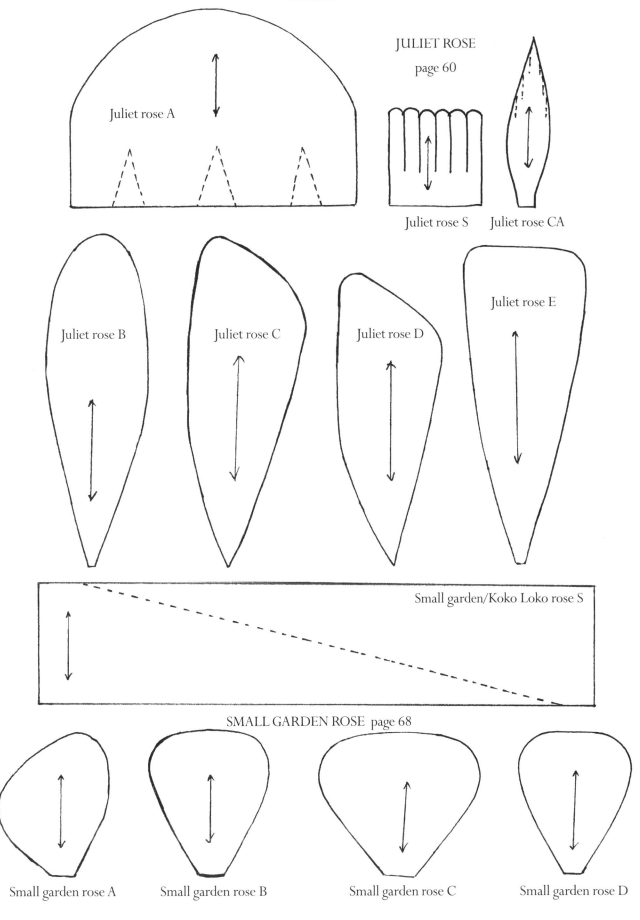

Juliet rose A

JULIET ROSE
page 60

Juliet rose S

Juliet rose CA

Juliet rose B

Juliet rose C

Juliet rose D

Juliet rose E

Small garden/Koko Loko rose S

SMALL GARDEN ROSE page 68

Small garden rose A

Small garden rose B

Small garden rose C

Small garden rose D

245

KOKO LOKO ROSE page 76

CORAL CHARM PEONY page 82

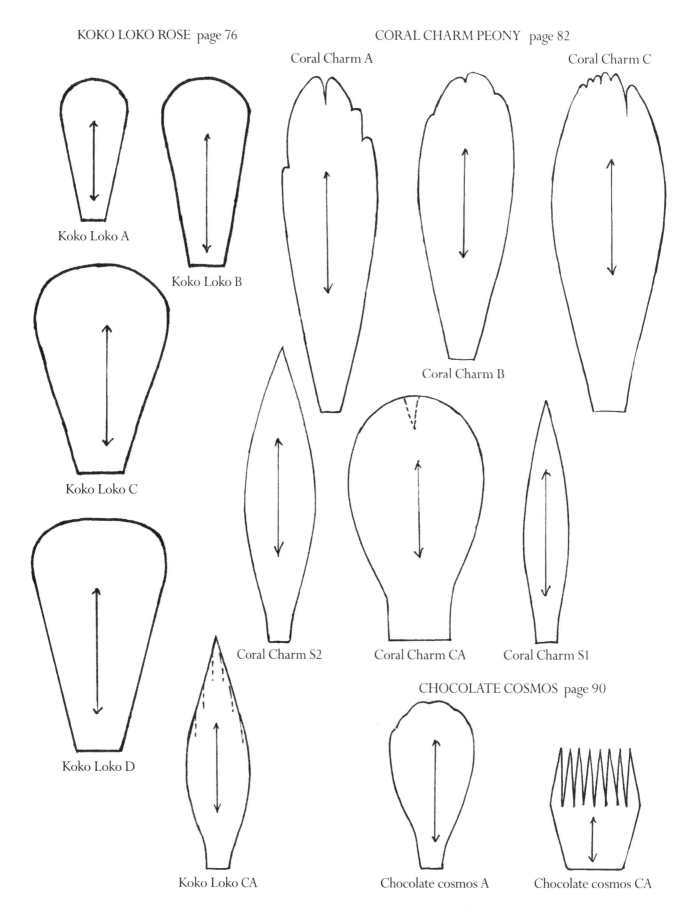

Coral Charm A

Coral Charm C

Koko Loko A

Koko Loko B

Coral Charm B

Koko Loko C

Coral Charm S2

Coral Charm CA

Coral Charm S1

Koko Loko D

CHOCOLATE COSMOS page 90

Koko Loko CA

Chocolate cosmos A

Chocolate cosmos CA

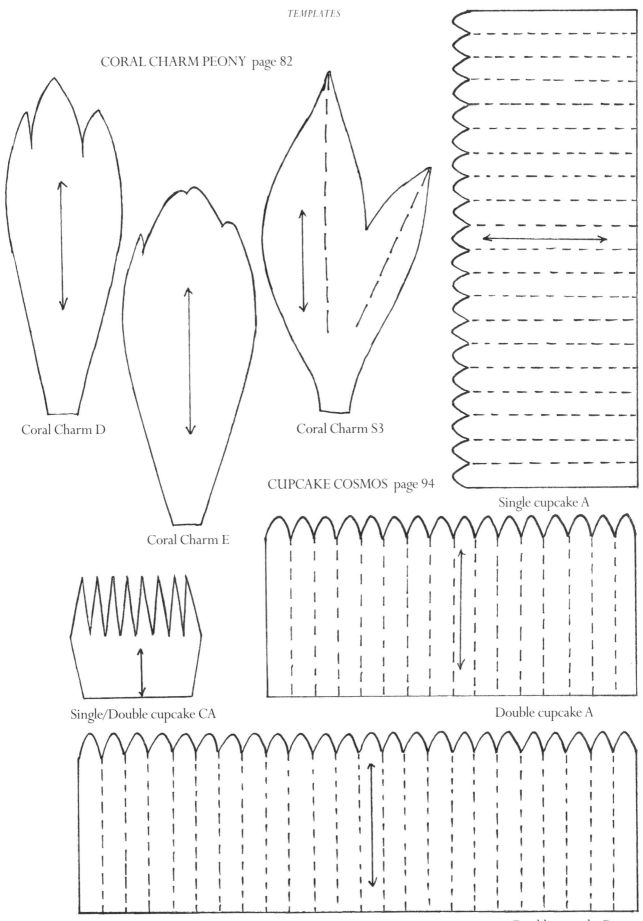

CORAL CHARM PEONY page 82

Coral Charm D

Coral Charm E

Coral Charm S3

Single cupcake A

CUPCAKE COSMOS page 94

Single/Double cupcake CA

Double cupcake A

Double cupcake B

COLLERETTE DAHLIA

page 100

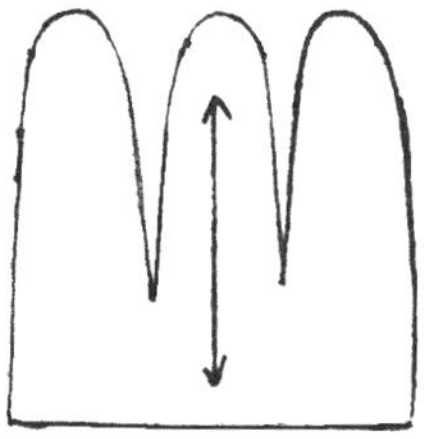

Collerette dahlia A

Collerette
dahlia BR2

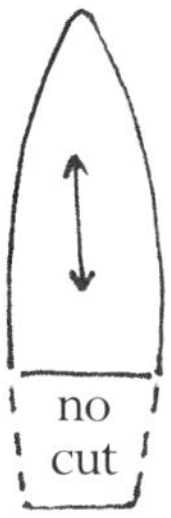

Collerette
dahlia BR1

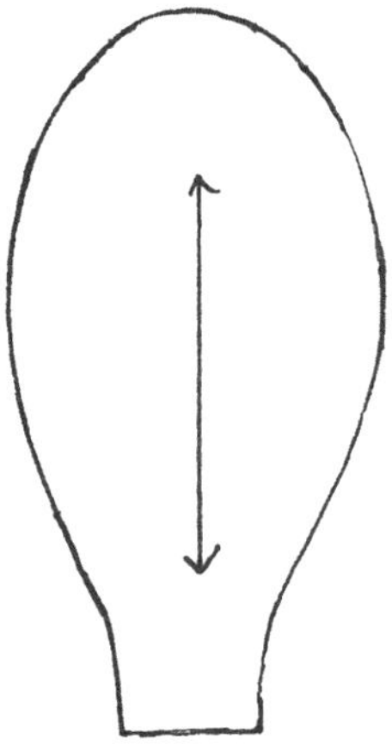

no
cut

no
cut

Collerette
dahlia B

BALL DAHLIA

page 106

Ball dahlia BR2

Ball dahlia BR1

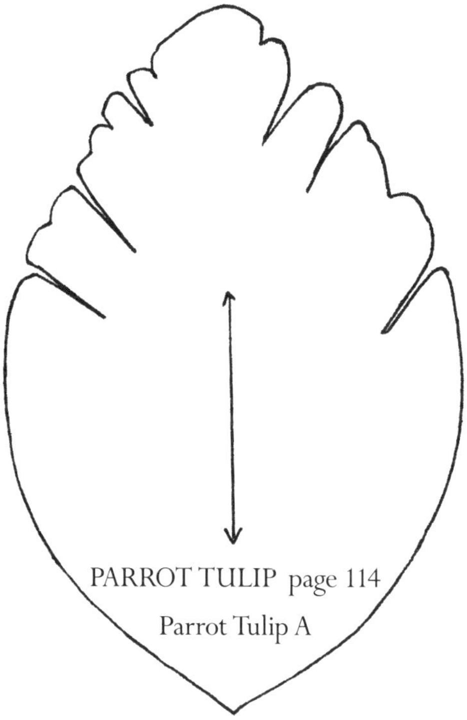

PARROT TULIP page 114

Parrot Tulip A

OPEN RANUNCULUS

page 122

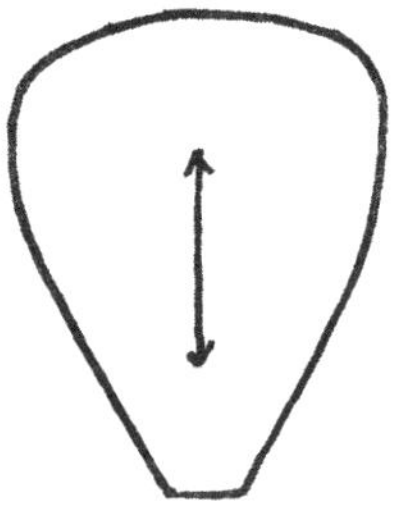

Open Ranunculus A

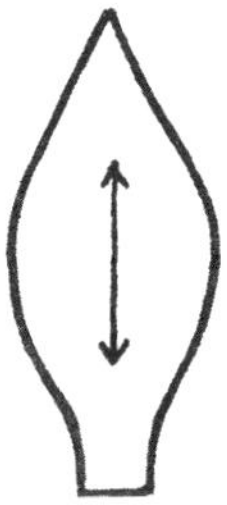

Open Ranunculus CA

CLOSED RANUNCULUS page 128

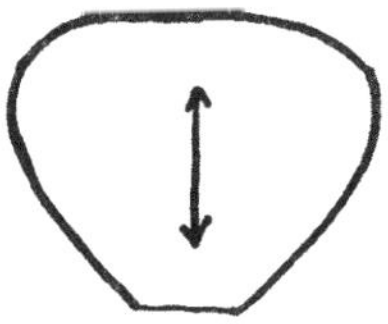

Closed Ranunculus A

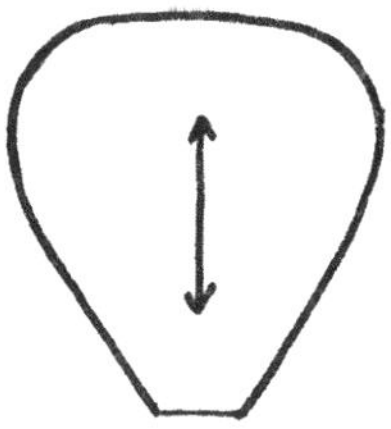

Closed Ranunculus B

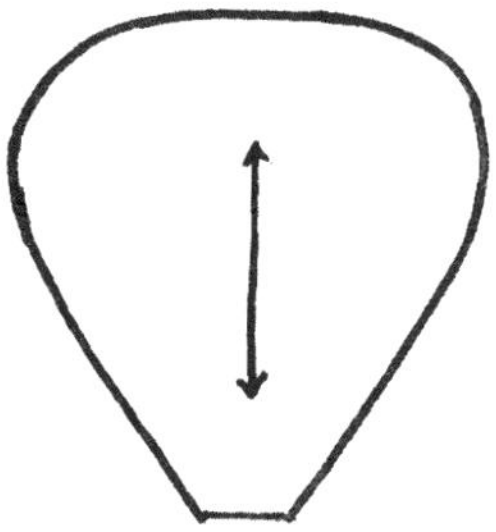

Closed Ranunculus C

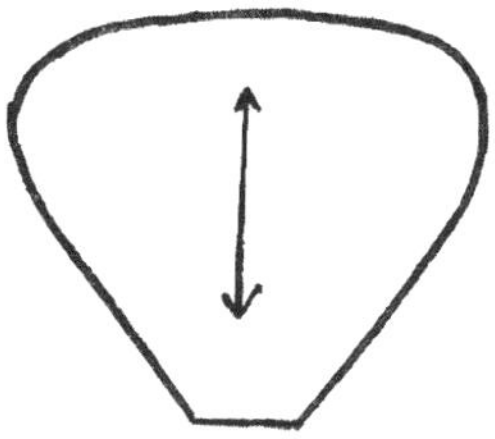

Closed Ranunculus D

PANICLE

HYDRANGEA

page 136

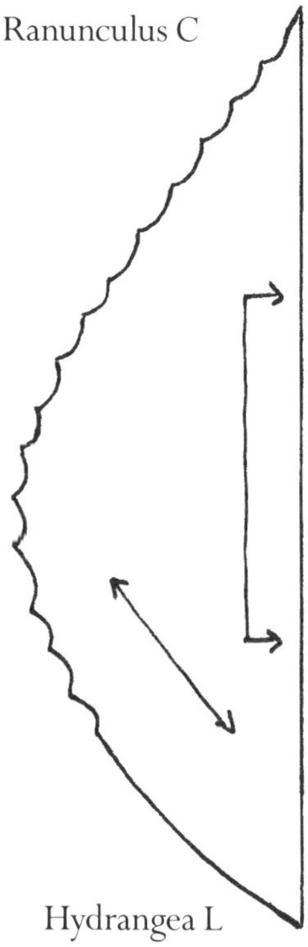

Hydrangea L

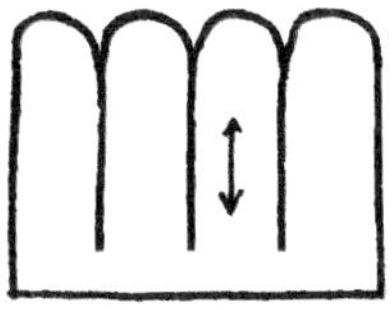

Hydrangea A

248

ROSEBUDS page 142

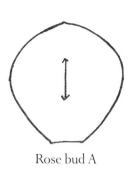

Rose bud A

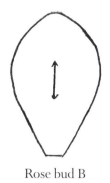

Rose bud B

Rose bud CA

PHLOX page 154

Phlox A

SWEET PEA page 148

Sweet Pea A

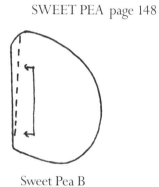

Sweet Pea B

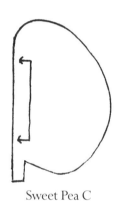

Sweet Pea C

CAMPANULA page 160

Campanula CA   Campanula L

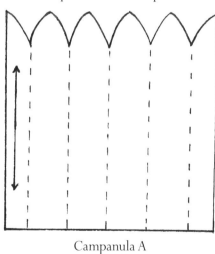

Campanula A

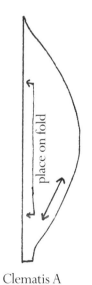

Clematis A

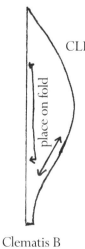

Clematis B

CLEMATIS page 166

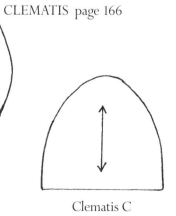

Clematis C

FRUIT BLOSSOM BRANCH page 178

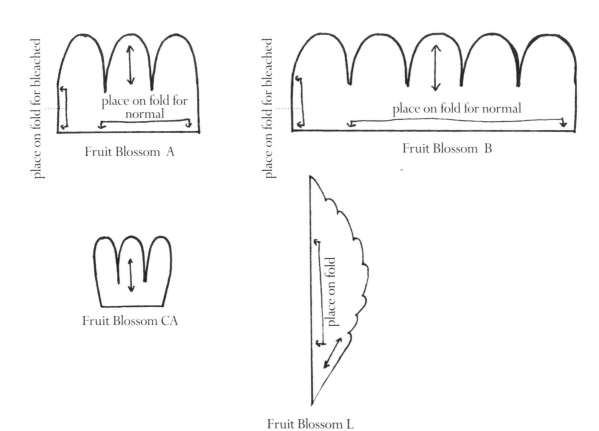

place on fold for bleached

place on fold for normal

Fruit Blossom A

place on fold for bleached

place on fold for normal

Fruit Blossom B

Fruit Blossom CA

place on fold

Fruit Blossom L

BASIC LEAF FOLIAGE page 184

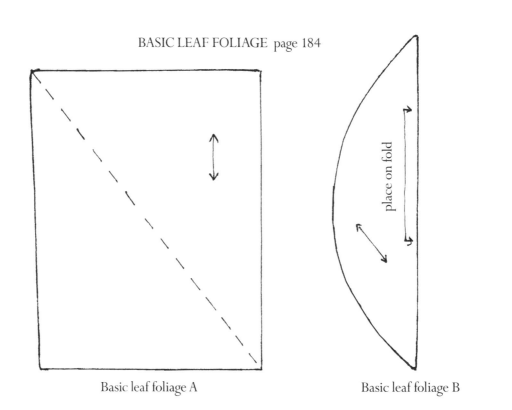

place on fold

Basic leaf foliage A

Basic leaf foliage B

250

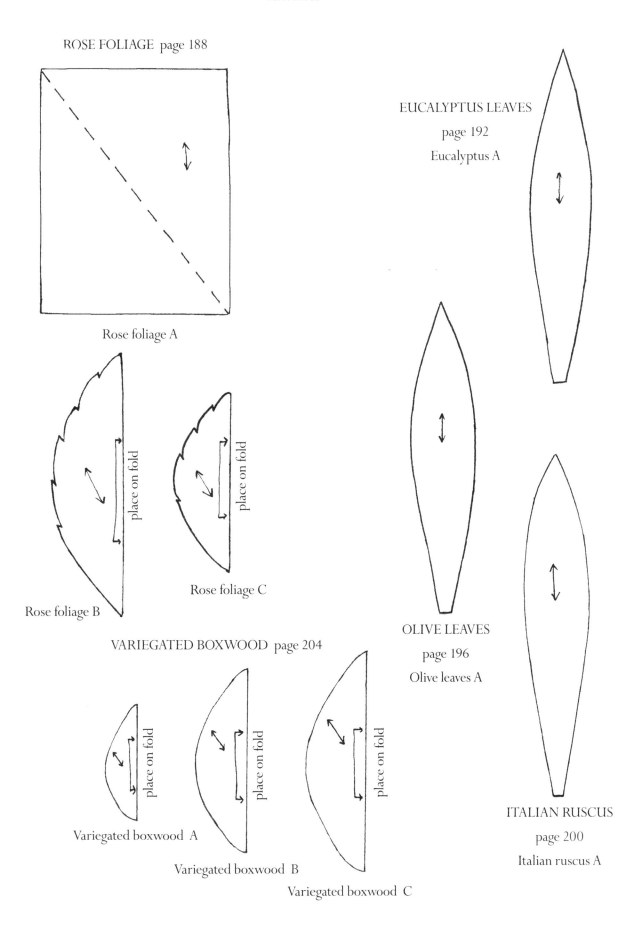

ROSE FOLIAGE page 188

Rose foliage A

Rose foliage B

place on fold

Rose foliage C

place on fold

VARIEGATED BOXWOOD page 204

place on fold

Variegated boxwood A

place on fold

Variegated boxwood B

place on fold

Variegated boxwood C

EUCALYPTUS LEAVES

page 192

Eucalyptus A

OLIVE LEAVES

page 196

Olive leaves A

ITALIAN RUSCUS

page 200

Italian ruscus A

Resources

CREPE PAPER

North America and UK

Amazon: Amazon.com

Carte Fini: www.cartefini.com

Crepe Paper Store: www.crepepaperstore.com

Lia Griffith: www.liagriffith.com

Paper Flower Supplies: www.paperflowersupplies.com

Paper Mart: www.papermart.com

Rose Mille: www.rosemille.com

The Paper Place: shop.thepaperplace.ca

Italy

Cartotecnica Rossi: cartotecnicarossi.it/eng

STEM WIRE AND FLORAL TAPE

North America

Daiso: www.daisojapan.com

Golda's Kitchen: www.goldaskitchen.com

Michaels: www.michaels.com; www.michaels.ca

Paper Mart: www.papermart.com

UK

Whittingtons: www.whittingtons.biz

Japan

Daiso: www.daisojapan.com

GENERAL ART SUPPLIES

North America

Curry's: www.currys.com

Deserres: www.deserres.ca

Joann: www.joann.com

Michaels: www.michaels.com; www.michaels.ca

Shades of Clay: www.shadesofclay.com

UK

Jackson's Art: www.jacksonsart.com

FLORAL SUPPLIES

North America

Design Master & Smithers-Oasis (International): www.dmcolor.com

Ezpots: http://www.ezpots.com/PINFROG.html

Michaels: www.michaels.com; www.michaels.ca

UK

Whittingtons: www.whittingtons.biz

About the author

Jessie Chui is a floral and botanical artist, educator, lawyer, and the creator of Crafted to Bloom. She started making floral paper art just before her son's birth and continues to do so during her son's naptimes. She is known for her realistic paper floral art and intricate floral paper compositions. Jessie's work has been featured in *100 Layer Cake*, *Lia Griffith*, *The Paper Place*, *WedLuxe*, *Holt Renfrew's Holiday Magazine*, and has been exhibited in a gallery in Toronto, Canada.

Jessie regularly teaches workshops and offers a series of online courses. She is highly involved in the paper florist community as one of the directors of The Paper Florists Collective, an international organization of paper florists. Jessie lives in Mississauga, Ontario, Canada, with her husband and young son.

Jessie's portfolio can be viewed at www.craftedtobloom.com or on Instagram @jessieatcraftedtobloom.

Author's acknowledgements

I could not have written this book without the support and encouragement of so many wonderful and generous people in my life.

First and foremost, I have to thank Warren Yee for being the incredible person and partner that he is. Warren, you've been so supportive of my creative journey from day one. At times, you have more confidence in me than I have in myself. You are the reason why I can pursue this dream. I will be forever grateful for your love and encouragement. I love you so much.

To my dear Tristan: when you entered our lives, you reminded me that life is precious and short. You are the reason why I decided to pursue this creative journey and change the trajectory of my life. I know I've missed many happy moments in your life this past year; I will try my hardest not to miss another one. Ugga Mugga.

To my parents and my brother: thank you for teaching me to be resourceful and encouraging me, always. I am grateful that I can share this part of my life with you. Love you.

To all of my clients/friends who have helped me build up my fine arts portfolio in the last few years and made this book possible: you placed your faith in me when I had very little to show for it. Words cannot express how much that meant to me and I cannot thank you enough.

To the following individuals who have supported me in one way or another to make this book possible (in no particular order): Heather Sauer and The Paper Place team; Lia Griffith and her team; the 100 Layer Cake team; Anna Chedid, Amity Beane, Laura Richey, Chantal Larocque, Jacqueline Butler, Lucia Balcazar, Wendy Middaugh, Susan Bonn, Stephen Brooks, Sheila Fisher, Alice Che. Thank you.

To Quynh Nguyen and Priscilla Park: it has been a joy to work with you in the past year and a half. Your friendship has made this creative journey less daunting and incredibly fulfilling. You are both amazing artists in your own right and I've learned so much from you. Thank you for understanding when I couldn't contribute more time towards our work together and for encouraging me all the way through this.

Finally, I have to thank all of the paper flower artists who came before me and taught me their techniques, shared their philosophy with me, inspired me to take the leap, and paved the way for me and so many others with this art form: Lia Griffith, Livia Cetti, Lynn Dolan, Kate Alarcon, Jennifer Tran, Margie Keates, Susan Beech and Tiffanie Turner. There are many other paper flower artists (and florists) who inspire me every day. Our paths have crossed in one way or another and I hope you know who you are. You have my gratitude.

First published 2019 by
Guild of Master Craftsman Publications Ltd
Castle Place, 166 High Street, Lewes,
East Sussex BN7 1XU, UK

Text © Jessie Chui, 2019
Copyright in the Work © GMC Publications Ltd, 2019

ISBN 978 1 78494 544 2

While every effort has been made to obtain permission from the copyright holders for all material used in this book, the publishers will be pleased to hear from anyone who has not been appropriately acknowledged and to make the correction in future reprints.

The publishers and author can accept no legal responsibility for any consequences arising from the application of information, advice or instructions given in this publication.

A catalogue record for this book is available from the British Library.

Publisher Jonathan Bailey
Production Jim Bulley and Jo Pallett
Commissioning Editor Dominique Page
Senior Project Editor Wendy McAngus
Editor Nicola Hodgson
Managing Art Editor Gilda Pacitti
Designer Wayne Blades
Photographer Jessie Chui

Colour origination by GMC Reprographics
Printed and bound in China

Index

To order a book, or to request a catalogue, contact:
GMC Publications Ltd, Castle Place, 166 High Street,
Lewes, East Sussex, BN7 1XU, United Kingdom
Tel: +44 (0)1273 488005   www.gmcbooks.com